Praise for
change your church for good

Change Your Church for Good is a great book! The truths and principles Brad gives in this book can be applied to any church or ministry, pastor, or leader as they transition from where they are to where God wants them to be . . . without compromise. This book provides inspiration, practical help and hope . . . a definite "must read" for the church today!

—**John C. Maxwell, Author, Speaker, and Founder,
INJOY Stewardship Services and EQUIP**

I believe the church is the hope of the world and its future is in the hands of its leaders. One of the great needs of church leaders is to learn the art of leading transition. Brad Powell and NorthRidge have taken this leadership art to a new level. I highly recommend the example of Brad and NorthRidge Church.

—**Bill Hybels, Senior Pastor, Willow Creek Community Church**

Brad Powell knows what it takes to reach people in the twenty-first century. His book *Change Your Church for Good* will blow your mind, open your eyes, and move your soul.

—**The late Dr. Jerry Falwell, Former Chancellor and President,
Liberty University, Lynchburg, Virginia**

Regardless of the size, age, location, or style of their church, all leaders know that transitioning a church is one of the greatest challenges they'll face. In *Change Your Church for Good*, Brad Powell not only equips pastors to lead their church into the transition process, but he also inspires and identifies with them through honest admissions of his own mistakes and trials he encountered as a new leader attempting to resurrect a dying congregation. If you dream of seeing your church transform into a community where people are meeting God, this book is a must-read.

—**Linda Lowry, Editor,** *Outreach* **Magazine**

I have known Brad Powell since he came to Temple Baptist Church in Detroit, Michigan, and began his ministry there. I have seen many changes—all for the good—which brought about renewal and growth in the church now called NorthRidge. Brad has his feet in the Word of God, yet his heart is attached to carrying out the Great Commission even though there are changes in society. He has suggested many outstanding ways to implement the Great Commission in the American church. May God use this book for His glory.

—**Elmer L. Towns, Vice President, Liberty University**
Dean, School of Religion, Lynchburg, Virginia

Brad Powell offers hope without hype for all leaders who want to transition their church to a fresh new place of vibrancy and health. Brad writes with honesty and experience. His leadership at NorthRidge is a model that is transferable and will encourage you to lead your church through positive change.

—**Dan Reiland, Executive Pastor, Crossroads Community Church,**
Lawrenceville, Georgia

I've been studying and analyzing the church and church growth for all of my adult life. The church desperately needs to change its ministry methods to engage culture without compromising God's Truth. I don't know of a more successful model for this than Pastor Brad Powell and NorthRidge. Leaders and churches should take advantage of the lessons and insights Brad has learned through the NorthRidge transition.

—**John Vaughan,** *Church Growth Today*

change your church for good

Revised Edition

brad powell

THOMAS NELSON
Since 1798

NASHVILLE   DALLAS   MEXICO CITY   RIO DE JANEIRO

Published in Nashville, Tennessee, by Thomas Nelson. Thomas Nelson is a registered trademark of Thomas Nelson, Inc.

Thomas Nelson, Inc., titles may be purchased in bulk for educational, business, fund-raising, or sales promotional use. For information, please e-mail SpecialMarkets@ThomasNelson.com.

Unless otherwise noted, Scripture quotations are taken from the HOLY BIBLE: NEW INTERNATIONAL VERSION®. © 1973, 1978, 1984 by International Bible Society. Used by permission of Zondervan Publishing House. All rights reserved.

Scripture quotations marked CEV are from THE CONTEMPORARY ENGLISH VERSION. © 1991 by the American Bible Society. Used by permission.

Scripture quotations marked NCV are from the New Century Version®. © 2005 by Thomas Nelson, Inc. Used by permission.

Scripture quotations marked NLT are from the *Holy Bible*, New Living Translation. © 1996. Used by permission of Tyndale House Publishers, Inc., Wheaton, Illinois 60189. All rights reserved.

Quotation in chapter 4 taken from R. Weber, ed., *Biblia Sacra Vulgata*, quartam emendatum ed. (Stuttgart: Deutsche Bibelgesellschaft, 1990).

Library of Congress Cataloging-in-Publication Data available upon request.

ISBN: 978-1-4185-4366-2

Printed in the United States of America

10 11 12 13 14 WC 5 4 3 2 1

To Roxann, my partner in life and ministry:
thanks for making me better at both.
Without your support, encouragement,
investment, and love, my life and ministry
would be in black and white, rather than
in living color. Thanks for saying, "I do."
And to my kids: you fill my life with
joy and meaning. I love you all.

Contents

Acknowledgments

No successful leader (or writer) stands alone. The truth is that I stand on the shoulders of many people. Though the words in this book flowed out of me, I am ultimately a product of the investment that others have made in me through their teaching, writing, example, and support. I owe them profound thanks. I'm both privileged and grateful to have such great people investing in me.

I also want to acknowledge those in our world who desperately need to see Jesus and discover His hope . . . I wrote this book for them. It is my prayer that God will use this book to help many churches become what God intends: a clear and compelling reflection of His love and truth . . . the hope of the world.

Finally, with love and thanks, I acknowledge my NorthRidge family, especially those who, in the face of significant loss, chose to take the journey of change with me. It really has turned out to be "Change . . . for Good."

Introduction

Churches Are Dying . . . but There's Hope!

The church had been built with a deep desire to honor God and help people. It had been beautiful: a white stone building with the cross placed atop the bell tower to be seen for miles. It had once stood proudly as a guiding light and symbol of hope. Then something went horribly wrong. In the end, it was abandoned, boarded up, and left as a symbol of disappointment and shattered dreams.

As was typical of many older churches, there was a cemetery on the church property. Yet one gravestone in that cemetery wasn't typical. They buried their church! The gravestone reads:

IMMANUEL LUTHERAN CHURCH

1906–1963

The church is supposed to be a place that gives evidence to the resurrection power of Jesus Christ, where people find life and hope. It's supposed to overcome death and destruction, not submit to it. Yet this church was buried. It's not supposed to be like this. It doesn't fit what Jesus said about the church in Matthew 16:18: "I will build my church, and the gates of Hades will not overcome it."

Though you won't often find the blatant honesty of the people of Immanuel Lutheran Church, many churches are dead or dying. They aren't reaching people with the hope of Christ and haven't for a very long time. Their congregations are getting older and smaller every year. Though the people inside are often sincere and love their church, the church appears to offer nothing of value to outsiders. They may not have etched the church's gravestone yet, but signs of life are quickly diminishing or have already disappeared.

As a result, multitudes of people are giving up on the idea of attending church. And in their defense, many churches aren't worth attending. When compared with everything else people can choose to do with their time, some churches are quite frankly second-rate, substandard, and shoddy. By most people's standards, they're dull, uninspiring, and mind-numbing. Though churches are in possession of the most profound and life-changing truth the world has ever known, the way many of them present this truth is superficial and boring. Because of this, most people have concluded that church has nothing to offer them. If it isn't going to encourage, strengthen, inspire, benefit, and fill them with hope, why would they attend? They have enough turmoil in their lives without adding a depressing church experience to their weekly schedule. In light of the negative reality in so many churches these days, who can blame people for making the choice to stay away?

Telling the Truth

Most people wouldn't expect this kind of material to be written by a pastor, especially one as committed to and in love with the church as I am. For many, it probably sounds more like sacrilege than devotion. And yet I've written it for all to see. Why?

I believe in both being honest and facing reality, so I have to acknowledge the truth. Like it or not, the majority of people feel this way about church in general and their church in particular. If you're honest, odds are this is exactly how you feel, though perhaps you'd never say it out loud. Just to clear the air, this doesn't make you a bad person. It means that you think church has become irrelevant, unpleasant, and meaningless. And sadly, more often than not, you're right.

Though some would call you sacrilegious for your honesty, as they have me, you're not. It's not blasphemy to tell the truth. It's God-honoring. (Heard of the Ten Commandments?) That it seems sacrilegious to honestly assess churches reveals the problem. Christians and churches have begun cherishing, valuing, and fighting for and against the wrong things. In so doing, they are more like the religious Pharisees of Jesus' day than like Jesus Himself. The Pharisees fought against and ultimately rejected Him. Why? Because in spreading God's truth, helping the hurting, healing the sick, and providing hope for the hopeless, Jesus was messing with their cherished and valued traditions, and it ticked them off.

> **Christians and churches have begun cherishing, valuing, and fighting for and against the wrong things.**

In Matthew 15:2–3, we find an example of this sad and destructive reality. The Pharisees asked, "Why do your disciples break the tradition of the elders? They don't wash their hands before they eat!" Jesus replied, "And why do you break the command of God for the sake of your tradition?"

The same is happening today. Like the Pharisees with Jesus, some Christians attack and condemn others simply because they're telling the truth about the present condition of the church and trying to do something about it. It was wrong for the Pharisees. It's wrong for people today. They, too, have misplaced their love and passion, choosing traditions over truth. But it shouldn't stop us from following Jesus' example. We should be "speaking the truth in love" (Ephesians 4:15).

Now, of course, to speak of Jesus Himself in critical terms *would* be sacrilegious. Jesus' character and teaching is the only secure foundation for our lives. As He said in Matthew 7:24, 26, "Therefore everyone who hears these words of mine and puts them into practice is like a wise man who built his house on the rock. . . . But everyone who hears these words of mine and does not put them into practice is like a foolish man who built his house on sand." To denigrate or dismiss the ultimate value and role of the church would be and is equally foolish. After all, Jesus loves and gave Himself for the church (Ephesians 5:25). He is committed to building the church, and it is the only force on earth that can prevail against the onslaught of hell in people's lives (Matthew 16:18). It is the one source of light in a world filled with darkness (Matthew 5:14–15).

However, to fear giving an honest assessment of how local churches are or are not living up to their God-given assignment is contrary to Scripture. First and Second Corinthians are almost exclusively devoted to correcting the believers in Corinth for messing up the church. A good summary of what Paul was saying in these two books of the Bible, in my parlance, would be: "Your church is second-rate, substandard, and shoddy! It isn't even close to what God intended."

If a church is:

boring, irrelevant, tired,

talking about loving the spiritually lost but doing nothing to reach them,

living for tradition at the expense of truth,

experiencing great conflict and little love,

talking about money and the budget more than life change and ministry,

giving to missions in foreign lands but having no mission of its own,

more concerned about clean carpet than helping messed-up and
hurting people,

> committed to comfort over sacrifice,

> celebrating yesterday and mourning today,

> focusing exclusively on the next life rather than
> living this one,

soft-pedaling people's sin rather than helping them
understand its destructive power,

> judging people for their failures rather than
> helping them find God's forgiveness,

condemning other churches for what they're doing
while continuing to do nothing,

filled with contempt for those who are different,

> treating the church more like a historical museum
> than a present-day ministry . . .

> then that church is *messed up*. It's not what God
> intended.

It may or may not be your fault . . . though more than likely,
if you're a Christian, you should take part of the blame. After all,
the church isn't a building, a program, a tradition, a denomination, a pastor, a board, a committee, or any other such thing. The
church is people, the family of God. Any given church is simply a
reflection of those who attend. Each church reflects the ideas and
principles that the people who attend genuinely value and love.
If they value tradition, the church will focus on tradition. If they
value the building, the primary focus will be the building. If they
value a certain style of music or preaching, these will become the
focus. If they value a small, comfortable environment that keeps

them safe from the world, this becomes the picture of that church. If they value politics, their focus will be political.

Though certainly influenced by leadership, the church is ultimately an expression of what the congregation values and is willing to fight for and against. If you're a believer, whether you realize it or not, you play an important role in shaping the church. Therefore, your level of involvement or uninvolvement, as the case may be, is helping to determine the character, quality, and direction of the church. This makes assessing what you personally cherish, value, and champion as essential as assessing the church leaders' role in shaping the church to be what it is today. And all believers need to make the choice to become part of the solution.

Any given church is simply a reflection of those who attend.

Loving and Hating the Church

Admitting that your church is ineffective in no way indicates that you don't love your church. In fact, very possibly, it indicates you love it immensely. And you need to know that you're not alone. There are many who both love and hate their church at the same time. Though these sound incompatible, they're not. Think about it. We all experience these dueling emotions. For example, I love and hate my house at the same time. I love how comfortable it is as a home. There is nothing like driving up to it after being away. But, at the same time, I hate all the work it demands.

Likewise, many love the history, familiarity, people, traditions, location, and memories of their church. But they hate that its services are boring, irrelevant, and predictable. They hate that they are no longer being inspired. They hate that it's not reaching anyone or making any significant difference in the world. They hate that they don't want to invite their friends. They hate that, when their kids are young, they have to drag them to church, kicking and screaming. And they hate that, when their kids grow older, they leave the church. They hate that it feels more like a museum than a church.

I received this e-mail from a person who is obviously battling with this very issue in his life. He wrote:

> I have watched each of my grown children walk away from the church. They all pray and have some sort of belief, but do not have a use for the church. I now think I am beginning to understand why. It is irrelevant to them. I am a leader in a church and lead a small home group each Sunday night. It, for the most part, is a church of older dying members who are the main financial support . . . I pray for God to use me and bring more families to serve Him, but it is not happening.

This man represents a lot of people. He is deeply discouraged by and disappointed with his church, even though he still loves it.

Though I don't like to admit it, this is exactly how I felt about the churches I've pastored when I first went to them. Some of you reading this right now are pastors or church leaders. Let me encourage you. You're not alone in your feelings about the church. In the past, my wife and I would comment on the fact that, if I weren't the pastor, we would never attend that church. If you're a pastor or church leader feeling this way, there's nothing wrong with you.

Admitting that your church is ineffective in no way indicates that you don't love your church. In fact, very possibly, it indicates you love it immensely.

The truth is that *there's something right with you*. You care enough about the church to be honest about its condition, and you're desperately looking for answers and hope for changing it. With all my heart, I believe this book can help you. You're not reading this by accident.

Of course, there are also people who hate the church . . . without loving it. Most of these were the kids brought to church kicking and screaming. Many have long since left. If this is you, I relate. This was me growing up. I hated church! Passionately. The fact that church attendance was a mandated part of my family life added fuel to an already out-of-control fire. Unfortunately, my passion motivated some bad decisions.

On one occasion when I was young, as we were driving to church, dressed in our Sunday best, I leaped from the car and made a mad dash for freedom. I was eventually caught. The great escape won me nothing but more grief. As I recall, I was still forced to endure church with the added bonus of an embarrassed and unhappy father's wrath.

Why Do People Disdain Church?

What would motivate a person to disdain church to that degree, regardless of age? For me, there were two primary issues driving my disdain, and I have found that the same holds true for others.

The first was my problem. I had no interest in God, others, or eternity. I was a self-absorbed taker. I was only interested in the moment and whether I was enjoying it. The Bible talks about this kind of shortsighted, self-centered attitude . . . though the churches I attended weren't communicating Scripture in a way I could relate to or understand. In Luke 12:16–21, Jesus told the story of a rich man who was consuming all of his wealth living for the pleasure of the moment and making no investment in others. And then, unexpectedly, he died. God calls him a fool for squandering his life in the moment rather than investing it for something eternally significant.

This was me. It may be you. The problem is that our self-centeredness keeps us from finding the fulfillment we're looking for and only God can give us. It ultimately leaves us empty and filled with regret. Though you feel that church has nothing to offer you, I encourage you to look further. You know that you're not finding what you're looking for when you live without God. I would encourage you to start looking for your fulfillment where I found it, in a personal relationship with God.

The second reason for my disdain was the church's problem. Though I'm sure the people designing the services and programs of the church were sincere, the reality is that everything about church was irrelevant to me. I didn't get the culture, the language, the thinking, or the point. It was like a club with secret hand-shakes, passwords, codes, and language. Somehow, I missed the orientation class. For me, church was a place that valued insiders. I was an outsider and, as a result, not welcome . . . in spite of what the sign in front of the building said. The reality is that the congregation's actions proved much louder than their words. In fact, because of their actions, I decided their words were both cheap and empty.

I believe this is true for many people today. They would love to know God . . . if He's real. They are interested in forgiveness, purpose, love, and hope . . . if they are really available. But they've checked out church and can't relate to anything. As a result, they've concluded that, if God is real, for some reason He can't or doesn't want to relate to them. This causes them to feel that God Himself is rejecting them.

The first problem that caused my disdain of church was solved when I discovered the reality of God in my life. I discovered not only that He was real but that He wasn't rejecting me at all. He doesn't reject anyone. In my self-centered focus on personal pleasure and fulfillment, I was rejecting Him. Though I thought He was the one hiding, I was wrong. I was hiding, and He was pursuing. Unfortunately, I didn't discover this reality in church. As I will explain later, I found this truth at a nonchurch event. Though it is, without a doubt, the greatest discovery of my life, through which everything that I now value and enjoy comes, it is extremely sad that I was unable to uncover God's reality in church.

> **I believe that the church is the hope of the world . . . when it's working right.**

Confronting the second problem, the fact that so many churches have become irrelevant to those who most desperately need God, has become my life's mission. Today, I'm as passionate in loving the church as I used to be in hating it. I believe that the church is the hope of the world . . . when it's working right. And therein lies the problem. Most aren't! Because of this, people aren't seeing the church as the hope of the world. They're seeing church as irrelevant to the world.

Though this reality is hurting a lot of people, keeping them from finding help, faith, and God, there is hope. The reason the apostle Paul wrote two letters identifying the problems in the Corinthian church was because, even in the most messed-up churches, there is hope. Paul said it best in Philippians 4:13: "I can do everything through him who gives me strength." In truth, though something may be impossible for us, nothing is impossible with God (Luke 1:37).

Hope for the Church

Though in this introduction I have clearly and honestly identified some negatives about the church, this is not a negative book. On the contrary, it is a very positive book . . . one about hope. However, just as people must first acknowledge their sin and guilt before they can, by faith, experience forgiveness and hope, so churches must first face their negative realities. When they do, they can then begin embracing and experiencing their hope-filled futures. The reality is that even the most irrelevant, boring, dying church can become relevant, exciting, and revitalized. After all, God identifies the church as "the body of Christ" (1 Corinthians 12:27; Ephesians 4:12). The truth of Christianity is that, though Jesus died, He now lives. A dead church is an oxymoron.

Therefore, if we unlock the doors of our churches by removing the chains of man-made traditions, terminology, and methods, and if we begin displaying and communicating God's love and truth in a way people can understand today, the church will once again live as the hope of the world.

As you will learn in this book, this is the real story of the church that I now pastor. In our journey from irrelevant to relevant; bound by tradition to freed by God's truth; unhealthy to healthy; dying to thriving, we learned a lot . . . much of it the hard way. God allowed us to experience our transition in order to provide help and hope for Christians who know that something is desperately wrong with their church; for pastors, leaders, and churches wanting to fulfill God's purpose in the world again; and for skeptics and seekers who, whether they know it or not, are desperately looking for God and His hope . . . which means they desperately need a church that's working right.

> **The truth of Christianity is that, though Jesus died, He now lives. A dead church is an oxymoron.**

While it's true that many churches are dead or dying, it is equally true that they don't have to stay that way. In this book, I show both the possibility and a way for churches to transition from what they are to what they can and should be. Your church can successfully *change without compromise*. This is a book about hope. Today, the church I have the privilege of pastoring is, while not perfect, living up to its God-given purpose to be the hope of the world. As you'll see in the opening chapter, it wasn't always this way. I believe every church has the same potential.

Read on and discover what you're looking for: hope . . . for you and your church.

PART 1

here is the church

CHAPTER 1

Failure Was Not Final

If It Can Happen Here,
It Can Happen Anywhere

I was broken. It was nothing like I had envisioned. I pictured myself as the effective new pastor of the church, riding a white horse to save the day. The church was not working, and I was going to fix it. Yet after two years, the church was no better, and all my effort had left me drained, discouraged, and defeated.

I was working harder than I ever had and was getting nowhere. I couldn't get traction. The church seemed to be in worse shape than when I arrived. Though a few positive things had transpired, the direction of the church was still downward . . . in every area. The attendance and attitude were declining, and it didn't appear that anything could turn them around. At this point, it became crystal clear that I had no white horse. In fact, in many ways, I seemed to be the problem. And I was.

It was during this time that God woke me up to the fact that I had been leading His church as if it were "my" church. I had been leading people to me . . . rather than to Him. I had been attempting to change the church by the force of my personality, and it wasn't working. I quickly put my finger on two reasons. The first was that this church was too large for one personality to make a positive impact. Though I was expending every ounce of energy I had in order to infuse this church with passion and excitement, I wasn't making a dent. The second reason it wasn't working was that they didn't like my personality. The congregation was used to older, refined, and staid pastors. I was a young, irreverent, and fun-loving one. Rather than being drawn to me, they were repelled by me. The prospects looked dismal.

> **I had been leading His church as if it were "my" church. I had been leading people to me . . . rather than to Him.**

In an attempt to get perspective, I took a short spiritual retreat to a church conference. I needed to get away, but, even more, I desperately needed to hear from God. At the midpoint of the conference, in place of a scheduled session, they inserted a time of worship. In the past, this would have ticked me off. I usually want to get as much information as possible. But on this occasion, it was exactly what I needed.

God used this moment to reveal Himself *and* my problem to me. I had never been in a place like this before. I didn't know what to do. I didn't have the answers. I was miserable and failing. And though it was difficult for me to admit, the problem was with me. I thought I could do anything, anywhere, at any time. God made it clear that *this* was the reason I was failing. I was trying to lead the church without Him. Though He was the only One who could build the church, I was shutting Him out. This realization broke me. I skipped most of the remaining conference sessions in order to spend time on my knees before God and His Word. This was a defining moment in my ministry. Finally, while alone in my hotel room, I was stripped bare of the self-sufficiency that had prevented me from experiencing the fullness of God's presence, power, and promises. Through brokenness, I was now becoming the man God had long been calling me to be . . . a genuine spiritual leader.

Leading from the Bottom

I came to this church when I was thirty-two years old and at the top of my game, or so I thought. In reality, I was at the bottom. It took two years of failing to realize that I couldn't successfully change the church because I couldn't change the hearts of people. Only Jesus could do this. I learned that the only way I could effectively lead the church through change was from the bottom . . . in full recognition of my weakness, inability, and complete dependence on Him. Of course, though I was learning it the hard way, the Bible makes this abundantly clear. "But he gives us more grace. That is why Scripture says: 'God opposes the proud but gives grace to the humble'" (James 4:6).

I was comforted to know that the apostle Paul had to learn this lesson as well.

To keep me from becoming conceited because of these surpassingly great revelations, there was given me a thorn in my flesh, a messenger of Satan, to torment me. Three times I pleaded with the Lord to take it away from me. But he said to me, "My grace is sufficient for you, for my power is made perfect in weakness." Therefore I will boast all the more gladly about my weaknesses, so that Christ's power may rest on me. That is why, for Christ's sake, I delight in weaknesses, in insults, in hardships, in persecutions, in difficulties. For when I am weak, then I am strong. (2 Corinthians 12:7–10)

As a result of this revelation, I repented of my past leadership and committed myself to leading the church to God and through God in the future. By grace, I was finally ready to lead, though the church I was called to lead would continually test my readiness.

Temple Baptist to NorthRidge

The church I had been called to pastor was Temple Baptist Church in Detroit, Michigan. It had an unbelievable heritage. In 1969, Elmer Towns had included it in his book *The Ten Largest Sunday Schools*. It had been led by a high-powered and innovative pastor from the South who came to the church in 1935. It was great timing. As a result of the booming automobile industry, there was a huge Southern migration to the Detroit area. Those working in the auto industry were leaving their families, friends, churches, and culture to work and live in the North. This Southern pastor was perfectly suited to reach them. Thousands accepted Christ and connected to this Southern-cultured church. It was like a little piece of home. As a result, it became a very large and impacting church, especially for the day.

Along the way, some insurmountable problems developed between this pastor and the church. In 1950, they decided to remove him and make his right-hand man their pastor. This man went on to pastor the church for twenty-five years. Though not the same kind of communicator or innovative leader, he managed the ministry with consistent excellence and relative success.

However, the world started changing. The influx of Southerners ended, and the culture of Detroit began to shift significantly. As a result, the Southern style of the church was slowly but surely becoming irrelevant to the changing community. The church began a long and painful season of decline. By the time Temple Baptist was included in Towns's book, it had already been in decline for fifteen years. The largest year for the church was in 1954. With the exception of only a couple of years, the church had been in continual decline.

The decline started slowly, but eventually the momentum of loss became unmanageable. Temple Baptist ultimately lost 75 percent of their attenders and 90 percent of their membership. The majority of these were lost in the ten years prior to my arrival. The average age of the attenders when I came was fifty-seven; there were very few young adults and even fewer children. It was clear that the church was facing a questionable future unless it experienced an unprecedented turnaround. Though many churches need *some* change, in order for this one to survive, it needed to transition in every conceivable way.

Cultural Transition

Our church needed to transition culturally. It was an early-twentieth-century, Southern-cultured church trying to reach late-twentieth-century people in a Northern-cultured area. There were banjos playing in the basement, an organ in every classroom, and ushers lining the back wall of the auditorium and staring at people through the entire church service. Though it made sense to those on the inside, it was like a foreign world to anyone from the outside. If this church was going to turn around, it had to transition culturally.

Generational Transition

The church needed to transition generationally. As I already pointed out, the average age of the church was fifty-seven. This church had literally missed two generations of people, and it was beginning to miss the third. They couldn't keep their own kids, let alone reach new young people. If the church was going to carry on, it had to begin reaching the younger generations.

Organizational Transition

Temple Baptist needed to transition organizationally. The church had been organized to support and sustain a ministry with very different needs and problems than it was facing at this time. In fact, most of its problems were being caused by a commitment to yesterday's solutions. They were committed to an organizational structure that was not equipped to offset the needs of a church heading into the twenty-first century. It was geared to support and sustain a vision that was no longer relevant. If this church was going to transition, it had to change organizationally.

Methodological Transition

Our church needed to transition methodologically. The methods being used by this church were relevant for an era that no longer existed. Yet they believed that these methods were the only appropriate way to do ministry. Over time, they had allowed their practices to supersede God's principles. In order for this church to become effective again, they would have to do the unthinkable . . . change their methods.

Philosophical Transition

The church needed to transition philosophically. It had become a defensive rather than an offensive ministry. As the result of three decades of decline, the church had directed its ministry toward not losing their own people rather than reaching new people. Quite simply, they were focused on insiders rather than outsiders. This would have to change if the church was to live on and be effective.

Spiritual Transition

Finally, our church needed to transition spiritually. There was a lot of anger and conflict in Temple Baptist Church. After three decades of decline, they began blaming and fighting one another. Though there were many wonderful people in the church, love wasn't always in evidence. There wasn't much light or hope being experienced or communicated.

This church wasn't working right in any way. There was a seemingly insurmountable negative momentum. If there was ever a church that could have written its own epitaph, it was this one. For this church to survive, it would require a miraculous turnaround.

With God, All Things Are Possible

Now, imagine me coming into this church thinking that I could save it . . . that I could perform this "miracle." It really was foolish. It was like Moses standing in front of the Red Sea, thinking he could part it. However, as foolish as that was, the idea that the church was worthy of and ready for saving wasn't foolish. After all, Jesus is the One who said, "With man this is impossible, but with God all things are possible" (Matthew 19:26). Though Moses couldn't part the Red Sea, God certainly could. And He did.

> **When I came to this church, my problem wasn't believing that the church could successfully transition. My problem was believing that I could do it.**

When I came to this church, my problem wasn't believing that the church could successfully transition. My problem was believing that *I* could do it. When I finally got my ego and self-confidence out of the way, God was then able to use me to do what He had always promised to do . . . "build the church" (Matthew 16:18). He was just waiting for me to get out of the way and trust Him.

Today, our church, now called NorthRidge, is experiencing what most had believed impossible. We are a healthy, growing, and culturally relevant church. The average age for attenders is around thirty years old. We've reached thousands for Christ. We're nearly three times larger than the church was in its biggest year before the decline began. We are no longer bound by cultural practices and entrenched traditions of the past. Rather, we are committed to living out God's purpose and values in the present. God's love, light, and hope are being experienced and communicated by many.

Why does this matter to you? It provides hope for your church! While there are some healthy and relevant churches in the world, there are far more that are unhealthy and irrelevant. More than likely, you are or have been part of one. Unfortunately, most people give up on these churches. Don't! God hasn't. Our church is living proof of this.

> **Here's the reality: if a successful transition could happen at our church, it can happen at yours. If God could use me to lead a transition, He can certainly use you.**

Here's the reality: if a successful transition could happen at our church, it can happen at yours. If God could use me to lead a transition, He can certainly use you. No matter what you or your church is presently experiencing, there is hope. In light of the resurrection, failure doesn't have to be final—not for people or for churches. After all, the story of a church is the story of people.

If you're part of a church that isn't all it should be, you should pray for, encourage, and offer help to your pastor and church leaders to begin the journey of change without compromise. If you're a pastor or leader of a stalled or declining church, I encourage you to hang in there. Commit to trusting God to use you to transition the church to health, relevance, and growth. While successful transitions are often difficult in the church, they're always worth it because the church, when working right, is the hope of the world. If your church isn't working right, please know that there's hope. You can draw great encouragement from us because if it can happen here, it can happen anywhere.

As I'm sure you can imagine, we've learned some valuable lessons in our transition . . . many of them the hard way. One of the reasons God allowed us to experience such a profound transition and learn these lessons is so that we can encourage and help other leaders and churches.

In the following pages, you will find the biblical truths and leadership principles that successfully guided us on our journey of change without compromise. If you will invest in reading and understanding them, I believe that God can use them to do the same for you and your church.

CHAPTER 2

Well Conceived

Hope of the World

I love the book of Acts. It shows the church exploding onto the scene in fairy-tale fashion. Though humans had always longed for it, for the first time in history, it appeared that there really was the possibility of a "happily ever after" ending. It was amazing. As the church burst onto the scene, the gospel began knocking down all the man-made walls of separation and began spreading a brand of love and hope that had never before been experienced. Groups who had thrived on mutual hatred for centuries began reaching out and accepting one another with grace. Though people in the past had buried the hatchet out of necessity for survival, this kind of transformation had never been seen. When the church was working right in those early days, lives were changed, hatred overcome, prejudice eradicated, failure forgiven, selfishness diminished, compassion expanded, and genuine hope, once only found in fairy tales, became a reality. The seemingly unbelievable words of Jesus became the true-to-life experience of people's lives. They really were enjoying life to the full (John 10:10). In a world such as ours, only God could have imagined something like this.

This is church as it *ought to be*! Doesn't the description of it make your heart beat faster? When you look deep down, isn't this the kind of church for which you've been longing? Of course, most of us have settled for so much less. If we're honest, though we believe the Bible, the church as described in the book of Acts seems no closer to our experience than a fairy tale. But it doesn't have to be this way.

God has envisioned and fashioned the church to be the hope of the world. Jesus made this abundantly clear in Matthew 5:14 when He said, "You are the light of the world." Of course, in a world where people are lost in darkness, light represents hope. In Matthew 16:18, Jesus said, "I will build my church, and the gates of Hades [hell] will not overcome it." The gates of hell won't prevail against the church. Don't miss this. In this passage, Jesus is revealing that He has come to change the world. Hell had been prevailing in the world since Adam and Eve made the choice to walk away from God. It had been blinding people to their God-given purpose and robbing them of the beauty and potential of life (John 10:10). But now, this was going to change. Rather than hell prevailing, the church would prevail. It would knock down the gates of darkness and evil, death and destruction, addictions and perversions, emptiness and loneliness, and sin and guilt. No longer purposeless and powerless, the church would be where broken people could be put back together, desperate people could find calm, fearful people could discover peace, empty people could be filled, and people gripped with sorrow could experience joy. The church was designed to be the hope of the world.

> **God has envisioned and fashioned the church to be the hope of the world.**

Of course, it doesn't take a rocket scientist to recognize that there's a problem. In general, churches aren't living up to this design. Hope certainly isn't prevailing in most parts of the world. The church is the hope of the world . . . when it's working right! The problem can be found in four simple words: "when it's working right."

What Is the Church Supposed to Look Like?

To avoid serious confusion, this is where we need to get on the same page with our definitions. When I write about the church in the singular, I am referring to all genuine Christians. Those who have acknowledged their sin and guilt before God and fully trusted in Jesus' death and resurrection for forgiveness and new life are the church. This is what Paul was referring to in Ephesians 5:25–27 when he wrote, "Husbands, love your wives, just as Christ loved the church and gave himself up for her to make her holy, cleansing her by the washing with water through the word, and to present her to himself as a radiant church, without stain or wrinkle or any other blemish, but holy and blameless." All genuine Christians and the church are one and the same. When I write about churches in the plural, I am referring to individual churches that have been developed by genuine Christians in order to locally reflect Christ and fulfill His purposes in a tangible way (Romans 16:3–4, 16; 1 Corinthians 16:19; Hebrews 10:24–25). Just as our human bodies provide a means for expressing our true selves, local churches are designed to be the physical expression of the one true church. Because God has called all those in His one true church to be part of a local church, the two can be spoken of synonymously. Local churches are envisioned and fashioned by God to be the tangible expression of all He has called the church to be. Therefore, all churches are designed by God to be the hope of the world.

Since there are no lasting alternatives for hope in this world, the fact that churches aren't working right is unacceptable. Churches must recognize the problem, accept responsibility, and do something about it. For this to happen, we must know what the church is supposed to look like when it's working right.

Alive, Not Dead

God intended the church to be alive, not dead. Romans 6:4 says, "We were therefore buried with him through baptism into death in order that, just as Christ was raised from the dead through the glory of the Father, we too may live a new life." A dead church is an oxymoron. In light of the resurrection, how could you have a dead body of Christ? Though we have a lot of dead organizations with "church" in their names, these aren't really churches. Genuine churches can't be dead. The church lives! Yet many churches today are reminiscent of a funeral. In case you missed it, the mourning and funeral were over three days after Jesus died, cut short by a resurrection. Churches are called by God to share the excitement and possibility of new life with the world.

Love, Not Hate

God intended the church to be love, not hate. As 1 John 3:14 says, "We know that we have passed from death to life, because we love our brothers. Anyone who does not love remains in death." How many churches does this describe?

According to God's Word, we know that we have passed from death to life, been freed from the prison of sin and guilt, because we love other Christians. The church is supposed to be filled with love, yet many churches are filled with hate. In the name of the One who lovingly asked God to forgive the people nailing Him to a cross, churches are often filled with hate over temporary issues that won't change anything. They use their foyer to sign petitions for the latest social outrage, which is an obstacle to offering God's hope to people on the other side of that political or social issue, the people who most need hope. This clearly causes the church to miss its ultimate purpose of reflecting Christ and His love to this world. As Jesus said in John 13:35, "By this all men will know that you are my disciples, if you love one another."

Forgiving, Not Condemning

God intends the church to be forgiving, not condemning. John made this clear when he wrote that "God did not send his Son into the world to condemn the world, but to save the world through him" (John 3:17). Jesus' ministry wasn't one of condemnation. Yet many churches claiming to represent Him are characterized by condemnation. No wonder so many people, believers and non-believers, have no use for the church.

> **The fact that churches aren't working right is unacceptable. Churches must recognize the problem, accept responsibility, and do something about it.**

In many ways, the church is embracing the compassionless ways of the Pharisees who wanted to have the adulterous woman killed (John 8:3–11). On the contrary, Jesus, with great compassion, encouraged her with the truth that her failures weren't final. He said, "Go now and leave your life of sin." The church was never intended to reflect man's hateful and hurtful condemnation. The church is to be a reflection of God's loving and healing forgiveness.

Truth, Not Tradition

God intended the church to be about truth, not tradition. In Mark 7:8, we find Jesus boldly asserting to a group of religious people, "You have let go of the commands of God and are holding on to the traditions of men." These religious people weren't just ordinary churchgoers. These were the religious teachers and leaders of Jesus' day, and they were becoming more loyal to their traditions than to God's truth.

Of course, this explains how they could promote hatred, condemnation, prejudice, and even murder in the name of God (Luke 19:47). Their traditions were *becoming* their God . . . what they lived for and worshiped. Unfortunately, the same reality seems to be seeping into many churches today. Though Jesus, in teaching and living God's love and grace, stood in stark contrast to this, many Christians and churches are more a reflection of the Pharisees than of Him.

Whether you're getting your first glimpse of what the church is supposed to look like or you're a seasoned veteran, you need to know that Jesus is angered by those who represent God in the spirit of hatred and condemnation. In fact, the only people Jesus ever blasted were these kinds of people. Look at what He said to them in Matthew 23:15, 25–28:

> Woe to you, teachers of the law and Pharisees, you hypocrites! You travel over land and sea to win a single convert, and when he becomes one, you make him twice as much a son of hell as you are. . . . Woe to you, teachers of the law and Pharisees, you hypocrites! You clean the outside of the cup and dish, but inside they are full of greed and self-indulgence. Blind Pharisee! First clean the inside of the cup and dish, and then the outside also will be clean. Woe to you, teachers of the law and Pharisees, you hypocrites! You are like whitewashed tombs, which look beautiful on the outside, but on the inside are full of dead men's bones and everything unclean. In the same way, on the outside you appear to people as righteous but on the inside you are full of hypocrisy and wickedness.

I think it's obvious that this is not the picture God wants His church to paint. He wants us to paint the picture of truth, love, and grace.

Freedom, Not Bondage

Tradition puts people in bondage. Truth sets people free (John 8:32). God intended the church to be about freedom, not bondage. Galatians 5:1 says, "It is for freedom that Christ has set us free. Stand firm, then, and do not let yourselves be burdened again by a yoke of slavery." The church is supposed to be setting people free.

Sadly, as I look around, I see many churches putting people in even more bondage. It's crazy. They are putting people in bondage to rituals, regulations, and traditions. They are force-fitting people into lifestyles designed by those who might not even know God, just like in Jesus' day. It's ridiculous. God created a world of diversity. When anyone or anything, the church included, seeks to limit that diversity by forcing everyone into the same cookie-cutter mold, it dishonors God and robs people of the joy and freedom of fulfilling their God-given design. It's like forcing people to crawl when they were created to walk.

Acceptance, Not Rejection

God intended the church to be about acceptance, not rejection. Romans 15:7 says, "Accept one another, then, just as Christ accepted you, in order to bring praise to God." Now, this is where many Christians and churches really start going wacko. "Oh," they ask in pious disdain, "are you saying we've got to accept everyone regardless of what they believe? We have to affirm their choices whatever they may be?" In condemning and arrogant tones, they ask, "So, is everything really okay?"

The simple answer is no. We're supposed to accept people like Jesus did. The truth is that Jesus embraced the adulteress while religious people condemned Him for it. But, in embracing her, He did not affirm her lifestyle. He said, "God loves you, but hates that you're destroying your life. Go and sin no more." And that grace changed her life (John 8:3–11; paraphrased).

The church is designed to reflect Jesus' grace and acceptance. Sadly, many don't. This explains why so few churches are seeing people's lives changed. Jesus taught and demonstrated that only grace has the power to genuinely change a life (John 3:16–18).

Desire, Not Duty

God intended the church to be about desire, not duty. The apostle Paul provided a profound example of this. As he vividly described in 2 Corinthians 11:23–29, he experienced some horrific troubles in his life and ministry.

> I have worked much harder, been in prison more frequently, been flogged more severely, and been exposed to death again and again. Five times I received from the Jews the forty lashes minus one. Three times I was beaten with rods, once I was stoned, three times I was shipwrecked, I spent a night and a day in the open sea, I have been constantly on the move. I have been in danger from rivers, in danger from bandits, in danger from my own countrymen, in danger from Gentiles; in danger in the city, in danger in the country, in danger at sea; and in danger from false brothers. I have labored and toiled and have often gone without sleep; I have known hunger and thirst and have often gone without food; I have been cold and naked. Besides everything else, I face daily the pressure of my concern for all the churches. Who is weak, and I do not feel weak?

In light of these, Paul was asked why he kept going. He gave a simple answer to the question: "Christ's love" kept him going (2 Corinthians 5:14). It fueled him with desire even in the face of all his troubles. Christ's love compelled him because He went to the cross for him. Paul had killed people because they followed Christ—only to discover His profound love and grace. In the wake of so much heartache, pain, and loss, a sense of duty could have never sustained him. But desire could and did.

The church was never conceived by God to be driven by duty; it was designed to be driven by desire. Love is the only motivation that will continue to drive us, no matter how difficult the circumstances. Love is what drove Jesus to the cross, and love is supposed to drive the church. Jesus made this clear in John 14:15: "If you love me, you will obey what I command." The reality is that God would rather have someone give a dime out of desire than a million dollars out of duty. Yet all around the world, pastors, churches, and Christians are preaching duty instead of grace. No wonder the church is repelling people rather than compelling them.

Transformation, Not Modification

God intends the church to be about transformation, not modification. Second Corinthians 5:17 says, "If anyone is in Christ, he is a new creation; the old has gone, the new has come!" In Christ, people go through such a metamorphosis that God declares the old gone and everything new.

In most cases, this is not the church I see today. I see churches accepting and encouraging modified behavior. The way Christianity is being taught in many churches today makes Jesus look like no more than a forerunner of our present-day self-help gurus. He has no power to genuinely change a life. He just laid out some beautiful platitudes that help us think more positively in the midst of our negative realities. The way many churches teach, you'd think Jesus authored the cliché "Fake joy is better than genuine depression." After all, when you boil it all down, this is what so many seem to be teaching. As a result, many people are living the Christian life as a charade rather than a reality. Though they are still wrestling with all the same darkness in their souls, they are looking very Christian on the outside. This is what Jesus labeled hypocrisy. And He despised hypocrisy above all else because it creates the illusion that God doesn't have the power to genuinely change a life.

The church must offer and accept nothing less than genuine transformation. What if Jesus had come out of the tomb paralyzed? I don't think Easter would be the celebration it is today, do you? Think about it. "Yeah, He rose from the dead, but He's still on life support." How much hope would that provide?

> **The church should be offering and expecting life change. It should settle for nothing else.**

The Christian life is not about modifying behavior. Every self-help program and motivational speaker in the country gives another plan for modifying behavior. And they can be very inspirational. However, the inspiration wears off. Generally, our natural realities get the better of us again. Not so with Jesus Christ. When we genuinely experience His touch, we are transformed.

The church has proven itself worthless to many people because while it has boasted the promises of Christ, it has, at best, provided only slight modification of behavior. Many churches say, in essence, "If you can adjust to a couple of outside rules and fit yourself to our standards, then, even though your heart is still filled with darkness, come on in. You can be one of us. Just make sure you keep the darkness hidden. And make sure you give financially. The more you give, the better. In fact, we'll name a building after you." No wonder so many people think the church is irrelevant.

The church should be offering and expecting life change, and settling for nothing else. I believe churches aren't seeing lives transformed today because they're not expecting people's lives to be transformed. The truth is that they've lost their faith in the power of God and His Word. So they declare the message of Christ in a benign way, with no expectation for changed lives. In this way, they pacify their conscience while avoiding disappointment.

Well, here's the deal from my perspective. We should never dumb down God's power to our level in order to protect ourselves from disappointment. We should determine to offer people what God has promised and willingly deal with the consequences. I would rather fail according to human standards, by offering people the hope of transformation God has promised, than to succeed by watering down God's truth, ensuring they never find it. Wouldn't you? I'd rather fail believing in God's promises and power than succeed by diminishing them. After all, it's impossible to please God apart from faith (Hebrews 11:6). Unfortunately, I believe a lot of churches, even those considered successful, are not pleasing God.

Imagine how the story of Moses would have changed if he had decided to lower the expectations of what God had promised in order to protect himself from disappointment or failure. In Exodus 14, as the leader of God's people, he was in an impossible situation. As a result of following God's direction, Moses had led the people of Israel into an inescapable setting. They were trapped by geography on every side but one. Unfortunately, the only way out was now blocked by the approaching army of the world's great superpower . . . Egypt. Egypt's goal was to humiliate the people of God, and God Himself. Trapped by circumstances beyond his control and ability, Moses had only two options: declare the audacious promise that God would rescue them by parting the Red Sea, or protect his leadership position (along with his salary and benefits package) by admitting the impossible and surrendering to Pharaoh and the Egyptian army.

Of course, adding to the drama and difficulty, the people Moses was leading wanted to surrender. "They said to Moses, 'Was it because there were no graves in Egypt that you brought us to the desert to die? What have you done to us by bringing us out of Egypt? Didn't we say to you in Egypt, "Leave us alone; let us serve the Egyptians"? It would have been better for us to serve the Egyptians than to die in the desert!'" (Exodus 14:11–12). They saw only the impossible circumstances.

Moses saw the same circumstances, but, unlike the others, he also saw the God who controls the circumstances. So with no thought of the disappointment or failure he could experience, he boldly declared the promise of God. In Exodus 14:13–14, "Moses answered the people, 'Do not be afraid. Stand firm and you will see the deliverance the LORD will bring you today. The Egyptians you see today you will never see again. The LORD will fight for you; you need only to be still.'" God did show up and fight for them, and the people were saved. The Egyptian army was destroyed. God's power and promise were seen and experienced, and Moses was celebrated by the same people who had just castigated Him. But the real reward was that he was honored by God.

Like Moses, Christians and the church are called to both believe and proclaim God's power and promises . . . at any cost. When they do, lives are changed, God is pleased, and the church experiences His blessing.

Authentic, Not Hypocritical

God intended the church to be authentic, not hypocritical. Second Timothy 3:5 says, "Even though they will make a show of being religious, their religion won't be real. Don't have anything to do with such people" (CEV). Yet many churches, in order to increase their membership, tolerate hypocrisy. They embrace and affirm people who put on the show of Christianity at church but don't live it in their everyday lives.

This pushes people away from and out of the church. When they see people who are living contrary to the teachings of Christ holding positions of power and being celebrated in the church, it turns them off. And it should. Yet, all too often, the church continues to put up with and promote it. This is tragic!

God wants the church to be authentic. The church should be a place where broken people can come in and find help, not a place that forces people to hide their hurts, temptations, addictions, flaws, and problems. It should be a place where they can find grace and healing. However, the way many churches are structured today, the kind of people Jesus came to help wouldn't be welcome and certainly wouldn't find grace.

It was the same in Jesus' day. The religious people didn't want anything to do with broken and hurting people. They heartlessly rejected them and scorned Jesus for accepting and loving them. One day, when Jesus was asked why He spent time with broken and hurting people, His answer was classic: "It is not the healthy who need a doctor, but the sick. But go and learn what this means: 'I desire mercy, not sacrifice.' For I have not come to call the righteous, but sinners" (Matthew 9:12–13).

> **The church should be a place where broken people can come in and find help.**

Interestingly, the people rejecting the "sinners" were no better than those they rejected. They were simply better at masking their offenses. The problem is that, no matter how hard they tried, the religious leaders of Jesus' day couldn't hide the truth of their own emptiness from themselves or Jesus. Though some of today's religious leaders are satisfied to hide their emptiness in a contrived image, most people aren't. No wonder so many have rejected God and the church in our world. They would rather be authentic in their brokenness than live a masquerade.

Relevant, Not Irrelevant

God intended the church to be relevant, not irrelevant. First Peter 3:15 says, "In your hearts set apart Christ as Lord. Always be prepared to give an answer to everyone who asks you to give the reason for the hope that you have. But do this with gentleness and respect." In other words, the church should be answering the questions about God's hope that people are asking. But most churches are wasting time answering questions nobody's asking.

The people coming into churches these days are asking honest, heartfelt, but tough questions. Questions like, "When everyone has rejected me, how can there be a God who loves me?" and "Where in this world of darkness can I find some hope?" The church, like Jesus, is supposed to honestly answer these questions.

Of course, the answer always comes back to people's need for God. As Colossians 1:27 says, "Christ in you, the hope of glory." In speaking of Jesus, John wrote, "Then you will know the truth, and the truth will set you free. . . . If the Son sets you free, you will be free indeed" (John 8:32, 36). There is hope in Christ, because He has made it possible for people to overcome the destructive power of failure and guilt. In Him, failure doesn't have to be final. The problem is that many Christians and churches are condemning failure rather than sharing the truth that failure isn't final in Christ. This is remarkable in that all Christians are themselves failures (Romans 3:23).

No wonder people avoid church. The real tragedy is that God is ultimately blamed for the failure of churches. When the church doesn't answer the questions people are asking or apply God's truth to the issues they're wrestling with, they think that God doesn't care about them. Of course, nothing could be further from the truth. As 1 Peter 5:7 says, "Cast all your anxiety on him because he cares for you." But the church is communicating the opposite by its inability or unwillingness to address the struggles, worries, hurts, and burdens that people are dealing with. When this happens, people have no alternative but to conclude that church is a waste of time and the God it represents is irrelevant.

People, Not Place

God intended the church to be about people, not place. Acts 8:3 tells us, "Saul began to destroy the church. Going from house to house, he dragged off men and women and put them in prison." This passage clearly communicates that the church was and is people. They didn't drag off the houses; they hauled off the people. Yet most churches tend to focus on place over people.

The church I have the privilege of pastoring has a beautiful campus and buildings. But the church is not about the campus or buildings. In fact, our campus and buildings are worthless unless used as a means to provide help and hope for people. People are what matter most to God and what should matter most to His people and church.

Sadly, some churches care more about their carpeting than people. Of course, they'd never verbalize it. But it's obvious. Keeping the carpet clean and protecting it from wear takes priority over people. In churches like this, "no" signs are posted everywhere. "No Food Allowed!" "No Drinks Allowed!" "No Running Allowed!" "No This!" "No That!" (They might as well hang a sign saying, "Why are you here?")

At our church, though we seek to maintain the buildings with excellence, we never let our property take precedence over people. For example, we invite people to bring drinks into our auditorium for services. In fact, we have cup holders on our seats to facilitate this. You wouldn't believe how many people, especially those who come to our church as nonbelievers, have

> **The real tragedy is that God is ultimately blamed for the failure of churches.**

told us that they were willing to come because they could dress casually and sip a latte or cappuccino while we told them about God.

Of course, it has its problems. Often, someone spills a drink in the back row. Since our auditorium floor is sloped, the spill slowly makes its way down front. It makes for cheap entertainment. People try to guess how far it's going to go. I think the record is twenty-three rows. But the facility team never complains. They know the drink was spilled by someone whom Jesus loves and died for. It was spilled by a person who needed and perhaps found hope during our service. Cleaning a spilled drink or replacing stained and worn carpeting is a small price to pay in order to show hurting or seeking people that they matter to God. Jesus certainly paid a far more significant price.

> **The goal of the church should be not to get people to fall in love with their traditions but to get people to fall in love with God.**

Relationships, Not Religion

Finally, God intended the church to be about relationships, not religion. As He was praying in John 17:3, Jesus didn't say, "Now, this is eternal life, that you keep all the rules and rituals as set out by church tradition and denominational hierarchy." In truth, that would be less like eternal life and more like eternal death. On the contrary, this is what He said: "Now this is eternal life: that they may know you, the only true God, and Jesus Christ, whom you have sent."

God never intended church to be about keeping rules and rituals or preserving traditions, liturgies, and calendars. God intended church to be about knowing Him and building a relationship with Him. After all, knowing God is the only thing that will ultimately count in life. As Jeremiah 9:23–24 says, "'Let not the wise man boast of his wisdom or the strong man boast of his strength or the rich man boast of his riches, but let him who boasts boast about this: that he understands and knows me, that I am the LORD, who exercises kindness, justice and righteousness on earth, for in these I delight,' declares the LORD."

The goal of the church should be not to get people to fall in love with their traditions but to get people to fall in love with God. This is the ultimate purpose of the church. Somewhere, many Christians and churches have gotten off track. This is the reason so many people believe that the church is irrelevant and avoid it at all costs. Our goal must be to get the church to live up to its billing . . . as the hope of the world. The church was well conceived. The problem is that it's being poorly executed.

CHAPTER 3

Poorly Executed

It's Not Working Right

Though I love reading the book of Acts, the church it pictures has seldom been my experience. In truth, as I view churches across our country and around the world, I see relatively few that reflect the church that God designed. So, more than likely, my experience speaks to your experience. In most settings, the walls of separation remain firmly in place and there are few signs of the unconditional love and unshakable faith that were introduced in the early days of the church.

As we've seen, the church is the hope of the world when it's working right. It's working right when it's everything God intended. Since most aren't, those who make up the church, all genuine Christ-followers, must come to grips with and take seriously their God-given responsibility to change this. Here's one thing I know: if you're a believer, God has given you the responsibility to make sure the church is working right. It doesn't matter who or what you are in church—(pastor, volunteer, staff, leader, attendee, nonattendee)—God's holding you responsible. The reason is simple: like it or not, *you* are the church.

If we're going to fulfill our responsibility to make sure church is working right, we have to know what's wrong. I have found that the best way to identify the problem is through the process of elimination. We have to identify all the possible problems and then determine which ones are keeping us from experiencing church like it ought to be.

God Is Not the Problem

Let's start with God. Could He be the reason the church isn't working right? Of course, many do blame God for all the problems in the world. Though it's convenient, this belief doesn't hold water. God is not causing the problem in the church. For Him to be causing the problem, it would require Him to have changed. And that isn't possible. He's the same today as He's always been. Hebrews 13:8 makes this reality clear: "Jesus Christ is the same yesterday and today and forever." In other words, His character doesn't change. If He loved the church yesterday, He still loves it today.

God's Passion Is the Same

God's passion was never for clean carpet, keeping traditions, singing the same songs, or boring people to death. In 2 Peter 3:9–10, we discover what was, is, and always will be His passion: "The Lord . . . is patient with you, not wanting anyone to perish, but everyone to come to repentance." His passion for reaching people is as strong today as the day He sent Jesus into the world.

God's Purpose Is the Same

In Luke 19:10, Jesus gave us His purpose: "For the Son of Man came to seek and to save what was lost." His purpose isn't to protect denominational identity, liturgies, dress codes, musical styles, ministry methods and programs, or particular translations of the Bible. His purpose is to seek and save the lost. If we care more about those temporary things than His clearly expressed eternal purpose, we're reflecting Jonah rather than Jesus. Jonah was a man called by God to help the Ninevites avoid judgment. God told Jonah to tell the people of Nineveh about His forgiveness and hope. Because these people were so vile and contrary to everything Jonah valued, He didn't want God to forgive them. He wanted them to be judged. Because Jonah's purpose was contrary to God's, he ran away from God's calling. Ultimately, after a miserable experience in the belly of a great fish, he obeyed God. And God's purpose was accomplished: the Ninevites repented and were saved. Yet Jonah was mad at God for saving these despicable people. Needless to say, Jonah didn't get a "Well done" from God. Unfortunately, many Christians and churches seem to be following Jonah instead of Jesus. As with Jonah, if they don't surrender to God's never-changing purpose, they will regret it.

> **If we're going to fulfill our responsibility to make sure church is working right, we have to know what's wrong.**

God's Promise Is the Same

"I will build my church, and the gates of Hades will not overcome it" (Matthew 16:18). This wasn't a temporary promise. It is as relevant and valid today as it was the day God made it. He will build His church.

God's Power Is the Same

As Luke 1:37 acknowledges, "Nothing is impossible with God." Yet I have found that many believers, church leaders, and pastors have a difficult time applying this truth to the church. Many believe that the decline of morality, constant attacks on the Bible and Christianity, and the culture's overall negative attitude toward the church have made growing a genuinely biblical church impossible. Many scoff at the concept of God bringing a revival into our world today. Though this belief develops as a rationalization for churches no longer reaching people, those embracing it ultimately believe that any church reaching people must be compromising or watering down God's truth.

While I'm sure most don't realize it, they are buying into the dangerous and deceptive lie that God doesn't have the power to build His church in a world like ours. Though there are many problems with this thinking, I want to point out three primary ones.

> **Because nothing is impossible with God, we can believe with confidence that no church, no matter how messed up, is beyond hope.**

First, *this thinking is rooted in the false idea that our world is more difficult to reach than the world in Christ's day.* Nothing could be further from reality. Without a doubt, the idea of reaching the world of Jesus' day was a far greater stretch than reaching our world. While the concept of one God is widespread today, it was held only by a small percentage of people in those days. Paul experienced firsthand the difficulty of presenting this concept in a world built upon a polytheistic, pagan philosophy (Acts 17:16–34).

The lack of value for life and compassion for the needy, infirm, and helpless in the days of the early church can't even be compared to our world. We have our problems, but, in most ways, we live in a world of light compared to the darkness of that world. Yet the church of Jesus Christ changed that world.

Second, this thinking *diminishes God and His power.* This view paints a picture of God as weak and unable to fulfill His promises. The reality is that there is no culture or power in the universe that can prevent God from fulfilling His promise. The reason Jesus took His disciples to Caesarea Philippi, a center of pagan worship, was to make His promise "I will build my church" in the heart of one of Satan's strongholds (Matthew 16:18). He was expressing with confidence what He wanted His followers to believe with confidence. God's power is more than adequate for the church to offer the same hope to our world that it offered that world. Because nothing is impossible with God, we can believe with confidence that no church, no matter how messed up, is beyond hope.

Finally, *God's presence is the same.* Jesus made this clear when He said, "And surely I am with you always, to the very end of the age" (Matthew 28:20). He's here. Many churches just aren't recognizing or claiming His presence. So the only reasonable conclusion is that, though there is definitely a problem with many churches today, God is not it.

The Message Is Not the Problem

Another target often blamed for churches' problems today is the message. It is common for people to cast aspersions on the authenticity, relevance, and power of the Bible. Many are calling for a change of message that would be more in keeping with the ever-changing culture. But the reality is that God's message isn't the problem.

Unfortunately, you'd never know this by the way many churches are changing God's message to appeal to today's culture. There are popular preachers who tend to leave out the absolutes of Jesus' teaching—the absolutes that are necessary for offering hope to a lost, dark, and hopeless world. Absolutes such as the sinfulness and guilt of all human beings (Romans 3:23); sin's eternal consequences of destruction, death, and separation from God in this life and the next (Romans 6:23); the perfect life, death for sin, and resurrection of Christ essential for forgiveness and new life (1 Corinthians 15:3–4; 2 Corinthians 5:17); Jesus as the only way to God (John 14:6); and faith in Christ as the way to forgiveness of our failures, experiencing the life we were created for, and knowing the hope of heaven (John 3:18; 10:10; Ephesians 2:8–10; 1 John 5:11–13).

God's Word is the power of God to transform people's lives and set them free (John 8:32; Romans 10:17). If the church is going to offer hope to this world, then we need to faithfully present His Word. Though many Christians and churches are avoiding it, changing it, and ashamed of it, God's message is not the problem. As Romans 1:16 says, the gospel "is the power of God for the salvation of everyone who believes."

The World Is Not the Problem

Though it almost always receives part of the blame, the world is not why the church isn't working right. Yet I often hear this from sincere and well-meaning Christians. More than likely, you have probably entertained this thought . . . at least to a small degree. Please know that I'm not criticizing or pointing my finger. I, too, have allowed this thought to seep into my view of the world at times. The world is an easy target when defending our inability to reach people. However, the world is not and never has been the problem with the church.

As we saw earlier in this chapter while discussing God's power, many believe that this world is too far gone to be reached for Christ and that growing a genuinely biblical church is impossible. I've heard many pastors blame the world for the stagnating or declining condition of their churches. They reason that the world is just too dark and hopeless for a relatively small group of believers to influence it with light and hope. I certainly understand their sentiment. The world is consumed with darkness. However, when we set aside self-defensiveness and emotion, we have to acknowledge that this idea doesn't hold up under scrutiny.

Think about it: the deeper the darkness, the brighter and more impacting even the smallest amount of light. The darkness of our present world provides an even greater opportunity for the light of God's truth to be seen and establish influence. Remember, the world wasn't a wonderful place in Jesus' day either. In the early days of the church, it was common for followers of Christ to be violently persecuted and even killed for their faith. By the eighth chapter of Acts, Stephen was killed for his faith by religious zealots. Persecution of Christians became so severe that they had to leave home, career, family, and friends in order to live in peace and, in some cases, survive. They scattered all around the known world of their day. The apostles were continually persecuted and every one of them, save for John, was ultimately killed for his faith in Christ and commitment to build His church. John managed to survive being boiled alive in oil and was then banished to an island away from all he loved.

If the church is going to offer hope to this world, then we need to faithfully present His Word.

People think it's tough to recruit people for ministry in our world. Imagine what it was like in their world! I can see the discussion now. "Hey, you should consider going into the ministry. It's an extremely rewarding career. You get to help people who despise Christ and will despise you. Though you'll reach some people, most will think you belong in a psych ward. You won't make any money. You won't have a place to call your own. But there's a great retirement benefit. In fact, most people serving Christ these days are experiencing retirement at a very early age."

Let's be honest. The selling point for being a follower of Christ and living for Him wasn't all that positive from an earthly point of view. Nero, one of the Roman emperors, actually impaled Christ-followers with a spear, poured oil on them, and set them on fire to illuminate his gardens. Clearly, the church was built in a violent and difficult world. In the face of unimaginable immorality and cruelty, the church was effectively offering light and hope to the world. It was reaching people and growing.

Because so many are confused about this issue and blame the world for their church's failures, I think it's important to understand some foundational truths. The world has always been dead in trespasses and sins (Ephesians 2:1). Though it has certainly dressed itself differently through the generations, the world has always been the same. The world has always loved darkness rather than light (John 3:19). And the world has never genuinely understood or sought after God (Romans 3:11).

Though the world is difficult and its cultures are always changing, the world is definitely not the problem with the church.

The Church Is the Problem

Since the problem with the church has nothing to do with God, His Word, or the world, there's only one answer left. The problem must be the church . . . Christ-followers themselves. And this isn't a modern-day phenomenon. In fact, it reminds me of a sad story in Luke 9:37–42.

In desperation, a hurting father brought his spiritually battered and broken son to Jesus' disciples for healing. Hearing about Jesus' compassion and power, he dared to hope again. Unfortunately, any hope he had was quickly dashed against the rocks of reality. To him, Jesus appeared to be no different than all the other religious charlatans. After all, as verse 40 says, he brought his son to Jesus' disciples for healing, "but they could not."

They all took a crack at it. Despite all their words of hope and fervent attempts to heal, they couldn't help the boy. You might be thinking, *Of course! Only Jesus had the power to deliver this boy from his spiritual torment.* But the passage tells us differently. Luke 9:1–2 says that "when Jesus had called the Twelve together, he gave them power and authority to drive out all demons and to cure diseases, and he sent them out to preach the kingdom of God and to heal the sick."

Think about this. Jesus had given the disciples the power and authority to heal this boy and, in so doing, to reveal God's love, power, and hope to their world. Yet, regrettably, they failed. In retrospect, the reason is clear: they were seeking to represent Jesus in the wrong way and for the wrong reason. In Matthew 17:19–20, Jesus told the disciples that they failed because they tried to heal this boy in their own strength. They were using this boy and his tragic circumstance in order to prove who was the greatest (Luke 9:46–48). They were using God's power to compete against one another. Of course, they failed. God resists the proud.

If Jesus hadn't come off the mountain and saved the day, not only would this boy have remained spiritually broken and defeated, but the idea that Jesus offered genuine hope would have lost all credibility with those who witnessed their failure.

Tragically, this is the picture many have of the church in our world today. Because so many have turned to the church for help and hope, only to find irrelevance and powerlessness, the genuine message of good news has lost credibility with multitudes of people.

How has this happened? The same way it happened for the apostles. We've been doing church the wrong way and for the wrong reasons. We've been doing church the way we like it, the way we enjoy it, the way we want it. If we're honest, we're all trying to prove that our way is the best way. Like the powerless disciples in Luke 9, we are competing to see which church is the greatest and want to condemn everyone who does church differently (Luke 9:48–50). We forget that "pride comes before the fall."

Church is not supposed to be about us. There are hurting people desperately in need of help. We forget that the world is looking to us for hope. We forget that we're the only Jesus some people will ever see. We forget that what they see and experience in our churches is the best they will ever see and experience of Jesus. We forget that eternity is hanging in the balance. And in the process, we've forgotten that only Jesus can build His church. Only God can genuinely transform a person. As a result, without realizing it, we've lost the power that God has given us to reveal His life-transforming hope in this world.

Coming to Grips with the Reasons

Though well conceived by God, the church isn't working because of our poor execution. If we don't commit to doing everything necessary for proper execution, our churches will never prevail against the gates of hell.

There are several possibilities as to why we've become an obstacle to the church revealing and releasing hope to this world.

We Have a Heart Problem

The first is that we have a heart problem. In Revelation 2:4, Jesus says to the church in Ephesus, "You have forsaken your first love." Unfortunately, this is true of a lot of churches. When a church loses its love and passion for Christ, it cannot function properly. A church that has forsaken its love of Christ begins loving and focusing on meaningless stuff that holds no hope for anyone. Instead of loving Jesus with passion and fervor, the congregation becomes passionate about buildings, denominational tags, church names, liturgies, traditions, and ministry styles. Though a common experience, losing first-love passion for Christ is both sad and dangerous. It's a heart problem that prevents the church from working right.

We Have a Focus Problem

The second possibility spills out of a focus problem. Like the disciples in Luke 9, all believers have the tendency to unwittingly turn the focus of life and ministry on themselves. In Philippians 2:3–5, the apostle Paul tackled this issue head-on: "Do nothing out of selfish ambition or vain conceit, but in humility consider others better than yourselves. Each of you should look not only to your own interests, but also to the interests of others. Your attitude should be the same as that of Christ Jesus."

This is tough medicine. After all, if we're honest, each of us is driven by selfish ambition. I have to put checks and balances on my motivations all the time. Even the disciples wrestled with pride and ambition. We all have the same internal engine that drives us to focus on ourselves.

It encourages me that Jesus never ridiculed the disciples when they battled with ambition. In fact, He simply sought to redirect their drive. Basically, Jesus would say, "Guys, there's nothing wrong with your drive for success and significance. However, there is something very wrong with your method. Selfish ambition is not the way up in God's economy. Serving others . . . focusing on others . . . is the way to experience true success and significance. Rev your engines in service, and you'll never regret it" (Mark 10:35–45; paraphrased).

Selfish ambition is destroying the church's ability to reveal God's hope to the world. People are vying for power and greater influence in the church. Church boards contend with their pastors. Pastors compete with their boards. Large contributors seek to leverage their giving for power. Members oppose church activities that don't directly benefit them. This is a significant problem in the church, and it's paralyzing our ability to reflect, reveal, and represent the unselfish love of Christ. It robs the world of the hope that the church is supposed to deliver.

> **We've been doing church the wrong way and for the wrong reasons.**

As Philippians 2 goes on to reveal, the church is supposed to reflect Jesus' attitude. Though He was God, He didn't grasp for the recognition He deserved. On the contrary, He was willing to take the role of a servant. He was willing to suffer and die undeservingly in order to protect those who deserved to suffer and die. In keeping with His teaching, this selfless attitude led to Him being highly exalted by God.

God exalts the greatest servants. And, as the church, we are called to focus on others, not ourselves. We are called to organize the church to reflect Christ by serving others' needs and interests rather than our own. Unfortunately, most churches are organized to serve the interests and well-being of the insiders rather than the outsiders. If the church is going to be the hope of the world, we have to fight this natural tendency.

We Have a Faith Problem

By nature, we want to see and touch before we'll accept. Of course, this is not always possible. There's much we can't see that we're forced to accept by faith. But we find it difficult to believe beyond our experiences. Yet for the church to work right, we must. As Hebrews 11:6 makes clear, "without faith it is impossible to please God, because anyone who comes to him must believe that he exists and that he rewards those who earnestly seek him." And 2 Corinthians 5:7 says, "We live by faith, not by sight."

When the church isn't working right, it is often a faith problem. As we've seen, Jesus promised that He will build His church and that the gates of hell will not prevail against Him (Matthew 16:18). In other words, He wants His church to be on the offensive. Gates don't attack; gates are attacked. So, according to Jesus, what's the church supposed to be doing? The answer is clear: the church is supposed to be attacking the gates of hell.

Yet most churches aren't playing offense. On the contrary, most churches are playing defense or worse . . . sitting on the bench. They're trying to keep people from leaving the faith and their churches rather than reaching out to new people. In light of Jesus' promise that the gates of hell couldn't and wouldn't overcome the church, it's both unbelievable and ridiculous for the church to be playing defense. If our main focus and worry is about people leaving, we're in a world of hurt. This is poor execution. Instead, churches should focus on people who need to find the forgiveness, purpose, love, fulfillment, and hope of Christ.

> **Most churches are organized to serve the interests and well-being of the insiders rather than the outsiders.**

In light of Jesus' promise, what causes His followers and churches to cower in fear of losing people? The only answer is that we aren't fully trusting or believing Jesus. Of course, this is common for His followers. Time and time again it caused His first followers to fall short (Matthew 6:30; 8:26; 14:31; 16:8; 17:20). In fact, few things evoked more sadness from Jesus than the failure of faith. In each case, He would ask why the disciples had such little faith or why they doubted. After all, they had seen His power. He had never failed. Why did they doubt Him?

The same question must be asked of us today. What causes our faith problem? We've seen Jesus' power. If not firsthand, we know the church exists today in spite of all of the attacks of hell in the past. Yet we just don't believe that He's really building His church today. So we play defense, protect our territory, and compete with one another over the relatively few people we have in our churches rather than going after the multitudes held captive by darkness. We're fishing in each other's half-empty goldfish bowls instead of in the vast, untouched oceans filled with people "without hope and without God in the world" (Ephesians 2:12).

How sad! No wonder so many people think the church is irrelevant. They're not seeing power; they're seeing weakness. They're watching churches cower in fear of the world rather than confidently charging and knocking down its evil strongholds.

Rather than believing Jesus' promise, many Christians are afraid of hell coming into the church. They do everything in their power to keep the world out of their churches. If Jesus had adopted this philosophy, He would have never come into the world. In truth, this isn't what those who are truly following Christ do. It's what those who are like the Pharisees of Jesus' day do. After all, their philosophy and practice was built upon the concept of keeping all the bad people out. As a result, they started condemning and ostracizing those whom they considered to be negative influences.

The problem with adopting this philosophy is that it contradicts the purpose Jesus has given the church. The church is supposed to be the "light of the world." How can we fulfill this calling in our churches if we isolate ourselves from those in darkness? We can't. For this reason, Jesus went on to say, "A city on a hill cannot be hidden. Neither do people light a lamp and put it under a bowl. Instead they put it on its stand, and it gives light to everyone in the house" (Matthew 5:14–15). Jesus made it clear that His people weren't to pull out of the world and isolate themselves. They were to intentionally infiltrate the world. In His words, the church is to "go into all the world and preach the good news to all creation" (Mark 16:15).

When we use the church as a place to hide from the evil influences of the world, we're demonstrating our lack of faith. The Bible is clear: "GOD is our refuge and strength, an ever-present help in trouble" (Psalm 46:1). When we genuinely trust God, we don't have to cower in the face of evil influences. It's a faith issue. In the wake of His disciples' fear when He was asleep in the boat, Jesus told them, "You of little faith, why are you so afraid?" (Matthew 8:26). Churches were never meant to be hiding places. When this happens, the opportunity for people to find hope is diminished because the church isn't working.

The book of Acts provides the picture for what the church can be when it's working right. The Acts of the Apostles is not meant to be a history of what the church once was; rather, it is a picture of what the church is to be today. The problem seems to be that most Christians and churches don't have the faith to act on it.

The story of Peter and John healing the lame man in Acts 3:1–10 provides a clear and powerful picture of this reality.

> One day Peter and John were going up to the temple at the time of prayer—at three in the afternoon. Now a man crippled from birth was being carried to the temple gate called Beautiful, where he was put every day to beg from those going into the temple courts. When he saw Peter and John about to enter, he asked them for money. . . . Then Peter said, "Silver or gold I do not have, but what I have I give you. In the name of Jesus Christ of Nazareth, walk." Taking him by the right hand, he helped him up, and instantly the man's feet and ankles became strong. He jumped to his feet and began to walk. Then he went with them into the temple courts, walking and jumping, and praising God. When all the people saw him walking and praising God, they recognized him as the same man who used to sit begging at the temple gate called Beautiful, and they were filled with wonder and amazement at what had happened to him.

Scripture often uses people with physical challenges to illustrate the reality of our spiritual lives and the condition of the world. In this passage, the lame man is a picture of our world:

he was without hope. The best he could hope for was the ability to survive. He wasn't looking for or dreaming of a better life. For him, this was outside the realm of possibility. His hope had been lowered to mere existence. His greatest hope was that someone would give him enough to get through another night so that he could beg again the next day.

This is the story of humanity. As Ephesians 2:12 describes it, we are "without hope and without God in the world." No matter how much people accomplish on their own, there is still an emptiness consuming their existence. Everyone is looking for something more.

> **The Acts of the Apostles is not meant to be a history of what the church once was; rather, it is a picture of what the church is to be today.**

One day everything changed for the man begging outside the temple courts. He went from down and out to leaping and praising God when Peter and John introduced him to the life and hope that only Jesus could give. He was hoping for some spare change to get him through another miserable day, but he got more than he could have ever dreamed. He went from existing to living, empty to fulfilled, miserable to joyous. This happened because Peter genuinely believed that Jesus was the one gift this man needed and the greatest gift he could offer. He believed that Jesus was the hope of the world. As a result, this man's life was forever changed.

This is the role the church is supposed to play in our world. The church is the hope of the world, when it's working right. The church is supposed to break into the lives of people who are merely existing day to day and reveal to them the hope of "life in all its fullness" (John 10:10 NCV). Unfortunately, more often than not, the church is only offering what people are asking for . . . just a little help to make it through another miserable day. They're offering a temporary fix, a safe place to hide. As a result, the world is still begging for bread.

We need to believe with Peter that we have the truth that can set people free. We have what the world needs. Rather than avoiding them or cringing when they ask for help, we need to reach out to them and give them Jesus. We need to confidently believe and proclaim that Jesus is what's missing in the world . . . that He still has the power to save. We need to get to where we can say with Paul, "I am not ashamed of the gospel, because it is the power of God for the salvation of everyone who believes" (Romans 1:16). One of the reasons the church isn't releasing hope into this world is the lack of faith. We don't genuinely believe that people can be transformed like that anymore.

We Aren't Speaking the Language of the Culture

There is one more possibility for why the church isn't working right. And this one can keep a church from fulfilling its purpose even when they have it together in every other area. A church can have the *right heart*, the *right focus*, and the *right faith* and still be totally ineffective at reaching people with God's hope. They are passionate about pleasing God and reaching those He loves. They are focused on serving others rather than themselves. And they really do believe in the power of God to change lives . . . even in our world today. Yet they aren't seeing any life change in and through their ministry. Their attendance is stagnating or declining. They just can't seem to attract people into their ministry or to the hope of Christ. It creates deep frustration, discouragement, and conflict.

Though it may be difficult for people inside the church to identify the problem, it's clear to anyone who visits. In fact, it's the primary reason those who visit don't come back. As sincere as the people in the church may be, the way they do ministry is irrelevant to anyone from the outside. They aren't speaking the language of the culture. No amount of passion, concentration, or faith can compensate for a language barrier. This is one of the reasons God gifted the disciples supernaturally to speak in languages they had never learned (Acts 2). If people were going to connect to God's truth, they needed to hear it in a language they could genuinely understand. As important as heart, focus, and faith are, they cannot eliminate the importance of language. I think this is one of the important lessons of Acts 2. Everyone heard the message in their own language. And as a result, thousands of people came to Christ.

> **No amount of passion, concentration, or faith can compensate for a language barrier.**

There is no stopping the church from reaching people and impacting the world when they communicate God's powerful truth and life-changing hope in the language of the culture with passion, focus, and faith. In order for people to benefit from and apply God's truth to their lives, they have to hear it in a language they can understand. If they can't understand, it's impossible for them to accept and embrace it.

The church really is the hope of the world . . . when it's working right. And because hope is in such short supply in our world, people need the church to be working right now more than ever. Simply put, the world needs the church to fix the problem. If you're a believer, you are the church. Regardless of your status in the church, you need to become part of the solution.

Though most churches need to shore up their hearts, focus, and faith, these aren't the primary reasons the church is executing the mission so poorly. The primary problem facing the church today is the culture barrier. The church is not making sense to people because it's not able to connect to them. If we are going to properly execute God's plan for the church, then we must do what Jesus did. Jesus was so committed to providing hope for the world that He left heaven and came to earth. This was a major change. The solution for the problem in the church today is the same—major change. As Jesus demonstrated, change is not wrong when it's done for the right reasons and in the right way.

CHAPTER 4

It's All in the Delivery

Change Without Compromise

It was the worst moment of my young life. I was standing frozen in front of the phone. I had just been expelled from the same high school for a second time. What made it significantly worse was that this school was fifteen hundred miles away from home. My parents had sent me the first time hoping to help me start over. The choices I made in my early high school days were the kind of choices that could destroy a life forever. Regrettably, the change of circumstances didn't change me. The first day at this new school, I became best friends with the most rebellious kid there . . . at least he was before I arrived. As I'm sure was easily predicted by any sane observer, I was kicked out of the school within one semester.

Approximately a year later, I decided on my own that I wanted to go back and give it another go. Because hope springs eternal, my parents supported this decision with excitement. I'm sure they had high hopes for a breakthrough. Though this second attempt started positively, you already know the conclusion. It ended in the same way as the first, only with a deeper sense of disappointment and discouragement for my parents.

Standing at the phone and dialing their number was a nightmare for me. As it turned out, what I imagined as I dialed the number paled in comparison to what I experienced after we were connected. The profound disappointment in their voices was startling. As a parent myself now, I can't even imagine dealing with a child as prone to trouble as I was. Yet in keeping with their proven character, they responded with unconditional love. They made the arrangements for me to come home and, since it was my senior year of high school, figured out a way for me to graduate on time. Though hurt beyond comprehension, they did everything they could to continue positively investing in me.

Though it's a longer and more complicated story than I'm sharing, the consequences of this repeated failure stirred a significant change in me. For the first time, I fully embraced and experienced God's love, forgiveness, and hope. As God promised, when I turned to Him, He transformed me. Though I certainly continued to take some backward steps, I was finally leaning forward. My life was taking on a very different reality. Following graduation, I was privileged to take a summer mission trip to Ireland. On this trip, I began to engage my relationship with God in life-changing ways. He became my primary value and first priority, and, as always happens, my life was transformed. On this trip, I learned to love and personally benefit from spending time in God's Word, and I led a person to Christ for the first time. It was during this experience that I was clearly called to ministry and decided to go to a Christian university. My life was significantly and forever changed. It was the answer to every prayer my parents had ever uttered . . . and more. I can only imagine how they thanked God for the change.

Change Isn't a Four-Letter Word

My story proves an important though often forgotten point: change isn't a four-letter word. Though many usually see changes as a negative, as my parents discovered, change is the basis for hope. The single person hoping to get married is hoping for change. The same is true for the couple hoping for children, parents hoping for their baby's first steps, the student hoping to graduate, the sick person hoping to get better, the financially bankrupt person hoping to make money, and the addict hoping to overcome addiction. Change is the basis for hope.

Likewise, the hope of Christianity is founded upon the possibility of change. For example:

- "Do not conform any longer to the pattern of this world, but be transformed by the renewing of your mind. Then you will be able to test and approve what God's will is—his good, pleasing and perfect will" (Romans 12:2).
- "Do you not know that the wicked will not inherit the kingdom of God? . . . And that is what some of you were. But you were washed, you were sanctified, you were justified in the name of the Lord Jesus Christ and by the Spirit of our God" (1 Corinthians 6:9, 11).
- "Therefore, if anyone is in Christ, he is a new creation; the old has gone, the new has come!" (2 Corinthians 5:17).

It's this hope of change that made possible the transformation of Saul of Tarsus (the angry and merciless persecutor of Christians), to the apostle Paul (a fervent and faithful servant of Jesus Christ). It's this hope of change that has given a new beginning to each of us who has trusted in Christ. Though once defined by failure, we are now defined as "more than conquerors" (Romans 8:37). Though once far away from God, we're now called His children. Though we once walked in loneliness, emptiness, fear, insecurity, guilt, and darkness, we're now walking in joy of God's presence, purpose, peace, power, potential, and promises. We've experienced the hope that is only experienced through change.

In light of this, why do so many Christians have a negative perception of change when it comes to the church? More often than not, they see change in the church as synonymous with compromise. But the reality is that change is not compromise unless it involves compromising character or truth.

God Himself provides a great illustration of this truth. In one sense, God never changes. He never changes in character. He never betrays a promise or an established principle. For this reason, He can always be trusted. However, while He never changes His character (who He is), God consistently changes His conduct (what He does). He is unchanging in principle and ever-changing in application. The Bible is filled with this reality. In regard to character, God says, "I the LORD do not change" and "Jesus Christ is the same yesterday and today and forever" (Malachi 3:6; Hebrews 13:8). In regard to conduct, God says, "See, the former things have taken place, and new things I declare" and "See, I am doing a new thing" (Isaiah 42:9; 43:19). If God ever changed in character, we could not trust Him. Yet if God never changed in conduct, there would be no Jesus, cross, resurrection, redemption, church, hope, or future.

> **This book is about changing the church in its conduct (practice) without compromising the character (principle) of God's truth.**

This book is about changing the church in its conduct (practice) without compromising the character (principle) of God's truth. It's about allowing the church to be a clearer reflection of who God is and what He does.

The Church Must Be Relevant

In order to work right, the church must be relevant. It must communicate God's truth and hope in the language of the culture in which it's situated. Unfortunately, many consider cultural relevance a compromise for the church. Though they may be sincerely motivated, they're wrong. As an incontrovertible example, let me share some words from Jesus Himself on this:

Videns autem turbas ascendit in montem et cum sedisset accesserunt ad eum discipuli eius et aperiens os suum docebat eos dicens beati pauperes spiritu quoniam ipsorum est regnum caelorum beati mites quoniam ipsi possidebunt terram beati qui lugent quoniam ipsi consolabuntur beati qui esuriunt et sitiunt iustitiam quoniam ipsi saturabuntur beati misericordes quia ipsi misericordiam consequentur beati mundo cordequoniam ipsi Deum videbunt beati pacifici quoniam filii Dei vocabuntur beati qui persecutionem patiuntur propter institiam quoniam ipsorum est regnum caelorum beati estis cum maledixerint vobis et persecuti vos fuerint et dixerint omne malum adversum vos mentientes propter me gaudete et exultate quoniam merces vestra copiosa est in caelis sic enim persecuti sunt prophetas qui fuerunt ante vos . . .

Wasn't that awesome? It defines the foundational message of Christ and explains His life and ministry, doesn't it? You just read a portion of the greatest sermon ever given by the greatest preacher in history . . . the Sermon on the Mount (Matthew 5). The truths you just read are a part of the foundational hope that Jesus Christ came to give us.

Let me ask you: how much hope did you experience as a result of reading the words of Jesus above? How relevant were they to your life? If you're honest, unless you're proficient in Latin, it was totally irrelevant. And the reason it was irrelevant is because you couldn't understand it. It didn't make any sense. Your inability to understand it rendered it inoperative in your life. Though it contains powerful truth, reading it was boring and a waste of time. More than likely, either you didn't try or you quickly gave up.

We need to realize that this is the experience of lost and unchurched people when they attend a church that communicates God's truth in what I call "Christianese." Whether they know it or not, this is the language most churches all over the world are speaking. "Christianese" is the language of any given church's culture and tradition. As with all languages, it is understood clearly by those who have been raised with it. The problem, though, is that only insiders can understand and appreciate it. When unchurched or different-churched people attend a church that speaks its own unique form of Christianese, they don't get it. They have no clue what's being said. It's like a foreign language to them.

In my youth, my parents took me to churches like this. I couldn't understand a word they were saying. I couldn't understand the secret codes. I felt like an unwanted outsider and considered the church experience worthless.

This is how many unchurched people feel when they come into tradition-based churches: unwanted and unwelcome. They feel like the church is out of touch and worthless. It literally disconnects them from the truth we've been assigned to share with them. Even if they want to get something out of it, as you tried to do with the Latin passage, they quickly give up.

Irrelevance Is the Compromise

Relevance, speaking in the language of the culture, in no way compromises God's truth. Irrelevance is the compromise. After all, God has called Christians to be ambassadors of His kingdom in this world. An ambassador's job is to learn the language and culture of the nation to which he or she has been assigned. While the ambassador doesn't have to adopt the culture or beliefs of the country, he must understand the country, the culture, and the language in order to well represent his own nation.

This is the purpose of the church. The church is to represent heaven, hope, and Christ on this planet. If we're going to be good ambassadors, we must understand and speak the language of the people in our small part of the world. We don't have to adopt the values of the culture. But, as Jesus did, we must learn to relate to the people in it.

If we do not communicate God's truth in the language of our culture, we will fail to fulfill God's expressed purpose for the church. This is the ultimate compromise. By fighting change, I believe churches today are compromising what Jesus Christ sent us into this world to do. He sent us to follow in His footsteps. He left heaven, His comfort zone, in order to "seek and to save" those who are lost. Unfortunately, many churches would rather stay in their own comfortable world, speaking their own private language, than do the hard work of leaving their comfort zones to reach people who are without God and without hope in this world. When the church fails, it is because it refuses to be like Jesus. Jesus didn't force people to learn the language of heaven before He was willing to tell them the truth. He adopted the language and successfully related to the culture of His day. It's time the church today starts following Christ again.

> **If we do not communicate God's truth in the language of our culture, we will fail to fulfill God's expressed purpose for the church. This is the ultimate compromise.**

More often than not, we tend to see this issue through our denominational, traditional, or historical lenses, because this is where our experiences are and where our significant relationships exist. This generally causes us to miss the positive impact and hope that change could bring to people presently outside of the church. Instead, we tend to see how those inside the church will be negatively affected by changes. Of course, this creates stress, tension, and even fear. Who wants to lose friends when reaching out to strangers? In view of our nature, no one does. However, in view of Christ's nature, all believers should be willing. He gave up everything to reach outsiders. Exposing ourselves to the reality of people's lives outside of our church settings can truly help us gain perspective. Seeking to understand their thoughts can motivate us to care about reaching them.

These are the questions that many without Christ are asking: *Is there anything about God, anything about the church, that can genuinely help me in my life? Is there any hope out there?* When you think about the needs that people with and without God are wrestling with and then look at how the average church does ministry, it's easy to understand why many don't bother. Why should they? If the church isn't going to show them how God is both real and relevant to their lives in this messed-up world, why would they waste their time going? Even the Bible affirms this logic. In 1 Corinthians 15:32, Paul wrote, "If the dead are not raised, 'Let us eat and drink, for tomorrow we die.'" If there is no meaning or hope beyond this moment, then God is irrelevant. Though it doesn't solve any of our problems or fill our emptiness, we might as well live it up in the moment and not waste our time on church.

In order to reverse this sad reality, the church must change without compromise. If we are going to fulfill the purpose that God has assigned to us on this planet as believers, as His church, we need to communicate God's truth with doctrinal integrity and cultural relevance.

We cannot corrupt God's truth. We cannot water down God's truth, as so many are doing, to try and reach people by making the truth less offensive. The truth is the truth. It's the only hope that people have to find freedom and forgiveness. We cannot change the truth. We must present God's truth with doctrinal integrity (Romans 1:16; 10:17; 2 Timothy 3:16–17).

But the truth will not help or impact people unless we present it in a culturally relevant way. The Bible assigns the responsibility of both doctrinal integrity and cultural relevance to the church (1 Corinthians 9:19–23). While cultural relevance is non-negotiable when fulfilling the purpose of the church, it's vital to understand that the truth has the value, not the culture or relevance. The language we speak isn't valuable; the truth is valuable. Yet many Christians are fighting to preserve the culture and language in which they found Christ more than the truth itself. As a direct and predictable result, they consider it compromise to make any attempt to change the language or culture of the church. They see relevance as compromise. But the reality is that, by valuing the church's language and culture more than the truth itself, they are the ones compromising. They are displaying greater value for their preferred culture, language, and traditions than for the people Jesus loves and died to save. For the sake of their traditions, they are keeping the church from effectively communicating God's truth to those who desperately need it. This is compromise.

Essential for Life

Cultural relevance is not a bad thing for God's church. Cultural relevance is simply a means for delivering the truth to people who are locked in any given culture and time. This reality is beautifully symbolized by water. The Bible uses water as a symbol of truth. And this makes sense. We cannot live without water. We cannot live without truth. Without truth, we're dead in our trespasses and sins.

Water provides a wonderful illustration for truth. Though water has the power to promote and sustain life, it is useless if a person can't get the water. The fact that there's water in the world doesn't help the person dying of thirst in the desert. Therefore, water must be accessible to a person in order for its value to be experienced. As important as water is to life, it is worthless without an effective delivery system. This is why, throughout history, humanity has sought better and better ways to make water conveniently accessible to people.

The Hand Pump Versus the Faucet

In the early days of humanity, people knew they needed water to live, so they chose places to settle based upon the proximity to water. Of course, even though they located near a natural water supply, they still had to develop a means of delivering the water from where it was to where they needed it. So containers were invented. The containers could only hold so much water, and water gets heavy in large quantities. Transporting the water wasn't convenient. However, water was essential for life, and this was the best delivery system available in those days.

Times changed and technology advanced. Mankind put God's gifts of creativity to work and came up with a very different means of delivering water. They found water deep beneath the surface of the earth, drilled wells, and then extracted the water with a creative device called a hand pump. Without exaggeration, this was one of the most awesome inventions in the history of mankind. It allowed people to have freedom of mobility. No longer were they limited to living near natural water supplies. They could live almost anywhere. They would just drill a well, outfit it with a pump, and build themselves a dwelling close to this brand-new water delivery system. Imagine how life changed. You could have water for all of your needs, right outside your house.

But it didn't stop there. It got even better. Mankind's ingenuity advanced so far that they were able to drill a well, build a house near the well, and then position a pump in the center of the kitchen sink. Imagine the convenience and time savings. Families could have water in their kitchens. It was no longer necessary to walk to the town center or even outside to get water. To have all of the life-giving water necessary, you only needed to walk to the kitchen and prime the pump. People could live almost anywhere with convenient access to water. What could be better than that?

As always, mankind's resourcefulness kept advancing. Soon it became impractical and inconvenient to have only one source of water in the house. Though it was certainly better than having to go to a community well, it became labor intensive to go to the kitchen sink and pump by hand all the water needed to run a household. So, with the invention of electricity, a new and far better way was developed. An electric-powered pump was fitted to the well and was able to force water through pipes that led to sinks, bathtubs, and showers strategically placed in rooms throughout the house. Of course, this also allowed for the advent of indoor restrooms. Through these technological advancements, the world was changing.

Of course, the point here becomes obvious. Though water is delivered in a very different way today than in the past, there is nothing different about the water. Our modern faucets are just a different delivery system from yesterday's hand pumps. The water is the essential value. We need water to survive. Because both systems provide the means for people to have the water needed for life, neither system is right or wrong. However, it is obvious that one system is preferable to the other.

As we've seen, water beautifully represents the truth. Both are essential to life. And just as water needs a delivery system, so does truth. Culture is the delivery system for truth. If we don't understand this, we start worshipping and valuing the wrong things. As we saw in the water illustration, the delivery system can change, but the water doesn't change. Likewise, the truth doesn't change.

The delivery system doesn't matter. What matters is that the truth, like water, gets to people in the most effective way possible. The truth is vital to their survival. As water is useless if it is unreachable, God's truth (with the power to produce and sustain spiritual life) is useless if a person can't reach it. Therefore, truth must be accessible for its value to be experienced.

There is absolutely nothing about water that comes from a hand pump that makes it better than water that comes through a faucet. Nothing. The same is true in regard to truth. There is nothing better about the truth delivered through older cultural expressions. The reality is that culture is only a means for delivering truth. As long as the truth remains pure, the delivery method does not matter. The only value in the delivery system is its effectiveness at delivering the truth to people.

So if the church is concerned about getting God's truth to people, they should ask, what is the best delivery system available today? However, it isn't this easy for many churches. They believe that the way the truth is delivered is as important, if not more so, as the truth itself. If we're honest, this thought process is crazy. Think about it. Wouldn't it have been ludicrous for people, when the pump was invented, to say, "No! You can't use the pump to deliver water. In fact, it's wrong. You must deliver water the way God intended. We're supposed to get down on our hands and knees in the mud and put our faces down in that water. If we don't do that, I'm quite sure we'll go to hell because of it"?

> **Truth must be accessible for its value to be experienced.**

Or can you imagine, after the invention of indoor plumbing, somebody saying, "I will never use that newfangled contraption. I'm a pump guy. If it was good enough for my parents, then it's good enough for me. In fact, I believe that anyone who uses that indoor plumbing stuff is anti-God"? This would be laughable.

Yet this is exactly how many Christians and churches, in the name of Jesus, think about delivering God's truth. They're basically saying, "If you move from the pump to the faucet, it's wrong!" How sad. Think about how ridiculous it is that people think it's wrong to deliver the truth through a different delivery system—through a different culture. It's not wrong. The only possible wrong could be in refusing to get God's truth to people through the best available delivery system. Yet some Christians and churches continue to attack, judge, and condemn other Christians and churches simply for using an indoor faucet instead of a hand pump to spread the water of God's truth.

J. Hudson Taylor: Change Without Compromise

A famous missionary, J. Hudson Taylor, had to face the same skewed thinking in the late 1800s. He started the China Inland Missions in order to help open up China to God's truth and hope. He had originally aligned himself with a typical mission society of his day. However, he found that they were seeking to deliver the truth through an ineffective delivery system. They were trying to reach the Chinese as they would reach the English. The missionaries were dwelling in compounds among the English rather than living among the Chinese people. They dressed, spoke, ate, and acted English. J. Hudson Taylor found this to be ridiculous. He thought it was vitally important, if they were going to reach the Chinese, to become like the Chinese. So he started growing his hair out and dressing like them.

As a result, he was not accepted by many of his fellow missionaries. It seems bizarre that people claiming to love, follow, and serve Jesus would reject a fellow believer for doing what Jesus did. After all, Jesus left heaven, took on the nature of the people

He came to reach, and adopted the culture and language of those people to effectively deliver God's truth. But the religious people of Jesus' day had Him killed for it. Come to think of it, maybe it doesn't seem all that bizarre that people would be critical of J. Hudson Taylor.

In the end, he started his own mission to reach the Chinese people. It became the policy of the mission to speak their language and identify with their culture because that was the appropriate delivery system for truth in that world. And, though he was maligned by many, his mission became unbelievably successful.

> **We're missing generations of people who desperately need Christ. And it must stop!**

Of course, this explains a lot of the junk that's going on "in the name of Jesus" today. A lot of traditional Christians are criticizing churches that seek to communicate God's truth in the language of this culture. The amazing thing is that many who are doing the blasting would proclaim love and admiration for J. Hudson Taylor. But if they had lived in J. Hudson Taylor's day, they would have blasted him.

This shouldn't surprise us. We have to understand that this is a common problem. By nature, we tend to focus on and value the wrong things. We value the delivery system that was used to reach us with God's truth. We start loving the hand pump, and when someone tries to take the pump out and put in faucets, we started screaming in bloodcurdling fashion, "Don't take my pump from me!" We might as well be singing "Great Is Thy Faithfulness, O Pump, to Me" or "Amazing Pump, How Sweet the Sound." When we do this, we're valuing the delivery system more than we value God and His truth. This is hurting a lot of people and churches. We're missing generations of people who desperately need Christ. And it must stop!

Jesus Was Culturally Relevant

Though these concepts may seem new to you, they aren't. Jesus dealt with the same stuff we're dealing with as we try to communicate truth in the language of the culture. He was called Satan. He was despised. He was hated. He was rejected. He was put on a cross and left to die. Why? Because He took God's truth and delivered it to people through a different system than the religious leaders who were bound by tradition. He sought to communicate God's truth in the language of His culture. Jesus communicated God's truth with doctrinal integrity and cultural relevance. He never changed or polluted the truth, but He significantly changed the way it was being communicated. He communicated in the language of the people of His day. He was culturally relevant.

In John 14:7–9, Jesus told Philip and the other disciples, "Anyone who has seen me has seen the Father." This was His purpose. He came to reveal the Father. So how did Jesus accomplish this?

He Left His Comfort Zone

First, Jesus left His comfort zone, heaven, and came to earth. Talk about a change in culture. Jesus left His paradise—everything He knew, deserved, and enjoyed—in order to communicate and reveal the Father and truth to us. He changed His entire world to reach out to those who had rejected Him. Wow! But the church today isn't willing to give up their comfortable world in order to deliver the message of His love and hope to their peers in this world. It's unforgivable.

He Dressed Like the Culture

Second, Jesus chose to reveal the Father by becoming culturally relevant to the people of His day. He dressed like those in His culture. Remember, we're talking about God here. Yet He didn't dress up in clothes that set Him apart as different or unapproach-able, as the religious leaders of the day did. He dressed in a way that clearly identified Him with the common man.

Unfortunately, many Christians and churches today have decided to mold themselves after the religious leaders of His day rather than Jesus Himself. They insist that spiritual people dress up, wearing suits and ties, fine dresses, or even robes. Of course, there is nothing inherently wrong with any of these. But there is noth-ing inherently right about them either. Our wardrobe decisions should never be influenced by historical or traditional expecta-tions. As long as the principle of modesty has been addressed, what we wear should be influenced by what best helps us to com-municate God's truth to the people in our sphere of influence.

He Spoke the Language of the Culture

Jesus spoke the language of those in His culture. He didn't insist on speaking heaven's language or some religiously accepted language. He came to reveal God to mankind. The world already thought that God was aloof, distant, unapproachable, and difficult if not impossible to know. He wanted to correct those misnomers. He wanted to break down the barriers. Why would He have cho-sen to communicate in a way that upheld them? But this is exactly how many Christians and churches present God—in a language that makes Him seem aloof, distant, unapproachable, and difficult if not impossible to know. No wonder people have concluded that God is irrelevant and the church is a waste.

Jesus walked, talked, worked, and lived with those in His culture. Of course, more often than not, Christians today isolate themselves from those who don't know God. They only know and associate with other Christians. Unfortunately, this makes it impossible for them to be "light in darkness." Of course, Christians do have to be aware of their own weaknesses. (Yes, we do have them.) The Bible makes it clear that "bad company corrupts good character" (1 Corinthians 15:33). It also warns us about joining ourselves too closely to those who don't embrace Christ and His values (2 Corinthians 6:14). However, this is speaking of our most intimate and influential relationships. This isn't a command for us to isolate ourselves from all who don't know Christ. The reality is that there's no way to do this and follow the example of Christ. Jesus revealed the Father's love to those who were broken, guilty, and far from God. He didn't isolate Himself from them, nor should His followers today.

The fact that Jesus dressed like those in His culture, spoke the language of those in His culture, and walked and lived with those in His culture, ticked off the Pharisees. They didn't condescend to the level of common men. They were better than that. It was beneath their indignity. Isn't that interesting? The One who had dignity chose to walk with those who had no dignity. Those who had been born in sin and had no dignity of their own chose to feign dignity. Unfortunately, many who claim to represent Him today tend to do the same. When this happens, the charade destroys their ability to reveal God's love and hope to real people desperately in need of it.

Unfortunately, the comparison between the religious leaders of Jesus' time and much of modern-day Christianity doesn't reveal much discrepancy. An eerie example of this is seen in Matthew 9:10–13: "While Jesus was having dinner at Matthew's house, many tax collectors and 'sinners' came and ate with him and his disciples. When the Pharisees saw this, they asked his disciples, 'Why does your teacher eat with tax collectors and "sinners"?' On hearing this, Jesus said, 'It is not the healthy who need a doctor, but the sick. But go and learn what this means: "I desire mercy, not sacrifice." For I have not come to call the righteous, but sinners.'"

Sadly, this is the same kind of attitude that many Christians and churches have today about those who are seeking to reach out to the lost, hurting, and broken people of our world. As Jesus Himself said, the Pharisees were committed more to their traditions than to God's truth. Regrettably, many churches are in the same place today. If we're going to be used by God to get the church working right, we can't follow them—no matter who they are. We have to follow Jesus.

Paul Was Culturally Relevant

This is certainly what the apostle Paul did. He clearly patterned his ministry after Jesus. Paul communicated God's truth with doctrinal integrity and cultural relevance throughout his ministry and teaching. As I've already expressed earlier in the book, Paul clearly taught this value in 1 Corinthians 9:19–23. However, a great example of how he practiced it is found in Acts 17. In this passage, Paul proclaimed Christ to the philosophers in Athens. He spoke to them on their level and in their language. He was clearly relevant in the way he addressed them. But his purposeful relevance didn't water down his message. They listened to him and understood, and some of them accepted Christ. They were eternally changed because he spoke God's truth relevantly and without compromise.

The Church Is to Be Culturally Relevant

Christians today have no excuse for not communicating God's truth in a culturally relevant way. Not only do they have the example of Christ and Paul, but it's the clearly expressed command God gave us in 2 Corinthians 5:18–20: "All this is from God, who reconciled us to himself through Christ and gave us the ministry of reconciliation: that God was reconciling the world to himself in Christ, not counting men's sins against them. And he has committed to us the message of reconciliation. We are therefore Christ's ambassadors, as though God were making his appeal through us. We implore you on Christ's behalf: Be reconciled to God." According to this passage, we're called to help people reconcile to God. Our God-given assignment is to be ambassadors.

Therefore, when the church doesn't do everything in its power to communicate God's truth to real people in a relevant way, as Jesus did, it is committing a crime against all those for whom Jesus died. It's committing a crime against Jesus Himself. Jesus died on the cross to provide hope to the world, the hope that all Christians experience by grace, and the church is called to reveal it to the world. When we don't, we are criminally negligent.

Though this may sound harsh to some, it is God's truth, not mine. In Ezekiel 3:18–19, God said, "When I say to a wicked man, 'You will surely die,' and you do not warn him or speak out to dissuade him from his evil ways in order to save his life, that wicked man will die for his sin, and I will hold you accountable for his blood. But if you do warn the wicked man and he does not turn from his wickedness or from his evil ways, he will die for his sin; but you will have saved yourself." And Paul, in Acts 20:26–27, clearly revealed this truth to the church: "I declare to you today that I am innocent of the blood of all men. For I have not hesitated to proclaim to you the whole will of God."

> The Pharisees were committed more to their traditions than to God's truth. Regrettably, many churches are in the same place today.

In today's terms, if we don't share with people about their need for God's forgiveness and hope, God will hold us accountable. In light of this truth, I believe blood is on the hands of many churches today, because they care too much about their beloved "hand pumps" to deliver God's truth to people in a way they can honestly understand. We will be held accountable.

There are a lot of obstacles that keep Christians and the church from doing everything possible to share God's truth and hope with the world. The fear of loss seems to be the most common. Pastors feel they will lose their jobs, church members, and even friends if they press the church in ways they aren't comfortable going. Christians fail to share Christ in the marketplace for fear that they'll lose their position, respect, or status. Church people don't seek to move the church forward by reaching people because they're afraid they'll lose their comfortable church to strangers and strange ways. But to be honest, I'd rather lose all these things and have Jesus celebrate me than to keep them all and hear Him tell me that I blew it.

Intersecting Responsibilities

When the church is following the example of Christ and fulfilling its God-given assignment to share God's truth, lives will be changed. As John 8:32 makes clear, when people know the truth, the truth sets them free. However, in order for people to know the truth and experience this life change, they must first genuinely hear and understand the truth. And then they must personally apply and act upon it.

The process of life change stems from the intersection of a twofold responsibility: the church's and the nonbeliever's.

The Church's Responsibility

The first responsibility falls to the church. The church must help them to hear and understand the truth. All Christians, and thus all churches, have been given the responsibility to help those who don't know God's love, hope, or truth to hear about and understand them. As Romans 10:14 says, "How, then, can they call on the one they have not believed in? And how can they believe in the one of whom they have not heard? And how can they hear without someone preaching to them?" Simply put, there's only one way for people to discover God. Those who know Him must do whatever it takes to introduce Him to those who don't. The church must organize itself to make God's truth both clear and understandable to those who don't yet know it. The church must follow Christ in doing whatever it takes to make this happen, even if it means leaving their comfort zone. This is the clear responsibility of the church.

Regrettably, for most of my Christian life, I believed differently. Through the words and actions of those who had spiritual influence in my life, I was led to believe that it was the church's responsibility to isolate itself from culture rather than to integrate with it. I was led to believe that being culturally relevant was wrong, even sinful. As a result, when I first went into ministry, I started proclaiming and practicing this myself. However, as I started studying God's Word and the life of Christ, I realized that much of what I'd been taught was contrary to everything God said and Jesus did. In fact, what I'd been taught was closer to the Pharisees than to Jesus. So I decided to stop believing what I'd been told, and I recommitted myself to becoming a student and follower of Christ Himself. I wanted my life and ministry to be an extension of God's truth rather than the Christian culture I had inherited. In so doing, I found that truth and Christian culture were often in serious conflict. Rather than being driven by love, forgiveness, freedom, desire, faith, and hope, many churches appeared to be driven by contempt, blame, bondage, duty, doubt, and despair. It was and is sad. It was a clear indication that these believers weren't genuinely experiencing the truth of Christ that set people free. And this being the case, how could they effectively share that truth with others?

As I dug into the reasons for this disheartening circumstance, I found that it was the simple result of misplaced values and priorities. Rather than valuing and aggressively seeking to help others know and understand the truth, they had become enamored with their means of delivering the truth. They had fallen in love with the hand pump.

The problem with this is clear. The truth, like water, is essential to life. The value is not found in the way it's delivered; it's found in making sure it is delivered. By whatever means, it's the church's responsibility to help people hear and understand God's truth. This, of course, demands that we have genuinely heard and understood it. I believe, unfortunately, that too many haven't. On the contrary, they're spouting what they learned twenty years ago as an extension of their Christian culture, instead of genuinely sharing the truth that God's Word is still relevant today. For the church to be what God intends, the hope of the world, this must change.

> **We must leave our comfort zone and go to those who need God's hope.**

The Nonbeliever's Responsibility

The second responsibility falls to the nonbeliever. Even when the church faithfully discharges its responsibility, there is no guarantee that people will experience God's love, forgiveness, freedom, and hope. After all, the nonbeliever still has a choice. Once the truth has been made clear and understandable, it becomes the nonbelievers' responsibility to apply it to their lives. As James 1:22 says, "Do not merely listen to the word, and so deceive yourselves. Do what it says." Once they hear and understand it, they must act on it.

Four Keys to Cultural Relevance

Here's the issue that the church doesn't seem to understand: the church's responsibility comes first. Some churches expect people to become acceptable to the church before they are willing to share the truth with them. This is inexcusable. Imagine if Jesus had done this to us. We would have never discovered His hope or known His forgiveness. The truth is that Jesus had to leave heaven, become relevant to us, and then seek us out; or we would have never had a chance. The same is true for the church—we must make the first move, just as Jesus did. We must leave our comfort zone and go to those who need God's hope. We must communicate God's truth to their lives in a relevant way. We must deliver the water to the desert where the people are living without water. The world is dying of thirst, not because there is no water, but because the church refuses to deliver it to them in a way they can get it.

This needs to change. For the church to work, it must embrace and employ a relevant delivery system for making God's truth clear and understandable in the twenty-first century. In other words, the church must learn to communicate God's truth in a relevant way, which it can do by following four major keys.

Key #1: Environment

The environment that people find and experience in a church is vitally important to whether or not they consider it relevant. There are many aspects that go into creating the environment of a church. Décor, dress, attitude, mood, excitement, and expectancy among the people all play a huge part in shaping the environment. One of the things I love to hear from guests in our church is, "I have never been in a church that obviously cares so much about strangers as this one does." Wow! Talk about relevance. And this is an environment issue. I have walked into some churches where I immediately knew that not only was I not accepted but I wasn't welcome. More than likely, you've had the same experience. Environment has a lot to do with relevance.

Key #2: Style

When it comes to the matter of styles of worship and service, I strongly believe that it's up to the mature Christ-followers to sacrifice for the lost, rather than the other way around. But this isn't how most churches are structured. Most churches are built around pleasing the most mature Christians. Why? Because they're the ones who do the giving. But playing to the money, instead of our God-given purpose, kills the church every time. It keeps people from seeing the real Jesus. Remember, Jesus gave and sacrificed Himself for those who gave Him nothing. The church must do the same. The insiders must give and sacrifice themselves for the outsiders. When they do, eventually the outsiders find the hope of Christ and become insiders themselves. But this cannot happen without the sacrifice of the current insiders. This is the reason the church needs to organize and structure to please Christ and Christ alone. There are several ways a church can become culturally relevant in style.

Music. The style of music used in a church tells a person whether the message is relevant to them. This is the reason young people often feel that church is irrelevant. Their music language is not represented in the church. This is a big deal because the language of the culture is significantly influenced by the younger generation. The church must work hard to make sure they are utilizing music that is relevant to the younger generation and that they have young people performing it. Because musical styles are perpetually changing, churches need to be consciously and consistently transitioning musically. If they don't, they will find that they're not reaching the younger generation, the future of the church.

Many Christians don't like this idea. I've actually heard professing Christ-followers say, "If people want to come to our church, let them learn to like our music. Why should we have to use their music?" Once again, I'm thankful this wasn't Jesus' attitude. Can you imagine Him saying, "Father, if people want to come to heaven, let them find their own way here. Why should I have to go down to where they are?"

Presentation. Style also has to do with presentation of ministry. For example, we're living in a very visual age. We're no longer an auditory age. Television has totally transformed the paradigm for communication. Having grown up with *Sesame Street* and MTV, the younger generations have developed a need for constant and rapidly changing visual stimulation. The majority of people today learn visually. Therefore, if we're not stimulating people visually, we're not connecting with them. The world and its learning style have changed. If the church is going to fulfill our obligation to help them both hear and understand the truth, we must help them to see the truth.

Story. Story is another aspect of style. Once again, because of the significant influence of television in our lives, most people now learn more through stories than lectures. Therefore, if a teacher utilizes story, she will more than likely create a deeper and more significant connection of the truth in people's lives. Of course, this fits a biblical paradigm because the Bible is filled with stories. In order to build off of this, our church uses drama, personal stories (both live and with video), and, at times, relevant and appropriate film clips.

Passion. Style is also seen in passion. Yet many churches today seem absolutely dispassionate. This explains why people think church is irrelevant. If it's not worth getting excited about, then it's not worth attending. How sad that people paint their faces, wear bizarre outfits, and make fools out of themselves to support and cheer on their favorite sports team. But when it comes to supporting and celebrating the One who died and then came back from the dead, churches can be so dispassionate. What's really distressing is that these dispassionate churches tend to condemn the passionate churches.

In the church I pastor, the one unmistakable characteristic is passion. In fact, it sets us apart. People who attend our church know we genuinely believe the message we're communicating. We leave no doubt about it. Doesn't this make sense? If Jesus genuinely rose from the dead, how could those who follow Him be dispassionate? I can only believe that God wants His church doing what He and the angels are doing in heaven. Luke 15:7 says, "I tell you that in the same way there will be more rejoicing in heaven over one sinner who repents than over ninety-nine righteous persons who do not need to repent." He wants us passionately celebrating . . . even partying.

Just before a recent baptism time in our church, we performed the song that is often played in sports arenas to celebrate the home team: "Let's Get It Started." As I'm sure you can imagine, there were interesting reactions to such a high-energy song. Following the song, I introduced baptism this way: "I imagine for some of you that was the most unexpected experience you'd had in church. In fact, some may even wonder about its appropriateness. And yet, all over the world in sports arenas, that song is used to celebrate an event that will mean nothing ten seconds after the event is over. Whereas what we're celebrating today, lives eternally changed through faith in Jesus Christ, will have significance for all eternity. We passionately believe that this event is more worthy of high-energy celebration than any sporting event in any arena around the world. So, let's get it started in here . . ."

After that, the mood changed significantly and people started celebrating that which God celebrates. Though I'm sure not everyone leaned into our service that day, they had no doubt that we were passionate about our faith. Passion really does relate to the need for meaning in life, and it draws others to consider whether Christ might be able to generate the same passion for them.

Method of Relating to People. Style is also reflected by how we relate to people . . . relationally or authoritatively. In the post–World War II years, we lived in an authoritarian culture. Partially because of the significant military influence, people were used to a vertical structure of authority in almost every arena of life. Generals told soldiers what to do, and bosses told employees what to do. Few people thought in terms of shared ownership. They expected to be told what to do and how to do it. And they knew better than to ask why.

This vertical or authoritarian approach to life was carried into the church. Pastors tended to preach at people rather than talk to them. The message usually told them what to do, but never addressed why it was important to do it. The church had a top-down structure. This style is obvious in the design of many church buildings. When I was originally called to the church I now pastor, I inherited a building designed for an authoritative style of relating to people. The auditorium was designed to preach at people. It was narrow and long with a significant space between the people and the pastor. The platform was high so the pastor could stand above the people. When the pastor mounted the platform and stood behind the large, cross-shaped pulpit, he immediately had authority. The pastor also sat on the platform, looking out at the people until it was time to speak. This clearly set him apart and gave the appearance of authority. All of this made cultural sense in that day. It was a relevant style.

However, our world is very different. We live in a more relational or horizontal world. So when I had the privilege of participating in the design of our new auditorium, I envisioned a different kind of space. I wanted to communicate with people rather than speak at them, and we designed the auditorium to be wide and shallow. Though a large auditorium, it allows me to see every eyeball in the place. We also lowered the platform to a more reasonable height. Though it's raised in order to provide sight lines, it isn't designed to impress. And, of course, I would never sit on the platform during a part of the service I wasn't involved in. This would create an unneeded distraction and wrongly communicate that I was the center of attention.

But this doesn't mean that I'm better than the pastors who led in the past. It's a simple issue of style. It's vital that we communicate in a style that is relevant to the culture in which we're living. Sadly, many churches cling to the authoritarian style as if it were biblical. It's not. The real issue is effectively communicating God's truth.

> **Most people today need to be talked to rather than preached at.**

If your church's style is one of preaching at people, this may explain why people aren't listening. By virtue of their culture, most people today need to be talked to rather than preached at. Of course, there will be those who say, "This is the way Jesus did it." They are wrong. The truth is that Jesus used a far more relational style. In fact, He never stood on a platform. He wasn't known for screaming. He didn't talk over people's heads. On the contrary, He generally used stories from their everyday lives to which they could relate. He didn't put Himself over others. In fact, He made it clear that He came to serve. Even though He was God, He led with love and by example. Jesus was relational. And He called us to be the same. Think about His words in John 13:35: "By this all men will know that you are my disciples, if you love one another." By moving toward a more relational ministry, we're becoming more like Christ. In our culture, we're certainly becoming more relevant.

Key #3: Language

Along with environment and style, language is another key to communicating with relevance. If we're going to genuinely reach people, we have to speak in the language of the day. I have to be careful to not use the language of generations gone by, my religious upbringing, or my education. I need to use the language of today. As with Jesus, I can't speak the language I'm most comfortable with. I must speak the language that's going to be most effective at making God's truth clear and understandable.

Now, if my goal in preaching were to impress people, then I would use words that no one understood. Words that made it clear I was smarter and better educated than most others. However, that's not my goal. In light of Jesus' example, my goal is to reveal God to people. It's my job to help make God more real and understandable. If I use language that's irrelevant to or over the heads of people, I'm making God more difficult to comprehend. I'm making God appear to be aloof, out of touch, or irrelevant to their lives.

The church needs to speak the language of the culture, so they will think about Jesus and their relationship with Him. But with language changing as quickly as it is, this requires a significant commitment. As with the learning of any new language, you may occasionally make a fool of yourself. When I visited Korea, I was taught a couple of key words. Though difficult for me to pronounce, I tried. Of course, more often than not, I blew it. However, it was obvious to me that the people appreciated the effort. I have found the same to be true in seeking to learn and communicate in the language of today's culture.

For example, one time I decided to use a popular phrase in today's language. I don't remember exactly what I was talking about, but it involved something that pertained to perpetual activity. So I said, "This is a 7/24 issue, man." Of course, the whole church started laughing . . . not with me but at me. My kids shrank down in their seats and wanted to disappear. After the service, they told me, "Dad, it's 24/7, not 7/24. Get with it."

It's difficult to continually learn and grow in our understanding of the language of this culture. Yet if we're going to connect with people today, we need to speak their language. And, for those who think this is pandering to the masses, let me remind you of two realities. First, Jesus died for the masses (John 3:16). Second, God gave the majority of the New Testament to us not in classical Greek but in common Greek—the language of the masses. Was He pandering? No. He wanted His Word accessible to everyone. And so should His church.

Though it makes ministry more difficult, at our church we go to great lengths to make sure we're communicating God's truth in the language of our culture. The reason for this is simple. Our purpose is not to make ministry as easy as possible; it's to make it as relevant and effective as possible. Because the language of this culture leans so heavily on the visual, we spend a great deal of time creating relevant video support for our services and message. Since music is a huge part of language, we work hard to use music to communicate to the issues of the message being presented. In talking about style, I mentioned that we do drama. It allows people to experience the importance of the truth that I'm addressing in any given talk. We spend a great deal of time developing stage designs that create a visual context and support to the metaphors that I highlight as I'm speaking.

This takes a lot of work and a lot of time. Obviously, I can't be writing my talks the night before I'm going to give them. We have to work weeks and sometimes months ahead. It's not easy. Many of us sacrifice a great deal to make this happen. And, of course, we've been asked, "Why in the world would you go to all this trouble?" to which I answer, "Because one of the problems with the church is that it isn't going to enough trouble to introduce people to God's truth. We believe all of this work is worth it if we can get people to focus on and understand the fact that God loves them, Jesus Christ came to save them, and there is hope." We will go to almost any length to connect this truth to people's lives. We do this because we're Christ-followers and Jesus went to the greatest length to make this truth possible. We do this because the stakes are eternal.

Key #4: Need

There is one last foundational key to relevance: need. Simply put, a church service, ministry, or message is not relevant unless it is helpful or meaningful in real life. It must address or meet a need that real people are facing. One of the reasons so many churches are irrelevant is that they're off track. They don't design services or speak to what's happening in people's lives; they are concerned with a church calendar or a predesigned liturgy. They follow traditions without consideration of today's problems. The sad reality is that in churches all over the world, the services and messages are answering questions that nobody is asking.

Think about it. When the adulterous woman was thrown at Jesus' feet, He didn't follow some predetermined Scripture-reading format or liturgy. He addressed the issue at hand. He spoke to the religious leaders' arrogant condemnation, and He spoke to her need. He spoke the perfect words that she needed to hear: "Woman, where are they? Has no one condemned you?" "No one, sir," she said. "Then neither do I condemn you," Jesus declared. "Go now and leave your life of sin" (John 8:10–11). She listened, and her life was changed.

God Is Relevant to People's Needs

The church needs to clearly communicate how God's Word addresses the meaningful issues of life people are experiencing today.

A church that is working right must communicate God's truth in the language of the culture. To fail in this is to compromise.

People need to know that God is relevant to their need . . . whatever it is. This is one of the reasons we use secular music in our church. We don't use it because we think it'll make us cool or more acceptable. We use it because it helps us to address in powerful and relevant terms the needs that people have when they're living their lives without God. You see, those who write and perform secular music were created and gifted by God to express, in artistic and powerfully engaging ways, what they're communicating. Yet more often than not, they're living lives of emptiness without God. No one is better equipped to communicate the conflicts and hurts of life on this planet without God than these artists. By using their songs, we're able to identify the needs, conflicts, emptiness, hurts, and loneliness of life without God. Then I'm able to step into that need with the solution—God's truth. The reality is that God's truth provides the answers for all of the conflicts that humans experience without God. We use the music to introduce the conflict, and we use God's Word to communicate the solution. The impact is astounding.

Though we must speak the culture's language, we must never buy their message.

In one particular service, we used Joan Osborne's song "(What If God Was) One of Us." In this song, she's crying out in disillusionment for a god that she can relate to and that relates to her. From the lyrics, it's clear that religion has hurt and disillusioned her. Religion has made God seem distant, unapproachable, uncaring, and irrelevant. So, in the context of the song, she ponders the idea of a God that is close and understands our pain. It's a song of desperation. It's a song that relates to most people's desire for God. After the song was performed in one of our services, I talked about the one true God and how different He is from the god of religion. The one true God is not distant, unapproachable, uncaring, or irrelevant. In fact, He did become one of us. With absolute relevance, I was able to address that common need and to relate to that shared desperation by pointing them to Jesus. This was a powerful moment because it allowed for us to contradict the normal misconception about God. It was powerful because it was truth addressing a genuine need. It was relevant.

However, it's equally important to know that, though we must speak the culture's language, we must never buy their message. On the contrary, we need to use their language to condemn their message. As 1 John 2:15–17 says, "Do not love the world or anything in the world. If anyone loves the world, the love of the Father is not in him. For everything in the world—the cravings of sinful man, the lust of his eyes, and the boasting of what he has and does—comes not from the Father but from the world. The world and its desires pass away, but the man who does the will of God lives forever."

Relevance Is Different for Different People

The church's purpose is to reveal God's truth and hope to a lost and dying world. In order to do this, the church, like Jesus, must be relevant. But it must be understood that relevance is going to be different in each culture and in every generation. It's also going to be different to the various groups, personalities, and generations of people in the same culture. Often, the church misses this reality. In every given culture, there are many different segments of diversity. So, in any given church, there must be ministries that seek to communicate and connect relevantly to the many different groups.

In order to illustrate this, let's go back to the water metaphor. Water is essential to life, but it needs a delivery system. The only value the delivery system has is in its ability to deliver the water.

As we've seen, this is a wonderful metaphor of the truth. God's truth is essential for life, but it needs a delivery system. Culture is that delivery system. Therefore, in order to successfully deliver God's truth to people, the church must choose a relevant delivery system. For this reason, we use different delivery systems for the different groups of people in our church.

The "Sippy Cup"

The "sippy cup" is perfect for kids. If we genuinely desire to make God's truth clear and understandable for children, then we must communicate it in a relevant way for them. Kids require a very different delivery system. We have a kids' ministry at our church that connects God's truth to kids. In fact, more often than not, kids are begging their parents to come to church instead of parents begging their kids to come. Why? Because we do kids' ministry on their level. It's relevant to them. In order for the church to deliver God's hope to kids, it must have a relevant kids' ministry. And in case you haven't read any of the recent trade reports, flannelgraph boards aren't the latest technology.

The "Big Gulp"

The "Big Gulp" approach seems perfect for our middle school and senior high students. Teens are different from any other age group. Something happens in the brain during those years to encourage aberrant behavior. Because of this, we have found that for even a little bit of truth to be absorbed into their lives, teens need a Niagara Falls–sized dose of truth. Thus, the best delivery system for them is the "Big Gulp." This is a relevant conduit for students. Our team just keeps pouring out the truth with free refills and, with God's help, we're trusting that some of it will stick. The important point to capture is that ministry to students must be different. The truth is the same, but the delivery system is different.

The "Starbucks Cup"

Then there are adults. There's probably not a more relevant delivery system for adults than Starbucks. Who needs water when there's Starbucks? After all, there's water in there somewhere, right? And you can get your coffee the way you like it. Because adults also come in all shapes and sizes, they need to have ministries shaped to their diverse needs. For this reason, our church has developed diverse ministries for each adult life stage represented in our community, including those who are single, married, divorced, hurting, seeking, grieving, dealing with addictions, faced with special needs, and so on. Because our assignment is to reveal God to people in a way that is relevant to their needs, we have developed ministries that are relevant to all of the potential circumstances of adults in our area. Though it takes a lot of effort and resources, we believe this is our God-given responsibility.

The "Drinking Hat"

Finally, in every culture, there are those unique people who are just a little different from the rest. This group's uniqueness isn't age-based or culture-based. They're just—dare I say it?—bizarre. They range from sports fans to scrapbookers to motorcycle enthusiasts. We've got ministries for these and many more. Since Jesus also loves and died for these people, we have the same obligation to provide a relevant delivery system for their lives. We've found that the double-twelve-ounce "drinking hat" is the perfect metaphor.

Whatever It Takes

There are many possible ways to effectively deliver truth into people's lives. The question should never be, "How do we want to deliver the truth?" or, "How are we most comfortable delivering the truth?" The question should always be, "How do they need the truth delivered?" If someone needs truth delivered in a certain way, remember that Jesus would deliver it that way! However, the depressing reality is that many Christians and churches are proving to be unwilling to follow Jesus. In light of what Jesus has done for us, this should never happen. He said it best in John 13:15–17: "I have set you an example that you should do as I have done for you. I tell you the truth, no servant is greater than his master, nor is a messenger greater than the one who sent him. Now that you know these things, you will be blessed if you do them." Since it's what Jesus did, the church's assignment is to do whatever it takes to relevantly deliver God's truth to people. Whatever it takes.

Whether the church succeeds or fails in helping people to relevantly hear and understand God's truth is vital. It will form the basis for people's view of God. Unfortunately, because so many churches are failing to reveal God for who He is, many are concluding that God is irrelevant to their lives. I can't think of a worse legacy for a Christian or a church. This certainly won't measure up to a "well done" from Jesus.

Think about the seriousness of this. Churches that fail to help people hear and understand God's truth don't get to help them apply it to their lives. In light of Jesus' effort to give people the opportunity to receive forgiveness, a new beginning, fulfillment in life, and hope in death, the church should never fail to force people to make a choice one way or the other. We should create forks in their roads. They should never be able to walk by us and not notice. They should never be able to walk away saying, as I did as a young person, "I don't get it." The church is to be light in darkness, ambassadors revealing God and helping people to hear and understand God's truth. Because so many of us are failing to fulfill our assignment, we need to commit to change the church without compromising God's truth.

The Takeaway

Here's the important takeaway from this chapter: if churches are going to fulfill their God-given purpose of helping people experience life change and hope, then they must fully devote themselves to communicating God's truth with relevance to this world. As Colossians 3:23 says, "Whatever you do, work at it with all your heart, as working for the Lord, not for men."

> Unfortunately, because so many churches are failing to reveal God for who He is, many are concluding that God is irrelevant to their lives.

The evidence suggests that churches are too often devoted to and working for the wrong people and/or the wrong things. It's wrong to be devoted to and/or working for anyone or anything other than God. God has made it clear what He wants His church to be and do. When churches don't measure up to this clear assignment, whatever else may be true of them, they're not devoted to or working for God. And it has to stop. The church is the hope of the world, when it's working right. But it can only be working right when God's purpose for the church is being fulfilled. For this to happen, there are a few decisions that must be made.

Apply God's Truth to Your Life

First, we must decide to continually give our hearts to hearing, understanding, and applying God's truth to our own lives. This is an ongoing and never-ending requirement. I'm in my third decade of pastoring, and I need as much growth today as ever. In fact, the more I grow, the more I understand that I need to grow. Every day of my life I need to get into God's Word and allow it to shape my thinking. If I don't, then my thinking will begin shaping it. This is one of the significant reasons that the church is not working right. Too many Christians, pastors, and church leaders allow their thinking to shape their understanding of God's Word instead of allowing the Word of God to shape their thinking.

This was my problem for many years. I used to fight against some of the very issues I've been promoting in this chapter. Though God's Word and Jesus' example embraced them, my Christian culture rejected them. And I, for a while, was afraid to change my teaching. I was afraid of what people would think of me. This changed when I began reminding myself daily that I am responsible only to an audience of One—the One whom I will one day stand before and give account for my life and ministry. This helped me to get over the fear of rejection by family, friends, or the church I pastored. It no longer mattered. What mattered was fulfilling the assignment that God had given me. Make sure that you're not allowing your thinking to shape the way you live your life and perform your ministry. Allow the Word of God to shape your thinking.

Establish a Culturally Appealing Environment

Second, we must decide to continually give our hearts and energy to shaping the church to communicate God's truth in culturally relevant ways. Since Christians are the church, this is the responsibility of all believers. For this to happen, we need to establish culturally appealing environments, culturally engaging styles, and culturally connecting languages. And we need to make sure we're connecting God's truth to people's needs. When we're doing these things, the church will be relevant. The church will be the hope of the world because it will be working right.

Because of the impact God is allowing our church to make in people's lives, I receive a lot of correspondence. The number one thought shared in these letters is that the church is finally making God and His truth relevant to them. Many of these people had given up on church or even God because of their experiences in an irrelevant church. Now, because they are in a church that strives to communicate God's truth in the language of their culture, they're falling in love with God. Their lives are changing. The only difference is that they finally understand what's being said. To me, this is the point of church. I can't imagine anything less.

Of course, there are a number of key disciplines necessary for learning to communicate God's truth in a culturally relevant way. We must become honest students of God's truth. We can't allow ourselves to continually accept and embrace what we've been told. We must honestly investigate God's truth on our own. We must become students of people. This is the only way to ensure that your ministry is connecting to the genuine needs of people. And finally, we must become students of the culture.

Value God's Truth More than Cultural Forms

Third, we must be careful to not confuse our cultural forms with God's truth. In keeping with our water metaphor, we have to be careful never to confuse the artesian well, hand pump, or faucet with the water. For example, we should understand that hymns and hymnals are a delivery system, not the truth. We are to value the truth but not the delivery system. In the early days of my ministry, when we replaced hymn books with video, I had people sitting me down and passionately proclaiming that I was sinning against God. In response, I would kindly ask what part of God's Word I was violating. Though they continued to call it sin and me a compromiser, they could never identify where it violated or compromised God's truth. They were sincere people who had fallen in love with the "hand pump." Unfortunately, too many church leaders are surrendering to those who have misplaced their values. In so doing, they are compromising for the sake of comfort, peace, or their jobs.

There are so many examples of Christians and churches valuing their cultural forms over God's truth. Though very incomplete, the short list includes the "appropriate" clothing for church, church names, organizational structure, music styles, and service times. There are churches who genuinely believe that not meeting at 11 a.m. on Sunday morning is a compromise. The same is true for many churches with the Sunday evening service. Of course, there's nothing inherently wrong (or right) with either.

If the church is going to live up to its billing as the hope of the world, we must return to our first love.

The reason that 11 a.m. Sunday morning became a popular time for church was so the dairy farmers could attend. Any earlier and they couldn't make it. The question is: how many dairy farmers are in the average church these days? The Sunday evening service was extremely relevant when the church was one of the first buildings in the community to have electric lights. Going to church gave people something to do when it got dark outside. Of course, since the lightbulb, there have been a couple of new inventions to entertain us in the evenings. While there's nothing wrong with a Sunday night service, the original draw is no longer relevant. It is no violation of truth to choose different, and perhaps more effective, times for doing ministry. Since the church has the natural tendency to value its cultural forms more than God's truth, we must be careful to never confuse the two.

Return to Your First Love

Fourth, we must never allow ourselves to love our way of doing ministry more than we love God and seeing lives change. Unfortunately, many churches have fallen in love with the wrong things. As a result, those churches aren't working right. If the church is going to live up to its billing as the hope of the world, we must return to our first love (Revelation 2:4).

Commit to Following Jesus

Finally, we must commit to following Jesus, leaving our comfort zones, and doing whatever it takes to "seek and to save what was lost" (Luke 19:10). Though many Christians and churches protest that we're compromising when we begin changing the church to make it relevant to today's culture, the truth is just the opposite. Those adapting the church culture and language in order to live up to God's truth are not compromising. The compromising is done by the Christians who aren't willing to follow Christ in communicating God's truth in the language of the culture. For comfort, convenience, or fear, they are disobeying God's Great Commission to the church. We are to be going into the world, not isolating from it, in order to make disciples (Matthew 28:19–20).

My prayer is that the church will once again be what God designed it to be—the hope of the world. For this to happen, those of us who love and follow Him must commit to better execution. This will require changing the church without compromising God's truth. It can happen. I've experienced it. Though it's not easy, I can assure you that it is worth it.

However, this is where the fight for the soul of the church begins. There are many who refuse to consider the legitimacy of the truths I've presented in this chapter. They will fight to keep the church everything they want it to be without thought for what God wants it to be. They will fight the changes in the church as fiercely as my old friends tried to fight the changes in my life after I followed Christ. But this is no reason to pull back.

The good news is that there is hope for any church, regardless of the circumstances. Our church's transition story proves it, and if it could happen at our church, it can happen anywhere.

PART 2

start the wave

CHAPTER 5

You Gotta Be Crazy

The Right Leader

Through my experiences, I have realized that transitioning a church is like turning around a huge ship. This has helped me maintain the patience required to give change a fighting chance. Too many people try to change the church in the same way you turn a small automobile—quickly. You cannot turn a church like that. As with a huge ship, the structure of a church can't handle a quick turn. Rather, it requires a long and intentional turn. The ship's wheel must be held in the turn position until the rudder is finally able to get the traction necessary to totally turn the vessel. If you've seen the movie *Titanic*, you can picture the problem. They were headed for an iceberg. They tried to turn that ship as quickly as possible in order to miss it. The problem was that they didn't start the turn with enough time to successfully negotiate the turn. It takes time to turn a huge ship. When you attempt to turn it too quickly, the odds are that it will end in disaster.

The same reality is true with the church. What so many miss is that transitioning a church that is failing to one that is succeeding requires an intentional process. Too many pastors and church leaders, when they realize they need to change, start spinning the ship's wheel and making quick changes. They attend a conference or see a successful church model and decide to start doing church that way . . . overnight!

Though predictable, they're surprised when it ignites World War III in the church. Instead of helping the church, the swift change hurts it. In fact, more often than not, these sincere attempts to help do irreparable damage. It usually ends with the church seeing change as the enemy and going on the defensive. As a result, they put on a full-court press against any suggestion of change in the future. After all, they've tried it and it doesn't work. Seeking change without working the essential principles for successful change will almost always result in a church entrenching itself against change. This robs the church of God's pleasure and the world of God's hope.

Therefore, when seeking to transition a church, we must do everything in our power to ensure success. The ten principles I present in the next three parts of the book are the principles for successfully turning the ship's wheel of the church. These principles have been learned through trial, error, and failure. I'm sharing them so that you don't have to learn them the hard way, as I did. Remember, the issue isn't speed. The issue is getting to your God-given destination. This requires getting your hands on the ship's wheel and turning the church toward God's clearly expressed destination. It's time to start properly executing His well-conceived plan. Applying these principles will help you and your church avoid becoming part of another disaster story. Of course, as a ship navigating treacherous waters requires the right captain, so the transitioning church needs the right leader.

Starting the Wave

When turning a ship or transitioning a church, there's nothing more important than momentum. I like to compare this with "the wave." Undoubtedly, you've seen people do the wave at a sporting event. Living near Ann Arbor, Michigan, I have the occasional privilege of attending University of Michigan football games.

Michigan Stadium is one of the largest stadiums in the nation and has been sold out for every home game for decades. Watching football in this setting is a blast. When the wave gets going, the energy in that place is thrilling. During football season, some people adjust their entire lives around being at these games. Who wouldn't want to be part of something that so positively stirs the emotions?

I can't sit in that setting without thinking of the church. In truth, as much as I enjoy and enthusiastically cheer for the Wolverines, the impact of football is temporary at best; whereas the potential impact of the church is eternal. If there is any setting that should be drawing masses of people and getting them jumping to their feet in celebration, it should be the church, the hope of the world. As I have watched and participated in the wave at football games, I have learned some lessons that I have applied in the church setting. And, not surprisingly, they've worked.

The first one is simple. It takes the right leader to start the wave of transition. The fact is that you've got to be a little crazy to start the wave. I've had a front-row seat to seeing the wave begin in a stadium of thousands of people. By watching the end product—a hundred thousand people cheering in a timed sequence almost as beautiful as synchronized swimming—you'd never know how difficult, discouraging, and even dreadful it is to attempt to start the wave. You must be willing to make a fool out of yourself in your attempt to get other people to join you. You also have to be patient. You have to continue hopping up like a mad person until others join you—whether by inspiration or pity. But, if you hang in there, it ultimately takes hold. And it's worth it all. Seeing the wave in action makes the work of starting it more than worthwhile. I have found the same to be true of starting the wave of transition in the church.

It takes the right leader to begin the wave of change without compromise. Of course, the right leader in one setting seldom looks like the right leader in another setting. Effective leadership comes in different forms, personalities, and styles. I've found that this makes identifying the right leader more difficult for both the individual and the church.

Characteristics of the Right Leader

Every successful leader, in the church and in the world, is different. This is one reason that churches have a difficult time determining the right leader for their setting. Although some successful church leaders may appear to be opposites, I have found that there are similar characteristics driving all those who eventually prove to be the right leader. The truth is that I didn't look like the right leader for the church I now pastor. From the outside looking in, I didn't fit. I was antithetical to what they were. I was from the North. They were a Southern-cultured church. I was an irreverent baby boomer who loved coloring outside of the lines. They were a builder-generation church that followed the rules. It didn't seem that I was the right leader. But, as it turns out, I was.

This principle is vital for churches and church leaders. Like it or not, much of what will happen or not happen in the church will stem from the leader. Therefore, if the church is going to transition successfully, it's vital that the pastor be the right leader. Though church leaders will be different from one another in almost every way, the right leader will always embrace some non-negotiable characteristics.

Calling

The first characteristic is *calling*. The right leader to start the wave of transition is the God-called leader. The right leader believes to the core of his being that God has brought him to lead for such a time as this. It's not the calling to fill a position. A position ultimately means nothing. The desire to have or fill a position is not the point.

I had this problem in the early days of my ministry. I thought that if I could be the senior pastor of a large church, life would be good. This was flawed thinking. I have learned that holding a position does not make life good. In fact, it can make life miserable. Just ask any former president of the United States. Position means little. Influence makes a person the leader.

> **It takes the right leader to begin the wave of change without compromise.**

I have found that, in the church, calling is a key to gaining influence. After all, God can keep the most likely person from gaining influence and expand the influence of the least likely one. This was clearly seen when Joshua followed Moses as the leader of Israel. God called Joshua to the task, and though Moses was a tough act to follow, God ordered the events that led to Joshua gaining all the influence he needed to lead. "So the LORD was with Joshua, and his fame spread throughout the land" (Joshua 6:27).

While it doesn't take a calling to lead, a calling is necessary to be the right leader. Now, this doesn't necessarily mean that you will automatically fit the church you're called to lead. Too often, leaders miss their calling because they're looking for the perfect fit. To be honest, the fit is seldom obvious. And this makes sense. The point of transition is for the leader to take the church to new and different places. If the leader appeared to fit the church in its present circumstances, this very likely wouldn't happen.

More often than not, at the time of the calling, the right leader won't appear to fit the church. This means that the right leader won't necessarily be instantly at home, accepted, or comfortable in the church setting. Though I always knew it was the right move, in the beginning I usually didn't feel as though I fit in with the churches I was called to lead.

This was certainly true when I first came to the church I pastor today. Though already the pastor, I was wrestling with the issue of calling. I knew God had called me to pastor this church, but at times I questioned it. I was very much like the father in Mark 9:24 who told Jesus, "I do believe; help me overcome my unbelief!" This incessant questioning of what I already knew was the result of how obvious it was that I didn't fit this church at that time. Though I was putting my entire soul into the church, things weren't going well. Nothing was working. I honestly started to entertain the thought that God was playing a cosmic joke on me.

As I mentioned in chapter 1, during this season of doubt and discouragement, I attended a conference where these thoughts reached their boiling point. I remember the speaker saying something that rocked my world. He made the claim that significant church growth (from a human standpoint) occurs when the story of the pastor fits the story of the church, which fits the story of the community. His claim was that when these three align, a church can grow exponentially. When they don't, the church will struggle.

This put me down for the "ten count." The reality was that I didn't match the church or the community. And the community and the church couldn't have been more at odds. If it wasn't so tragic, it would have been laughable. As I thought through these realities, my grief, misery, and doubt engulfed me. I allowed myself to get trapped in a couple of very negative thoughts. The first was that I was wrong about my calling to this church. This thought really messed me up. If I had been wrong in thinking that I had clearly heard God's voice by coming to this church, how could I ever trust that I was hearing from God in the future? The second was that God was messing with me. This thought had the potential to drive me away from God. I was miserable.

I'll never forget what happened in the wake of this circumstance. I skipped the next session and began doing battle with all of these thoughts. I remember crying out to God for answers. Though it doesn't happen like this very often for me, God spoke directly into my soul as clearly as I've ever heard Him: *Why do you think I called you to this church? I want you to transition it to fit you because I'm going to move the church into a community that will be a perfect fit for both of you. I've called you to lead the church to fulfill My purposes in this generation. So, lead.*

This moment changed my life, ministry, and view of leadership. It wasn't about me. I wasn't called to enjoy the privileges of having a leadership position. I was called to invest the privilege of leadership I'd been given to make a difference for other people. As Jesus said to the first disciples, those who don't know God use the privilege of leadership to benefit themselves. Those who do know and love God are never to do this. They are to use the privilege of leadership to serve others (Matthew 20:25–28). This was a life-changing lesson. God wasn't playing a joke on me, and I wasn't a victim. God was giving me the great privilege of being called to lead. This required that I step out and do just that—lead.

If God is genuinely calling a leader to transition the church, he will be driven from within to do it. It won't be a whim; it will be inescapable. This doesn't mean that the leader will always know what to do, have all the answers, succeed, or be perfect. What a joke. More often than not, the opposite was true in my life. However, the leader who is genuinely called will be driven to figure out what to do, to find the answers, to keep getting up when he fails, and to strive to be the best. This is why I've attended so many conferences and read so much on the church. This is why I'm writing this book and you're reading it. Though we don't know it all, we're driven to know as much as possible in order to successfully lead the church to fulfill God's purposes. And nothing is going to stop us. The right leader demands a calling.

Character

The second nonnegotiable characteristic is *character*. The right leader for successfully starting the wave of transition in a church has to have character. The right leader must be authentic, rightly motivated, and one of integrity.

Too many leaders are trying to transition the church for the wrong reasons. They want change for their own benefit, or to become "somebody" in the kingdom of God. Unfortunately, this will ultimately hurt the church and the leader. Paul beautifully addressed this in Philippians 2:3–9 when he wrote:

> Do nothing out of selfish ambition or vain conceit, but in humility consider others better than yourselves. Each of you should look not only to your own interests, but also to the interests of others. Your attitude should be the same as that of Christ Jesus: Who, being in very nature God, did not consider equality with God something to be grasped, but made himself nothing, taking the very nature of a servant, being made in human likeness. And being found in appearance as a man, he humbled himself and became obedient to death—even death on a cross! Therefore God exalted him.

If you are a child of God, you are already "somebody" in the kingdom of God. You don't need a big or important position to become "somebody." Christians are not somebodies because of what they do. Unfortunately, too many people are grasping at the brass ring of church growth for the wrong reasons. And I can tell you from experience, if you're wrongly motivated, church transition will reveal those motivations. And you won't last.

Wrongly motivated leaders generally leave in the middle of the transition because they can't stand the heat. Since they're in it for themselves, they tend to run away when the circumstances get ugly, which always happens in times of transition. The sad result of their leaving is that the church is ravaged. The concept of change gets blamed for the problems, and the church retreats back to the comfort of irrelevance. And more than likely, they will never take a run at change again. They will adopt the same philosophy in their church that the Israelites expressed to Moses in

If God is genuinely calling a leader to transition the church, he will be driven from within to do it.

Exodus 14:12: "Didn't we say to you in Egypt, 'Leave us alone; let us serve the Egyptians'? It would have been better for us to serve the Egyptians than to die in the desert!"

Character is essential in church leadership for two reasons. The first is that a leader without character will disrupt the church. The Bible is filled with this truth. Proverbs 16:18 says, "Pride goes before destruction, a haughty spirit before a fall." And James 4:6 says, "Scripture says: 'God opposes the proud but gives grace to the humble.'" Another example of this reality is illustrated vividly in the lives of the kings of Israel. Though certainly not perfect, kings who led with integrity ruled the nation better than those who led with conceit. Similarly, a church leader without character will ultimately take the church down with them.

Leaders and churches need to be keenly aware of this reality. It doesn't take character to enjoy the influence of leadership and the attention that comes with standing on a platform in front of people. You can enjoy doing both of these without loving Jesus or the church. You can do these with impure motives. The fact is that all of us have a sin nature that drives us to be the greatest. Yet if we're doing our job properly, people should think that Jesus is the greatest. The right leader has to consistently fight these impure, sinful drives. A leader without character can't and won't fight for integrity, however, and will hurt the church every time.

The second reason is just as critical. People won't follow a leader without character for long. A leader can fool people for a while, but eventually his real character will emerge. Here's the reality: people won't follow a leader they don't respect, and earning respect requires character.

Competence

The third nonnegotiable characteristic is competence. If you're going to be the right leader to lead change without compromise, you need gifts or abilities that lend themselves to leadership. From my experience, there are two primary gifts required for leading a church through transition: leadership and communication.

It is my impassioned belief that the church deserves the best leadership and communication in the world. The church is dealing with eternity. It is a huge pet peeve of mine that business, which only has a temporary influence and impact, expects and receives the most talented and best-trained people in the world. As well, businesses generally demand and fund continued growth for their leaders. On the other hand, the church, which is eternal in influence and impact, tends to get the leftovers and settle for ongoing mediocrity. This is wrong. In my opinion, if we're not continually bettering our leadership and communication skills, we're not the right leaders for the church. If we have less passion for the eternal mission of the church than the average business-person has for her business, we're at least part of the reason for the church's mediocrity.

If we're going to develop these gifts to the best of our ability, then we need to learn from others. This has been key in my leadership and communication. There is no way I would have been capable to lead or communicate at the level required in the transition of our church without others. Everything I know and do as a leader and communicator has been strengthened by others. In fact, I'm learning more now than ever. As our church has grown, the need for my competencies has grown exponentially. The same is true with all leaders. The good news is that there are a lot of helpful resources available for growing in our abilities to lead and communicate. The bad news is that unless we do the hard work of investing ourselves in them, they won't help us. The right leader must continue to develop competence in both of these vital areas.

Now, for those of you performing or contemplating church leadership who don't feel you have both of these gifts, there is still hope. The truth is that few people are built with both high-level gifts of leadership and high-level gifts of communication. This is a unique combination. Leaders tend to be strong in one and weak in the other.

While both gifts are essential to the right leadership existing in the church, they don't necessarily have to be embodied in one person. Often, pastors are more gifted at communication than leadership. In this case, a pastor with the right kind of humility is able to build a support team of leaders for the purpose of setting an appropriate course for moving forward. This works especially well in the church. God has designed it on the principle of one body made up of many people with different gifts. As Romans 12:5–8 says, "So in Christ we who are many form one body, and each member belongs to all the others. We have different gifts, according to the grace given us. . . . If a man's gift is . . . serving, let him serve; if it is teaching, let him teach . . . if it is leadership, let him govern diligently." In light of this truth, a pastor and church leadership team, with the character of genuine humility, can combine their abilities to achieve the kind of leadership and communication necessary to move a church through the whitewater of change. Under these circumstances, the pastor, as the primary spiritual influencer in the church, communicates the agreed-upon vision with appropriate values and passion. In this way, the church is still led well and moves forward.

> **Few people are built with both high-level gifts of leadership and high-level gifts of communication. . . . Leaders tend to be strong in one and weak in the other.**

However, as human nature is a powerful force even among spiritual people, this kind of partnership only works when the character of the participants is in check and commitment to fulfilling the God-given purpose of the church is the goal. For this reason, I strongly believe that there must ultimately be submission to the primary spiritual influencer of the church, the pastor (Hebrews 13:17). Whether this person is the most gifted leader or not, he must be the primary force in the final decisions of vision and direction. The reason is simple: if the pastor does not fully and passionately embrace and communicate the vision to the church, it will not become a reality. This is about practical reality, not power. Church structures that prevent the pastor from being a strong and positive spiritual voice and visionary to the people will not move forward in fulfilling God's purposes for the church.

Confidence

The fourth nonnegotiable characteristic is *confidence*. The right leader, in starting the wave of transition, needs confidence. As important as this quality is to leadership, there is a serious shortage of it among pastors and church leaders. This is a significant problem and explains why so many churches are failing to make a difference in the world.

The problem stems from a faulty, spiritualized view of confidence. Christians have been told that confidence is akin to arrogance. Though this view is absolutely wrong, it is taught in many circles and is robbing the church of the leaders it so desperately needs. In truth, every person who has ever done anything for God required confidence. Confidence in God is the only way to stand in the face of the enemy. At the same time, most of these people who stood confidently for God were accused of selfish ambition and/or arrogance. Moses provided a great example of this. Though obviously called of God and the humblest man on earth (according to Numbers 12:3), he was confident. Once he finally submitted to God's call on his life, he was confident in his leadership. As a result, he was accused of arrogance by other would-be leaders (Numbers 16). In this passage, the Lord clearly vindicated Moses.

The key for determining the difference is found by identifying the source of people's confidence. If their confidence is in themselves, then it is unhealthy confidence, or arrogance. If their confidence is in God, as with Moses, then it is healthy confidence. It is rooted in an understanding of their own weaknesses and faith in God's strength. In 1 Corinthians 15:58, Paul gave us a specific example of how to develop and maintain godly confidence: "Therefore, my dear brothers, stand firm. Let nothing move you. Always give yourselves fully to the work of the Lord, because you know that your labor in the Lord is not in vain." Our confidence should be founded upon God's character and promise. We don't have to cower in the face of anything or anyone, because God will never allow our decision to live for Him to be fruitless or go unrewarded.

When leading the church, especially in times of change, a leader must believe. It is the *only* basis for the needed confidence. The leader must believe that he's the right person, at the right time, doing the right thing. If he doesn't, the leadership will be marred by hesitancy, insecurity, and doubt. These are horrible qualities in a leader. This explains so much of what's happening in the church these days: people don't follow hesitant, insecure leaders into the unknown. They would rather stay put. And this is exactly what's happening in most churches today. They're just staying put. Better to do nothing and go nowhere than to follow an uncertain leader.

This reality became agonizingly clear to me at a pastors' conference I attended early in my ministry. A young pastor was invited to speak. For the first ten minutes of his talk, he basically apologized for being there. He said things like, "I can't believe you've given me the privilege of speaking. Every one of you is more deserving than I am to speak. You have so much more experience than me. I don't even know why I was asked. I should be listening to and learning from you. This is the honor of my very short ministry, and I want to thank you for coming. Though I'm not sure that I can say anything that you don't know already, I'm going to do my best."

I believe two things about what that young guy said. First, he didn't believe a word he was saying. He thought this false humility would buy him influence. Second, he blew any opportunity to make an impact. He lost his audience, because no one listens to a person who has no confidence in what he's saying. And he lost those who saw through his false humility, because no one listens to someone who is disingenuous.

If I've done due diligence in preparing, I always have confidence that what I'm going to say is worth hearing because God has an important message for the world and He's called me to communicate. I can also lead with confidence, because I know that God has called me to lead and has promised me wisdom if I ask believing (James 1:5). This is what Paul did as well. I love how he wrote it in 2 Corinthians 3:4–6: "Such confidence as this is ours through Christ before God. Not that we are competent in ourselves to claim anything for ourselves, but our competence comes from God. He has made us competent as ministers." It's okay to have confidence. It just has to be rooted in the right source—God rather than self. As Zechariah 4:6 says, "This is the word of the LORD to Zerubbabel: 'Not by might nor by power, but by my Spirit,' says the LORD Almighty."

Of course, a confident leader isn't a perfect leader. Even a confident leader makes mistakes. He just makes them confidently and then admits them confidently. The fact is that most of what our church is doing successfully today we learned from our mistakes. I made some bad leadership decisions during our transition. Arrogance would have pretended they weren't bad decisions. Confidence admits mistakes and seeks to learn and benefit from them.

Leaders need to understand that a bad decision doesn't make a bad leader. Otherwise, they will allow mistakes to rob them of their confidence. When this happens, they can no longer lead effectively. The right leader must humbly believe that he's the right person at the right time doing the right thing, and, when he blows it, he must be willing to say, "Oops!" and then keep leading with confidence. Otherwise, why would people follow? My heart breaks for churches that have no leader willing to claim God's wisdom for vision and direction. Until they find this kind of leader, those churches will never experience the joy of being a church that's working right.

Courage

The fifth nonnegotiable characteristic is *courage*. Being the right leader to transition a church demands courage. Significant transitions are almost always difficult. More often than not, it's like an intervention. In an intervention, people confront a person who is making self-destructive choices. They put significant pres-

> **Even a confident leader makes mistakes. He just makes them confidently and then admits them confidently.**

sure on this person to start making choices that will help or even save him. While those intervening are doing it in love, it isn't always received that way. In fact, it usually evokes anger, hostility, and promises to never forgive. It's tough. Because they genuinely love the person and want to save him, they are willing to put the relationship on the line. It takes courage. But when it genuinely saves the person, it's worth it. And in almost every successful intervention, the person rescued sings the praises of those they once condemned.

The same is often true for the person seeking to lead a church into and through a season of change. As with the intervention, it is not well received initially. The majority of people don't generally respond well to the idea, nor do they see the point. It can create a lot of tension and hostility. It takes courage. But, as I have experienced firsthand, when a church moves from dead or dying to alive and thriving, there is nothing like it.

I have also had the joy of reestablishing relationships with people who had rejected me out of hand. I remember one couple in particular who angrily and contentiously left the church. They attacked me from within and without, and they sought to negatively influence others to leave the church. But a few years later they apologized for treating me contentiously and for leaving. They shared with me that, through the transition that they had condemned, the church had become everything they needed. As a result of coming back into the church, they were experiencing and living for God in ways they had never thought possible. It was an affirming moment. It takes courage to stand in the face of rejection, but it's worth it.

Courage to stand alone. The right leader for moving a church through change without compromise must be willing to stand alone. Of course, this has been true of every godly leader who has made a difference in this world. Though they were different in many ways, leaders in Scripture who genuinely lived and led for God were all forced to stand alone. Moses, David, Paul, and Jesus, to name a few, all stood alone.

Godly leaders must have the courage to stand alone, because there's *always* someone waiting and willing to betray them. Those who desire to lead should take note of this reality. There is always someone waiting to betray a true leader. Often they are in the leader's small group and are leaders themselves. Heard of Judas or Absalom? How about Korah, Dathan, Abiram, and On? All of these betrayers were in the leader's small group and were leaders themselves. This is why, when I do small group, I am very careful about whom and how many I choose.

The right leader needs courage to stand up to the traitor. In churches needing transition, the Judases and Absaloms of this world have secured leadership positions or influence. It happens because there aren't courageous leaders to stand up to them. When these kinds of people are leading the church, the church will never be what Jesus wants it to be. It will be what those leaders want it to be. If the church is going to be light in this world, it desperately needs some courageous leaders willing to stand up to them.

I've been forced to play this role in every church I've pastored. I had a self-proclaimed "godly" board member in one church look me in the eye and say, "I just got elected to this board, and my mission is to fight you every step of the way." Surprisingly, he didn't say "in Jesus' name." Transition requires courage, because it demands going against the prevailing current. It's not easy, but it's necessary. And, of course, Jesus did it. Since the role of spiritual leaders is to be like Christ, we must do it as well.

Courage to love people without needing them. This kind of courage demands loving people without needing them. Jesus was this kind of leader. He loved people supremely. His entire life and ministry was motivated by sacrificial love. However, He was not held captive to needing people. Jesus evidenced this aspect of His character in John 2:23–25: "Now while he was in Jerusalem at the Passover Feast, many people saw the miraculous signs he was doing and believed in his name. But Jesus would not entrust himself to them, for he knew all men. He did not need man's testimony about man, for he knew what was in a man." This was the secret behind Jesus' courage to continue telling the truth when people started walking away from Him.

Unfortunately, those of us who choose to become pastors often do so because we both love and need people. We love making an investment in people's lives, but at the same time we enjoy people affirming and responding to our investment. We tend to have a deep need for people to accept, esteem, love, and positively respond to us. Though common for many people, it creates a huge problem for a leader. If you need people, you will do anything to get and keep people . . . including compromise. There is no way for an individual who needs people to lead courageously. When people respond negatively to what the leader is saying or where the leader is leading, they only have to threaten to leave and the leader will cry "uncle." If people threaten to pull their personal support or stop giving, the leader will surrender to their demands. Yet if a leader is going to be successful at effecting change, he cannot allow cancers to grow, gain influence, or rule the church. They must cut them out. Too many leaders are unable to do this, because they need people to love them. As a result, the cancer grows and destroys everything of eternal value. It helps to explain the reason so many churches are experiencing conflict and so few churches are living up to their God-given potential.

When I became senior pastor of NorthRidge, I was thirty-two years old. I inherited two assistant pastors who had been on staff at the church for a decade longer than I'd been alive. Though they were wonderful and faithful men, many of the changes my leadership created proved difficult for them. As a result, I had to confront them multiple times. Needless to say, this was never easy. I dreaded the long walk to their offices or the long wait in my office for the meeting where I would confront them with another tough and tense issue. But since I genuinely cared about them and wanted the church to be all it could and should be, I had to do it. Otherwise, I would simply be using my position to serve my own emotional needs for love, comfort, and acceptance. There was only one way that I found the courage to do this as a positive reflection of Christ: I had to genuinely love and desire the best for these men without needing them to love me back.

The right kind of courage. The right leader needs courage, but only the right kind of courage. Godly courage stems from calling and confidence rather than arrogance and stupidity. A leader can develop the right kind of courage by playing to the applause of the right audience. This is what Jesus did. Though He loved all people, He didn't need them to love or accept Him. As long as God the Father was applauding Him, He was good. This is seen throughout His life and ministry. It's clearly evidenced at the beginning of His ministry. In Matthew 4:8–10, "the devil took him to a very high mountain and showed him all the kingdoms of the world and their splendor. 'All this I will give you,' he said, 'if you will bow down and worship me.' Jesus said to him, 'Away from me, Satan! For it is written: "Worship the Lord your God, and serve him only.""" It's on display again at the end of His ministry. In Luke 22:42, as Jesus was preparing for the cross, He prayed, "Father, if you are willing, take this cup from me; yet not my will, but yours be done." Because He lived this way, He received God's pleasure: "While he was still speaking, a bright cloud enveloped them, and a voice from the cloud said, 'This is my Son, whom I love; with him I am well pleased. Listen to him!'" (Matthew 17:5).

The right leader never plays to the audience who pays him; he plays to the Audience who made him.

In order for a leader to effectively guide people through change, he must have the courage that stems from playing to the audience of One. The leader who needs people to love, respect, and accept him will never have the courage necessary to lead the people where they need to go. The right leader never plays to the audience who pays him; he plays to the Audience who made him. Too many church leaders live in fear of what their people might do. It takes courage to do right in the face of being wronged. But if the church is going to reflect Christ clearly, it must follow Him in doing just that. It takes courage to lead the church as and where Jesus would lead it.

In the early days of the NorthRidge transition, I got a phone call from another pastor. Like so many calls I received in those days, this wasn't going to be an encouraging call. This pastor, who had a history with the church and didn't agree with the direction of my leadership, said, "Brad, if you keep leading in the direction you're leading, you're going to lose all your money people." Of course, he was right. The sad reality is that people, when their hearts aren't in the right place before God, seek to use money in order to manipulate and control. However, the truth is that these threats can only work if the leader has an eye more on money than on God. So in response to this pastor's advice, I said, "Let me ask you a question. Do you think that God called me to the church to keep the money people, or do you think God called me to lead this church to fulfill the Great Commission?" The phone call was over. Though it took courage to stand up to this pastor, the truth is that the real courage was needed in standing up to the reality that "the money people" were leaving. It took the courage that only comes from playing to the right audience. I decided in those early days that God was truly God and that, as long as He was pleased with me, I didn't need the "money people." After all, He's promised to meet all of our needs (Philippians 4:19), and I was just naive enough to believe Him.

Moses could have said, "But God, You're leading us into the wilderness. There's no food or water." But he didn't. He trusted that God would provide wherever He guided. The same was true of Abraham when facing the loss of his son. He decided to trust that God would provide wherever He guided. The same must be true for those of us who undertake the difficult task of leading the church today. We must decide that we don't need the "money people" (though we need to love them and it sure doesn't hurt to have them), as long as we have God and His pleasure.

Courage wins respect. Though it's almost always tough to maintain this kind of courage, it's a significant key in leading people through transition. The right kind of people, the kind who will become a positive force in the church, ultimately respect a leader who leads by conviction rather than following the whims of people.

When I was being interviewed as a possible candidate for pastor at NorthRidge, there was a significant influencer in the church who appeared to disagree with me on almost every issue I addressed. If I was going to have any chance of becoming the pastor of this church, this man's approval was vital. Yet I found myself on the opposite side of him on most issues. Of course, the easy and common route during an interview is to soften the answers to appease the decision makers. I refused. If I won them to myself this way, I would either be compromising my ability to make the right decisions or be forced to compromise my integrity once I became the leader. Unwilling to accept either of these outcomes, I mustered the courage to not color more acceptable answers. I stood firm on all of my beliefs about the church and where I would lead it if called. When the meeting was over, I was convinced that I had lost any hope of this man's support. I was wrong. Not only did he support me as the candidate for pastor, but he put his influence behind his support. As it turns out, this man didn't want someone who would tell him what he wanted to hear. He wanted someone who would tell him the truth . . . no matter what. He wanted a leader. I believe this is what most churches are looking and longing for in their pastor.

Commitment

The sixth nonnegotiable characteristic is *commitment*. The right leader must be committed. If a leader isn't determined to stay for the long haul, he should not attempt to lead a church into a season of change. I believe that it's self-serving and pitiful to lead a church into a transition and then leave before it's done. The right leaders finish what they start—even when it's tough. After all, it's not supposed to be about the leader. It's supposed to be about God and those who so desperately need His love and hope.

Imagine Jesus in the Garden of Gethsemane, getting up off His knees and saying, "Guys, wake up. I've decided I don't need all this grief. Let's go fishing." What would have happened if Jesus had done this? Though it wouldn't have been apparent at the time, it would have robbed the world of any hope for light, love, and life. The same happens in the church when a leader quits in the middle of a difficult transition. Though it may not be apparent at the time, a quitting leader robs the church of any hope for becoming effective in the future, without a significant intervention by God. The vacancy tends to cause the church to retreat into their comfort zone and see change as something to be feared and avoided.

If there is one thing transition needs, it's a leader who sticks with it through thick and thin. In the middle of our transition, it seemed that nothing was going well. Throughout the ministry, even among those leaders close to and supporting me, retreat seemed to be the common rallying cry. It really did appear that we were in one of those "perfect storms" that could destroy the church if we didn't turn around. I had to hold on to the ship's wheel with both hands and continually encourage those who were with me in order to keep the transition going. It was intense.

During this time, I received a phone call from one of the most prominent and successful churches in the nation. The pastor, a man I had learned a great deal from and deeply admired, had recently left. They called me under the pretext of getting my counsel for finding this leader's replacement. I was honored and willing to help. At the conclusion of our lengthy phone call, they asked me a question I wasn't expecting: "Would you allow us to consider you as a candidate to become the next pastor of our church?" It floored me. I was experiencing the worst of times in a church that still appeared to have little or no hope of becoming a growing, relevant, effective church. This offer was coming from one of the flagship churches in the nation, and it was experiencing the best of times. I should also point out that the failing church I was pastoring was in Michigan, while this successful church was in one of the most desirable cities in the country. It appeared to be a once-in-a-lifetime opportunity. For most people, it would have been a no-brainer. "Yes. Let me pack my sunscreen, and I'll see you in the morning." And, indeed, it was a no-brainer for me . . . but in the opposite direction. I said, "While I'm honored by your request, I have to turn you down." I went on to tell this man that I thought it would be disingenuous for me to leave in the middle of a transition I had begun. This wasn't a tough decision for me because I had already made it when I committed to lead the church through the transition. If I hadn't, it would have been a tough decision . . . one that I very easily could have failed.

Because I was confident that God had called me, I wholeheartedly believed that there was no better place for me. If He couldn't use me where I was, He certainly wouldn't be able to use me in another church. So I stayed. As a result, I've had the privilege of being part of God doing an amazing work in our church. I wouldn't trade my experience for anything . . . not even the perfect climate.

Continuous Growth

The seventh and final nonnegotiable characteristic is *continuous growth*. The right leader for a transition demands continuous growth. The reality is that churches will never be able to grow any further than their leaders. Unfortunately, most churches are led by pastors, boards, and people who are experts in organizational structure, people management, and ministry programming that was perfect thirty years ago. For some reason, they stopped growing. As the saying goes, "if you always do what you've always done, you'll always get what you've always got."

My counsel to church leaders who refuse to keep growing and learning is to get out of the way and let someone lead the church who's willing to bleed for it. The right leader must keep growing because the circumstances and challenges never stop changing. I have found that the need to grow as a leader expands exponentially as time goes by and/or our ministries grow.

Church leaders need to continue learning because they become less and less in touch with the way life is for those outside of the church and faith. When we're younger, we have all kinds of natural points of contact with the world and culture. This tends to change as we lose ourselves in living the Christian life and leading the church. As a result, we can start living in a bubble of irrelevance without knowing it.

Church leaders need to continue learning as their ministries grow because the challenges change. Though it appears that I know what I'm doing and am successful as a leader, the reality is that I have never led a church the size and scope of the one I'm now leading. We have grown so rapidly that I now face different challenges than I faced before. If I fail to grow in my understanding of the new circumstances and challenges, I will face them in the same way that I faced past challenges. And, more than likely, I'll fail. I have never needed to change and transition as a leader more than I do now. Thankfully, because of the way I'm wired, I have never been so hungry to grow as I am now. I need to keep growing in order to be and remain a driving force in the church. If the church I lead starts outgrowing me, I will become an anchor rather than an engine. If I refuse to continue growing and learning, I will become a significant force in the church's failure to be what God intends . . . the hope of the world.

> **The only way a leader can ensure remaining at the top of his or her leadership game is through a commitment to continuous learning and growth.**

Not ending well is one of my biggest fears. I have seen so many people finish poorly. In whatever endeavor of human achievement, it appears to be a common flaw of those who become successful. They stay just a little too long. It happens in sports, business, and even the church. The only way a leader can ensure remaining at the top of his or her leadership game is through a commitment to continuous learning and growth.

One of the reasons relatively few leaders continue growing is because the onus is on them. Generally, there is no one standing over the church leader's shoulder, making him grow. If I stopped growing as a leader today, more than likely, I could continue pastoring NorthRidge for the rest of my life. And, because of its sheer size, most people would think I was successful. Given this scenario, I would be a failure. I'd be using the church, which was made possible through a cross, not through my own efforts, to make my life comfortable. If I'm going to stop being a driving force in the church, then I need to leave. Anything less is driven by selfishness, dishonoring to God, and destructive for the church. My passion for the church and its purpose drives me.

As 1 Timothy 3:1 makes clear, it's noble for you to be, or desire to be, a pastor or leader in the church. In my opinion, there's nothing better. After all, it puts you in the center of what our almighty God has chosen to invest Himself in. Added to this, leading the church puts you at the center of the only hope for the world. It's an awesome place to be. But, because of the importance, failure is not an option. Therefore, as you seek to become a part of the wonderful adventure of leading the church, it's vital to make sure you're the right kind of leader. Don't settle for anything less.

CHAPTER 6

Can't Do It Alone

Investing in Leaders and Building Teams

The right leader doesn't lead alone. For the right leader to successfully transition a church, he must invest in other leaders and build teams. The day this stops happening in a church is the day the church is condemned to plateau, stagnate, and decline. This need never diminishes, and the process should never stop. Though we are a large and relatively successful ministry, I'm investing in leaders and seeking to build teams more today than I ever have. In fact, I now see it as one of my primary jobs. I have also made it the primary job of our staff. This is a required reality for any leader seeking to move a ministry forward or change a ministry's direction. It must be done. I have found that when I back away from investing in leaders and building teams, the church begins to slow down and sputter.

Everything Rises and Falls on Leadership

Here's the first reality every leader and church needs to understand: everything rises and falls on leadership. Though there are some nice, sincere, and seemingly well-intentioned people who diminish the importance of leadership in the church, they are wrong. This view is dangerous because, if people believe that leadership isn't important, the church will begin structuring to limit leadership. And it will ultimately kill any potential for the church to become a force of help and hope in this world.

In my opinion, the church should be structured to let leaders lead, not to keep leaders from leading. Yet many Christians actually believe that strong leadership is unhealthy for the church. This is another significant reason so many churches aren't working right.

I pastored a church in Naples, Florida, for three and a half years. When I was first called to this church, there were three men on the board. The church had a Sunday morning attendance of about sixty people. My predecessor resigned as pastor of the church because, when the church went over fifty, he felt it was too large for him. He actually resigned with those words and declared his intent to find a smaller church to pastor.

Though I'm sure he was a wonderful man, he lives in a world immensely different from mine. I can't comprehend that kind of thinking. I arrived at this small, calm, and slow-moving Florida church proclaiming a vision of thousands of people attending our church. I'll never forget the reaction of the board. While sitting in one of our first meetings, they said in a shell-shocked way, "We thought the last pastor was a little too slow. We had to keep prodding him to do anything, but we see that we're going to have to bridle you." Though it's usually not expressed so openly and clearly, this is how many people think in churches today. Though it doesn't make sense, many Christians feel threatened by leaders who can actually change the church to make a difference in people's lives; so they organize it to ensure that the leader is rendered ineffective. How ridiculous. Needless to say, the board's opposition to change made my job as pastor very difficult. Though they were great people and God did some wonderful things in this church, it was structured to limit rather than to maximize impact.

Structure for Leadership

When God has gifted people with leadership, we should not only let them lead but also celebrate their leadership. As Romans

12:6–8 says, "We have different gifts, according to the grace given us. If a man's gift is . . . leadership, let him govern diligently." God says, "Let them lead."

Think about this. No duly elected committee would have ever voted with Moses, Jesus, or Paul. Thank God they didn't wait for a vote. They led. No wonder the church is such a mess. Many churches have to take a vote to determine what kind of toilet paper to purchase. It's amazing.

In the first church I pastored, one of the initial board meetings I attended was consumed with whether they were going to roast a pig or a turkey at that year's annual Labor Day event. This was a church that had shrunk from more than two hundred members to only eighteen in a community that was growing quickly. There was no talk about reaching people or resolving conflict. There was no examination of serious issues facing the church. There was certainly no seeking God's heart or wisdom for the church, even though the meeting began and closed with prayer. (As I recall, this was the only role they thought I should play in the meeting.) The entire meeting focused on roasting a pig or turkey. When they finally voted, the pig won or, from the pig's perspective, lost. After that first meeting, I clearly identified the problem in that church. However, when I attempted to take the lead in addressing the problem, the church was uninterested. They just wanted me to pray before and after they voted on things that didn't matter in the moment, let alone in eternity.

Structure for Positive Accountability

Leaders should have accountability. In my present ministry, because of the significant growth and impact we've experienced, I've gained a significant amount of influence. But when it was time to restructure our church constitution and bylaws, I led in structuring for accountability of my position. The reason is simple. I've lived long enough to know a little bit about humanity. I know my own humanity and I know other people's humanity. Leaders need clear and intentional accountability.

Churches need to have structured accountability for leadership. But those structures should not bridle or prevent leadership. They should be directed toward ensuring and encouraging that the leader is living a life of godly character, leading the church to fulfill God's purposes, and remaining true to God's Word in teaching and leadership. I believe strongly in accountability for church leaders. Churches should structure for accountability to the right things.

> **If churches are going to get unstuck and start making a difference, they must structure to let leaders lead.**

Churches should not restrain their leadership by requiring a vote or approval for every minor decision or every dollar they spend. While the church board should ensure that the budget supports the pastor's stated leadership priorities and that the overall amount is reasonable, they should not nitpick every issue or area. It is more important to evaluate how the leader's decisions have impacted the overall growth of the church than to dictate what the leader can and cannot do.

If churches are going to get unstuck and start making a difference, they must structure to let leaders lead. They should hold pastors accountable for faith, integrity, and truth, but they shouldn't try to bridle and control them.

Leadership Is Possible in Any Structure

With that being said, it's important to acknowledge that, generally speaking, the right leader can effectively lead within any church structure. I often hear church leaders blaming the church structure for their inability to lead. More often than not, the structure is only a hindrance, not the ultimate problem.

All four of the churches I've pastored have, in the beginning, had different and difficult church structures. As with so many churches, the structure had become a big part of the problem. Though it may have once supported the church's vision and purpose, over time the structure became the focus and an obstacle to the mission. Yet I was able to lead the church forward within each of those structures. In so doing, in every case but one, I was able to gradually transition the structure to more effectively support leadership. The right leader can lead in any structure. It just takes patience, commitment, and a customized kind of leadership. Just because a structure is difficult, the leader shouldn't think of running. Rather, he should work toward transitioning it. It is worth the effort because every church is the only picture of Jesus some people will ever see.

Every church will ultimately rise and fall on leadership. Therefore, as a leader attempts to lead a church into and through transition, I strongly recommend keeping integrity with the structure of the church. Until the structure is legitimately changed, working within the structure is an issue of character for the leader. If the leader violates the legal or binding structure of the church, the leader will forfeit the necessary influence required to lead legitimately through change. Since trust is only established through proving character, a leader must live by character to win the trust necessary for leading. Once trust is established, the possibility of legitimately leading the church to change structure becomes a reality.

In one of the churches I pastored, there was a woman who was a huge obstacle to the church moving forward. Though I don't believe she was mean-spirited in her intentions, her commitment to structure was a serious impediment to any kind of leadership. The way this church was organized required a business meeting and congregational vote for almost everything, and she controlled every meeting. As a result, she owned the direction of the church. I discovered her secret: she was a self-proclaimed expert on *Brown's Book of Parliamentary Rules and Procedures*. I knew that if I was ever going to lead this church, I needed to diminish her power over the business meetings. So I made it my goal to get to know that book better than she did.

Sure enough, at the next business meeting, she attempted to shut down the decision to move forward on some issue. It went something like this: "Excuse me, Pastor, you can't do that because . . ." She went on with her legal reason. When she was done, I went to work. "I appreciate your heart. I know you love this church and want to do the right thing. We're on the same page. But if you've read [this section, this point, and this subpoint of] *Brown's Book of Parliamentary Rules and Procedures*, you would know this is both acceptable and desirable. Therefore, we're going to move forward on it." She sat down in that meeting and never stood up in any business meeting again. She actually became a friend and supporter of my leadership. I received birthday cards from her for years after I left that church. As it turns out, she was looking for a leader with character. When she found one, she went from being a lion to a lamb.

One Person Can't Transition Anything

Here's another reality that every leader and church needs to understand: one person can't transition anything, but one person can be a catalyst for starting a transition. Too many church leaders attempt to be a one-person change agent. It doesn't work. The most any leader can expect to accomplish is to be used as a catalyst to get the transition started.

My first pastorate was a spectacular failure. I was twenty-six years old and, though I had been an assistant pastor for a short time, this was my first senior position. I was excited. I had been frustrated by the lack of enthusiasm and innovation in churches. I felt most churches were boring, stuck in the past, and paralyzed by unnecessary traditions. Finally, I had the opportunity to take the lead in changing the church. My wife and I jumped in with both feet and started doing everything we'd always wanted to do. She began working with, updating, and implementing new directions in the music, kids', and women's ministries. She also started updating the church décor. I placed a huge emphasis on evangelism and started an aggressive outreach ministry. We totally revamped the format of the church services and every other ministry. We significantly changed the church bulletin and all church literature. Everything at this church was stale, so we seized our new leadership opportunity to make it fresh.

People started making first-time decisions to follow Christ. The church immediately started growing. In fact, in six months, the church grew by 425 percent. My wife and I were excited. All the new people were excited. Unfortunately, the original church people were not excited. Though I didn't know it at the time, they had started their own visitation program. They were visiting all the members, including those who hadn't attended in years, in order to vote me out as their pastor.

I couldn't believe it. I literally couldn't comprehend how people who called themselves Christians could be so calloused. How could they not be excited about people coming to faith and the church growing? In light of all the great things happening, how could they want to get rid of me?

In retrospect, I understand perfectly what happened. It was the predictable outcome of how I went about the changes at that church. Rather than leading and transitioning those people, I did leadership and transition *to* them. I didn't take the people of that church into consideration whatsoever. I knew what needed to be done, and I did it . . . without them. As a result, it blew up in my face.

This spectacular failure led to one of the most important leadership lessons of my life. One person can't transition anything. But one person can be the catalyst for getting transition started.

Back to the Wave

I have a good friend in our church who is quite a bit older than me. He had been in the church for three decades prior to my coming. Though he was involved in an adult class, he was for the most part an observer in the church. As it turns out, he was a very keen observer. Several years after I arrived, I was privileged to have him join me in leadership. It was then that he shared some of his observations. He is the one who compared what he had seen me doing in the church to starting the wave. His objective observations were fascinating to me. He told me that during the first couple of years of my ministry, it appeared to him that I was trying to get the wave started, but no one was joining. Every week, I would mount the church platform and start pouring out positive energy and excitement. Without fail, it would land with a thud. Being a salesman, he told me that he couldn't believe that I kept showing up every week with the same positive energy.

> One person can't transition anything. But one person can be the catalyst for getting transition started.

Since he sat in the balcony, he had a full view of what was happening. After a couple of years, he finally started noticing a couple of people joining me. He could tell by the way they would respond to the music and my teaching. He said it amazed him that it took so long to get a few others to join me. Then, once I had others doing the wave with me, it doubly amazed him how quickly momentum took over, moving scores more to respond in a relatively short period of time. When I was doing it alone, it was easy for people to just sit and watch. But when others joined, the enthusiasm spread quickly.

As I mentioned in the last chapter, "the wave" is a great illustration of the need for leadership. One person doing the wave isn't the wave. It's just one person standing up and sitting down. It's at best a distraction. But one hundred thousand people doing the wave is awe inspiring. Yet the wave couldn't happen without the one person making the decision to become the catalyst for getting it started. However, for it to happen, this person can't just keep doing it alone. This person must inspire others to join him.

It's the same with leading a church through change. One person changing is barely noticeable. At best, as my friend illustrated, it's interesting to watch. But when that one person influences others to join, the changes can start gathering momentum. Everyone doesn't have to participate for the wave to get started or to be successful. The next time you see the wave taking place at a sporting event, take note of all the people who choose to not get involved. And yet, the wave is still spectacular. The same is true in leading a church through transition. Everyone doesn't have to participate, but you can still have a spectacular wave that moves around them.

Leaders Are the Catalysts for Transition

The sad reality in churches is that, quite often, the people who won't participate in the wave have leadership positions. When this happens, it's a problem. For good or for bad, leaders influence people. This brings clarity to the problem that so many churches are having in our world. A church doesn't get to the wrong place because it has all the right leaders and all the right people on all of its teams. The opposite is true. Therefore, in order for a church to transition successfully, the leader must start getting the best leaders and the best people on all of the teams. The greater the number of positive leaders investing, the faster the church will begin responding. I learned from experience that this doesn't happen by accident. If the leader is going to be the catalyst for getting transition started, he must begin by intentionally investing in positive leaders and building positive teams.

Invest in the Present Leaders

The present leaders and people with influence must understand the issues the church is facing. They must understand the reasons for what the church is presently experiencing. They must understand why the church isn't reaching new people, why so few are coming to faith or being baptized, why they're losing a generation, why they aren't seeing people genuinely changed, and any other reality facing their church. It's the leader's job to help them understand these issues, how they got into this mess, and what they have to do to get out of it.

When I came to NorthRidge, the church was in trouble. Because I was coming in as the senior pastor, I knew it was my job to understand the reasons for the church's decline and to help the church understand, especially the leaders. So I started immediately. The very first thing I did was start a ministry called Deacon Discipleship. The church had forty deacons. All but one were older than me. I told them we were going to begin meeting once a month to discuss the reasons behind the church's problems. They needed to understand why their church had been declining for thirty years; why no young people, including their own children, were coming to the church; and what had to be done to turn it around. Of course, for that to happen, I had to understand. This became my number one responsibility. I needed to research, identify, and understand these issues in order to help them understand. As the leader of the church, it was my job to become the expert on our church. Then, once a month, we would get together and I'd start sharing what I had been learning. This was vital in laying the groundwork for change and in building relationships with the present leaders.

As a result of the discussions that occurred in this setting, I was able to identify the positive and the negative influencers in the church. This proved invaluable. I discovered several different types of individuals on the deacon board. There were a few so frustrated with the church's problems they were ready to do just about anything to change the church. The discouragement of the church's decline was more powerful than their love for the past. They were with me. It was obvious to me that I needed to continue to invest in them and help expand their influence as leaders. They would help me start the wave.

There was another group of deacons who genuinely loved God and wanted the church to be reaching people for Christ, but, at the same time, they loved the church the way it was. Though these would be very slow to adopt change, if they could honestly see that change would help to please God and fulfill the Great Commission, they would begrudgingly support the change. Given enough time and success in reaching people and reinvigorating the church, they could eventually become supporters. Because of their history and influence with the church, their support would make a significant impact. Therefore, I decided that I should continue to invest in them and their leadership while monitoring their support level.

I also discovered a third group. These individuals loved and valued the church's traditions, culture, and methods so dearly that they would never contemplate change, for any reason. In their minds, God loved what they loved, and they would fight to preserve what they loved at all costs. Though they would never have admitted it, I knew that they would never allow themselves to be confused with or deterred by the truth. They could only see the truth through the lens of what they believed. All things being equal, what they believed could never be changed by any presentation of truth. These are the kind of people I wrote about in chapter 4 who wholeheartedly believed that removing hymnals from the church was a sin. Though no biblical truth supported it, this was their "conviction." Though I was in no way compromising the truth, I knew that there was nothing I could do to move these people to accept the changes I was introducing. They would be both vocal and aggressive in standing against any change. They would use their leadership position to negatively influence everyone they could. However, they wouldn't do it with integrity; they would do it subversively. They were a clear and present danger to the future of the church. If I didn't take measures to remove them from leadership and diminish their influence, they would continue to hurt the church.

Remove the Negative Influencers

As the leader, I was responsible for protecting the church. I needed to deal with negative influencers. Though this is never easy and actually feels unspiritual, it is the God-given responsibility of the leaders and the church to appropriately confront and deal with divisive people. Romans 16:17 says, "I urge you, brothers, to watch out for those who cause divisions and put obstacles in your way that are contrary to the teaching you have learned. Keep away from them." Titus 3:10 commands, "Warn a divisive person once, and then warn him a second time. After that, have nothing to do with him." Though it sounds harsh, appropriately confronting and removing these people is what God would have us do. He certainly wouldn't have us leave them in positions of leadership and influence. Though they matter to God, they are a danger to His church. They will use their influence to find and create more negative people. You've got to remove this kind of destructive influence, or they will start a reverse wave. The church is too important to allow a divisive person to hurt its ability to share love and hope with the world.

Oddly enough, most people believe that the primary group standing against change in the church is the older adults. Though this is certainly true of some seniors, I have found that fighting change isn't related to age. Rather, it's related to heart. In our church, many of the older people had a heart for the Great Commission. They desperately wanted to see people coming to faith through our ministry again. Many of them were willing to do whatever it took to make that happen. On the other hand, some of the younger adults in our church had a passion for power. They wanted to control the church. Age isn't an issue when it comes to a person's response to leadership and positive change. Character is the issue. And, if a person's character is questionable, they should not be allowed to represent God, the leader, or the church.

Though replacing negative leaders is both difficult and messy, the church is worth the sacrifice it requires. I've had to face this experience many times in order to see the church become a positive force again. On one occasion, while I was out of town, one of our leading church officers called a meeting of all the deacons and influencers of the church. He wanted to "innocently" poll them on how they thought things were going in the church.

In truth, there was nothing innocent about this. He disagreed with my leadership regarding hot issues like music. He was trying to create a surge of negativity against my leadership. He was trying to force me to submit to his agenda by creating a problem where no problem existed. Of course, he was doing it subversively. He was going behind my back rather than addressing it in a positive and productive manner. The reason was simple: he knew he couldn't get his way if he went about it legitimately.

This happens all the time in churches, and if it goes unchallenged, then it becomes common practice, moving the church further and further away from reflecting Christ. Unfortunately, because confronting can be uncomfortable, pastors allow themselves to be manipulated and controlled by it. In cases like this, I believe Jesus' words in Matthew 10:16 should be practiced: "I am sending you out like sheep among wolves. Therefore be as shrewd as snakes and as innocent as doves."

Though replacing negative leaders is both difficult and messy, the church is worth the sacrifice it requires.

When I arrived back in town, I was made aware of the meeting and survey. While seeking to keep my innocence, I became as shrewd as a snake. I immediately called this subversive leader for a get-together. He was in my office the next morning. I confronted him on the real issue—his character. Though he wanted to discuss his issues and pretend that he was trying to help and protect me, the charade couldn't stand up in the light of the obvious. He stepped down from his position and left the church. God's Word was honored. Respect for my character and leadership was strengthened. And the church was able to keep moving positively forward. Though emotionally exhausting and personally trying, it was the right thing to do. The church is the hope of the world, when it's working right. Without these kinds of confrontations, the church will never work.

As I'm writing, I can already hear what the common response will be to that story: "In my structure, I don't have the power to dismiss leaders." I didn't either. I didn't need it. He resigned. I called him out for who he was and what he was doing. I didn't need constitutional power; I had biblical authority. I held out God's character standards for leadership. Being a relatively intelligent guy, he knew he had no standing. If he had threatened a fight,

I would have laid out my plan for him. "At our next public service, I'm going to get up and teach the people about character. Then, I'm going to use you as the primary illustration of a leader in our church who is living in clear violation of God's standards." I would have made it clear that this was a fight I was willing to engage in and that I was willing to go down upholding God's standards.

Some leaders start sweating profusely just thinking about a confrontation like this. You need to know that I don't enjoy those circumstances. On the contrary, I'm a people person. I love people and like people to love me. But I value God's approval more than man's. I value the church's well-being above my own comfort. I am committed to people finding eternal hope more than I am committed to avoiding trouble. And I believe this should be true of every authentic Christ-follower.

Make the Effort to Work with People

These kinds of confrontations and removals aren't typical or frequent. Generally, with some attention and help, people who are being negative can become positive, or at least not as negative. The leader needs to be willing to work with people, even difficult people, as long as they can refrain from being a negative influence in the church. The leader should be willing to accept criticism, even if it's uncalled-for and harsh, as long as it is done behind closed doors and doesn't hurt or negatively impact church people.

As I mentioned previously, I inherited some staff who had been around for decades. Though some of them were very supportive, a couple had a very rough time, which only made sense. Had I been in their shoes, it would have been tough for me to have so much experience and longevity only to find myself reporting to a guy less than half my age. It would have been tough to have every comfortable practice questioned. So I tried to give significant grace. It was my goal to, as best I could, help these individuals finish well. I wanted to give them due honor, based not on how they treated me but rather on their years of faithfulness. Therefore, I made this determination: I would have no problem with their negative attitudes and criticism toward me as long as they didn't allow it to spill over into the church. If they could refrain from negatively influencing people in the church, I didn't care about the irritations they caused me. But if they started spreading negative poison in the church, I would have to call them on the carpet. Because the health of the church, not my comfort, was the value, this made sense to me. I strongly believed that honoring these men, if possible, would be a large positive for the church. Though there was tension for several years, and it wasn't the best of circumstances, this approach added great value to the church and to my leadership. These men retired with honor, and many of the people who loved them chose to follow me. Though it's not easy, this is what the church should look like when it's working right. As Jesus said in John 13:35, "By this all men will know that you are my disciples, if you love one another."

The Right People on the Right Teams

It takes time and patience to get all of the right people on all of the right teams. While navigating the tide of change, the leader must keep his hands firmly on the ship's wheel. The process of building teams begins with helping existing leaders to understand the issues facing the church and observing their response to identify the positive and negative influencers. At the same time, the leader needs to be developing new and positive leaders to have people ready to step into leadership positions as they become available. Genuinely positive people make an impact whether they hold a position or not; they make great cheerleaders. Investing in them will go a long way toward increasing momentum in starting the wave.

As the leader starts gaining influence, he can begin using that influence to move new leaders into positions of leadership. The easy way is by moving them into positions of leadership as existing leaders begin rolling off. This can be done regardless of the church structure. It just demands thoughtful use of the leader's growing influence. As this process continues to unfold, there will be a moment when the tipping point is reached. The positive influencers will begin outweighing the neutral or negative. When this happens, the wave is beginning to take hold. Because I am impatient, this process seemed to take forever in our church. However, we ultimately reached the tipping point. The change was unbelievable. I was able to drop my guard a little, play less defense in board and leadership environments, and start channeling their positive energy in appropriate directions. The leaders and I began working together rather than wondering, watching, worrying, and waiting. It was fun for a change.

Today, most of our church is doing the wave. As a result, those on the outside are wondering what all the excitement is about. So they come to check it out. When they arrive, we tell them about Jesus. Now thousands of them are doing the wave. Though it took a lot of blood, sweat, and tears, it was worth it. The same can be true in any church setting . . . if the leader will begin investing in leaders and building positive teams. If he does, the investment will one day reach the tipping point, and transition will happen.

For six years, church leaders and I invested our energy in the church with very little evidence of change. In fact, we were still in decline after six years. One of my good friends in the church and an active leader once told me that there were times when he questioned my sanity. He said, "You'd get up and start talking about all the great things God was doing, and I'd look around and watch three more families walking out the door. I was worried about you. I didn't know if you had any sense of reality." Then he looked me in the eye and said, "I'm so glad that you believed."

If I hadn't believed, if I had left at the six-year point in my ministry, I would have missed the incomprehensible work of God in this place. Though we worked hard for a long time with no evidence of a change, one day the transition happened. And it was worth the wait.

Positive Teams Don't Happen by Accident

This positive change would not have happened if we hadn't invested in leaders and built teams. Building teams of positive influencers will create pockets of positive movement in the church. While the leader is seeking to start the wave in one corner, others will be trying to energize the wave in another corner. It's vital to have other people helping to create the change. They will offset the leader's weaknesses, offload the leader's burdens, and help to eliminate the leader's loneliness. Positive teams are the leader's most valuable resource. But they don't happen by accident.

Foolishly, I did ministry alone for years, because I didn't make investing in leaders and building teams a priority. It was a mistake. For a church to work right, the leader must build into people's lives. He must build team. Paul made this clear in Ephesians 4:11–12: "It was he who gave some to be apostles, some to be prophets, some to be evangelists, and some to be pastors and teachers, to prepare God's people for works of service, so that the body of Christ may be built up." God created the church to work as a team (1 Corinthians 12).

CHAPTER 7

Give Them a Reason

Exposing the Necessity of Change

When I came to my present ministry, I marveled that many people didn't see any problem with the church. As I shared in the first chapter, they had experienced three decades of decline. In the ten years preceding my arrival, they had lost two-thirds of their people. In my mind, it was obvious that this church was in trouble. But my mind was definitely not their mind. Though some of the key leaders fully understood the trouble they were facing, the majority of people in the church honestly thought that they were still a great church.

Many of these wonderful people couldn't figure out why others were leaving. They certainly couldn't understand why guests only visited once. They couldn't figure it out because they loved every part of the church. They were comfortable there. To them, it was still a great church.

This is a common experience for people. I have visited some homes with furnishings and décor that was either unbelievably worn or three generations beyond the expiration date. But the homeowners thought it was still perfect. They were used to it. It felt right to them. However, the need for change was obvious to anyone who visited the home. Though outdated décor doesn't affect the functioning of their home, it does significantly impact the value. If they were to attempt to sell it in that condition, they would lose a great deal of their potential equity. In a case like this, a realtor would point out the problem to the couple. Though surprised and possibly hurt, the better part of wisdom would be to make the necessary updates in order to receive the full value of their investment.

The same reality applies to the church, but far more is at stake than financial equity. When a church is significantly outdated and irrelevant, it loses its ability to influence people for Christ and eternity. Though it seems fine to the insiders, the outsider comes in and receives the message loud and clear: God is old, tired, dusty, and irrelevant. "If this is what God is like," they conclude, "then I can't relate to Him. If this is what it means to be a Christian, I will never be a Christian." Of course, the style and décor of the church have nothing to do with God's nature or what it means to be a Christian, but this is the message that is clearly communicated.

> **When a church is significantly outdated and irrelevant, it loses its ability to influence people for Christ and eternity.**

Along with many other issues, this is exactly what was happening at our church when I first arrived. Like the real estate agent with the homeowner, someone had to point out the problem. Because the church members couldn't see it on their own, it took leadership to expose them to the necessity for change.

People Won't Fix What's Not Broken

This is a problem in most churches. Think about it from their perspective: it's not necessary to fix something you don't believe to be broken. Most faithful church attenders love their church. They're comfortable. They like seeing the same people. They love the music. They love the old décor and the stuffy smell. It gives them a warm feeling inside and keeps them connected to their history. It's a beautiful thing to have a retreat like this in a world that is moving so fast and changing so much.

What they don't understand is that outsiders don't have any connections to the place. Rather than a warm feeling, they feel as though they're getting the cold shoulder. They get the very real sense that this is a private club and new people need not apply. These are well-meaning people; they are just oblivious to the problem. Therefore, the leader has to help them see it.

This is similar to the problem in Jerusalem during the time of Nehemiah. The city was a broken-down mess. God's glory was no longer on display. God's people were living in squalor, and they didn't even notice. They didn't see the problem. They were used to it. It wasn't much, but it was home. Though they were God's chosen people in the city of God, they were living like rejects in a junkyard.

Nehemiah had to come all the way from the Persian Empire to point out the problem. He showed them the broken walls. He had to remind them that God's glory used to dwell there. When he started exposing them to the problems, they finally woke up to the necessity for change. They started working on the wall. As it turns out, the problem wasn't that they didn't care; it was that they didn't notice.

I have found the same reality in the church. Though sadly there are some who don't care, most church people just don't notice. So in order to lead the church into and through change, someone has to expose them to the necessity for change. Of course, as was true in Nehemiah's day, there will be those who attempt to prevent the church from experiencing renewal. Most people will get excited and involved when they see the problem and understand that they can become part of the solution. It just takes a leader, like Nehemiah, who is genuinely burdened about the problem and willing to make the necessary sacrifices to expose others to the necessity for change.

When I came to my present ministry, I already had a huge burden for the church. It had been a great church that reached thousands for Christ. But like Jerusalem, it had been broken down. Though I had the passion and desire to see this once great church become great again, if I was going to expose the church to the real problem, I had to fully understand it myself. I needed to fully acquaint myself with the problems facing the church, and I needed to understand what was causing them. Until I could figure this out, I would not be able to effectively help the church understand. So while performing all of the normal and necessary aspects of my ministry, my number one priority was becoming the expert on the issues facing our church. This is what every church needs: someone with a burden to see the church be all God wants it to be, a willingness to make it their job to understand, and a desire to share the reasons for change with others.

> **Most people will get excited and involved when they see the problem and understand that they can become part of the solution.**

Changing for the Right Reason

As I was examining the walls of our church, so to speak, I came to the realization that, in order for a church to change without compromise, *the change must be motivated by a core issue.* In other words, if I was going to successfully move people from doing church as they loved it to another way, I needed to connect the change to a fundamental issue.

As I worked to figure out the problems at our church, I discovered significant failure in two core areas. First, we were experiencing a failure of purpose. Though we had a lot of activities happening at our church, we weren't fulfilling the Great Commission: "Therefore go and make disciples of all nations, baptizing them in the name of the Father and of the Son and of the Holy Spirit, and teaching them to obey everything I have commanded you" (Matthew 28:19–20). With all that our church was doing, we were failing to fulfill the one purpose God gave the church.

As I began exposing the church to this problem, I was pleasantly surprised at many of the responses. I discovered that a high percentage of the people cared deeply about our church reaching people for Christ. Though they enjoyed all the church's activities, when they saw that they weren't helping to reach people for Christ, many began looking at what they loved differently. It was as if they were finally seeing their outdated home furnishings and décor against a new standard. Though nothing changed overnight, many of them were more willing to shop for new furniture.

> When a church isn't living up to the values that God has given, it's failing.

This is what should happen in every church facing the need to change. Someone has to help the church see what they're doing against the backdrop of the church's God-given purpose. If the church is reaching people for Christ and helping them to grow spiritually, then there is no need to change. If the church hasn't seen a person come to faith in a year or two, then there is a significant reason to change.

Second, it became clear to me that we were experiencing a failure of the values God had given to us, which I will discuss in the next chapter. Without a doubt, this was a core issue. When a church isn't living up to the values God has given, it's failing. When I was able to identify this reality in our church, it became crystal clear as to why we were in decline.

Once the core issue is identified, it becomes fairly easy to expose the problem to the church. It's just a matter of holding the church up to the lens of Scripture. The following are some of the examples I used in exposing our church to the necessity of change.

Offense Versus Defense

In Matthew 16:18, Jesus said, "I will build my church, and the gates of Hades will not overcome it." In other words, "My church is going to be offensive, not defensive." Jesus made it clear that the church was to be attacking the gates of hell, attacking the gates of darkness. With the rallying cry that "we are more than conquerors," the church is supposed to be knocking down the gates of hell in people's lives. Unfortunately, most churches today are playing defense by talking more about how to keep people than how to reach people. This is a failure of values.

> Most churches today are playing defense by talking more about how to keep people than how to reach people. This is a failure of values.

In a simple reading of Acts 2, it is obvious that no one had to convince believers to show up for church. Great things were happening. Lives were being changed. God's presence and promises were being experienced. People wanted to be part of it. This is what happens when the church is working right.

Years ago, while pastoring a different church, I received a phone call from a pastor of another church in the area. He asked if some of "his people" were coming to my church. He was trying to track them down and get them back where they belonged. In his perspective, leaving "his church" was unacceptable. I wanted to blurt out, "Buddy, the clue phone's ringing, and it's for you." While he thought the problem was with the people, the reality was that the problem was with him and "his" church. This pastor was playing defense: trying to keep people rather than reaching people. When this happens in a church, it is clearly a failure of values.

Truth Versus Traditions

Without knowing or meaning it, many churches, like ours when I first came, have begun valuing their traditions more than God's truth. As we've seen, this happened in Jesus' day with the Pharisees. Matthew 15:1–3 says, "Then some Pharisees and teachers of the law came to Jesus from Jerusalem and asked, 'Why do your disciples break the tradition of the elders? They don't wash their hands before they eat!' Jesus replied, 'And why do you break the command of God for the sake of your tradition?'"

This is common in churches today. People slowly but surely begin valuing the pump more than the water. They value their church name, structure, programs, liturgies, style, music, décor, and other traditions more than the truth. This is a failure of values, and it's killing the church.

Right Versus Wrong

Nowhere is the failure of values in the church more evident than in light of how God's Word says believers should live toward "one another." For example:

Love one another (John 13:34).
Be devoted to one another . . . Honor one another (Romans 12:10).
Live in harmony with one another . . . Do not be proud (Romans 12:16).
Accept one another (Romans 15:7).
Serve one another (Galatians 5:13).

These are the values of Christ Himself. What we do with these values determines the difference between right and wrong in the way we relate to others. When the church successfully exhibits these values, they become the light and hope of the world. When they don't, they aren't working right. Unfortunately, more often than not, churches are experiencing a failure of values in these areas. The result is that they're failing to honor God. As in Nehemiah's day, the church needs leaders who will start exposing the church to these core values. Those with good hearts will choose God's purpose and values over their own.

If you're a leader in the church, you can expose your church to the problem and reestablish God's glory in the church, as Nehemiah did in Jerusalem. You should embrace this as the point of your leadership.

In this section, I've introduced the principles for beginning the transition. It takes the right leader, investing in the right leaders and building the right teams, and exposing people to the necessity for change. When these are in place, the wave is getting started.

PART 3

paint the target

CHAPTER 8

Help Them See in 4-D

Developing and Implementing
a Ministry Charter

When I was young, Kmart was far larger than my known universe. But no matter. I've always been an activist. So, even as a preschooler, I was ready to take it on. My mom, ever the protective soul, was diligent about keeping close tabs on me. But one day, I decided it was time to scope out Kmart on my own and made the great escape. I had no fear. Somehow I thought that I knew where I wanted to go. So I went. However, like the proverbial dog chasing the car, I didn't know what to do with it when I got it. The aisles became a maze of gigantic proportions. I got lost in Kmart. It might as well have been New York City. Though I don't remember faces or words, I do remember fear. I started bawling. As always happens when children cry, I soon became the commander of a small army. Everyone in the store came to my aid. Usually all of this attention would get the engines revving. But the fear had too big a grip on me. I just remember a long, agonizing wait for my mom. When I saw her, everything was right with the world again.

It was then and there that I knew that I hated being lost. As a male, I shouldn't be this way. But I am. I hate being lost more than I hate humbling myself to ask directions. When I walk in a store, I immediately ask for directions. None of this walking around for hours, pretending I know what's going on. Same thing when I'm driving. The second I'm not sure where I am . . . I stop to ask directions.

This is one of the reasons I love the twenty-first century. I can now keep my manhood without getting lost. I have a Global Positioning System. It's awesome. I'd rather have my GPS than the latest computer game system. It has replaced the dog as man's best friend. I like to know where I am, where I'm going, how I'm going to get there, and how long it's going to take. And my GPS tells me without requiring me to feed or pick up after it.

My aversion to being lost has carried over into my leadership as well. Based on my experiences, most churches are lost. They have no clue where they are, where they're heading, how they're going to get there, or how long it's going to take. As a result, they're frustrated, confused, discouraged, scared, and wasting time. They just know they're supposed to get together at eleven o'clock on Sunday morning and talk about Jesus. And they wonder why more people don't show up.

This is a bizarre reality, given the fact that the church has been commissioned to help the lost find their way home. No wonder the church is having such problems today. The church will never fulfill its purpose or significantly influence the world as long as it is lost.

The Ministry Charter

This is the point of the fourth principle for successfully transitioning a church. If the church is going to transition to greater effectiveness without compromising God's truth, it must figure out where it is, where it's going, and how it's going to get there. The church must develop and implement what I call a "ministry charter."

Of course, it doesn't have to be called a ministry charter, but you do need one. A ministry charter sets the course. It identifies the ultimate destination. It clarifies the directions. It makes it easy to evaluate the church's effectiveness. At a moment's notice, you can know where the church is in relation to its purpose, if it's progressing, and at what rate. For a church to be moving in the right direction, it is essential to develop and implement a ministry charter.

Though there are many things I can't state emphatically, this I can. No church got to the wrong place following the right plan. Therefore, if a church is in the wrong place or floundering, either they have the wrong plan or they're not working the plan. This is as foundational as it gets.

> **If the church is going to transition to greater effectiveness without compromising God's truth, it must figure out where it is, where it's going, and how it's going to get there.**

In our lingo, a ministry charter represents a picture or description of what the church is about. A ministry charter is a foundational description of why a church exists and the ultimate intention of all its activities. If a church doesn't have this clarified in simple terminology, then it will never be able to move with precision toward a specified target. Anyone can shoot a gun, but few people can shoot a gun with precision. There is only one way to differentiate between an expert marksperson and a novice: it's called a target. The same is true with churches.

It's easy for a church to claim success as long as there is no specified target. But once the target is established, everything changes. This is the point of a ministry charter. The ministry charter at our church fits onto three simple cards that we make available to everyone. We call it a Value Pack. It puts the point of our ministry in the hands of anyone who wants it. It's not hard for leadership to evaluate how we're doing, nor is it hard for the guest.

We make the target clear. Because of this, while we might be off course, we're never lost. We may not be where we want to be, but we do know where we are and where we're supposed to be going. And so does everyone who has our Value Pack.

Our ministry charter simply defines the vision, purpose, values, and strategy of our church. It's our ministry in a nutshell. The ministry charter makes public the genetic code of our church. It serves as our church GPS—preventing us from getting lost, veering off track, and wasting time.

Over time, I have found that most churches enunciate their purpose one way but organize another. In other words, what they say has no relevance to what they are. If the church is going to impact the world, its activity must be consistent with its claims. Developing and implementing a ministry charter helps to accomplish this. We've developed our ministry charter around four words beginning with the letter *D*. Therefore, we encourage any church that wants to transition to effectiveness to "help their people see in 4-D."

Vision

Our vision *defines* us. For me, the best description for vision is "the picture of our preferred future." I think of vision as the picture of what we'll look like when we're working right. While the vision doesn't change, where a church is in relation to its vision can change constantly. One day the church can look exactly like the picture. But the next day it's out of sync. Because of this, vision is something you must always keep in clear view. Vision defines the church.

God gave us His vision for the church in Acts 2:41–47. This passage records the first day of the church. This is the perfect picture because it presents the church before people could get their grimy little hands on it and mess it up. Because this is the first day of the church, we can be confident that it's what God wants the church to look like. On the first day, the picture of the church captured three beautiful images. People were discovering Christ, developing in Christ, and experiencing Christ.

We have developed this picture and put it on the wall as our vision. Our vision is "to be a center for discovering, developing in, and experiencing Christ." A center where people from all different backgrounds come together and discover the purpose, potential, and promise found in Christ. Our vision defines us. Every church needs a vision defining its reason for existing. Otherwise, it will exist with no purpose. Unfortunately, too many of our churches are doing just that . . . simply existing.

> **While the vision doesn't change, where a church is in relation to its vision can change constantly.**

Purpose

Our purpose *directs* us. It directs the church to function in all the ways necessary to make us look like the picture. The purpose directs all of our activity in order to make sure that everything is lined up with our vision. It allows us to make sure that everything is working right.

We believe that, just as the vision of the church is given by God in Acts 2, the purpose is clearly given by Jesus in Matthew 28:19–20. These verses are commonly referred to as the Great Commission. Though we've stated the purpose in more contemporary terms, the purpose of our church is clearly the purpose that Jesus gave to all churches. We state our purpose this way: "We exist to lead people to a life of faith in Christ, and then on the journey to full devotion, one life at a time." This purpose directs all of our activities and decisions. It keeps all of us moving consistently forward in the same direction. Every church needs a clearly defined purpose. Because many don't have one, all of their activities and decisions are scattering them in a thousand different directions. It's depleting their resources and paralyzing their potential to make a difference in the world.

Values

Our values *drive* us. We believe that our values literally fuel all the positive activity of the church. Since I live near Detroit, it only makes sense that I would use an illustration from the car industry. Our church's vision is the beautiful picture of what our vacation would look like if it was going as planned. It's the picture on our wall that defines the perfect vacation. Since I live in a place that plays host to winter for nearly half the year, let's identify the vacation spot as Southern California. The purpose of the church puts the car in the right direction. The car needs to be pointing west. Even if the vacation picture is clear and the car is pointed in the right direction, there is no guarantee that we will actually experience the beauty of Southern California. In order to get there, we'll need fuel in the tank. The clearly expressed values of a church are the fuel in the tank. They drive the church to fulfill the purpose.

A lot of churches have the right vision. They know what they're supposed to look like when they're working right. They know their purpose. They can quote Matthew 28:19–20. They know their destination, and they have the car pointed in the right direction. Yet they're not moving. This is because they have no fuel in the tank. Unfortunately, they don't have the right values driving them.

Values Must Be Emphasized to Be Embraced

I spend a lot of time keeping our values before the church. In fact, I believe values are what ultimately move a church in the right direction. Our church is a great illustration of this truth. Values propelled our church to a unique impact in its early days.

Back in the 1940s and '50s, it was one of the largest churches in the world. They were reaching hundreds of lost people for Christ. This was clearly no accident. The pastor at that time poured the value of evangelism into them. It was his primary message. As a result, they were driven by this value.

As the years went by and that pastor left, the value of evangelism was slowly and subtly supplanted by different values. The values that began driving them were more about tradition and culture. They became very concerned about preserving the style, language, traditions, and preferences of their "Southern culture" ministry. As a result, this became an overriding value that drove the ministry. Though most of them didn't even recognize it, they were willing to miss out on winning people to Christ as long as they were doing ministry according to their cultural values. Values still drove them, but they had the wrong values.

When I came as pastor, I had to reconnect them to their original value so the church could start working again. As I poured the value of reaching lost people back into the church, it started driving them. They started loosening up on the issues of tradition and culture and began supporting the changes necessary to reach people for Jesus again.

Every Church Is Driven by Values

Every church is driven by values. The question is whether they are the right values. If a church is content not reaching people for Christ, they are being driven by the wrong values. Therefore, if a church is going to transition to effectiveness, the right values need to be poured into them. When a leader consistently pours scriptural values into the church, those values will begin lighting the fire of the people. With the right values driving them, they won't have to be pushed. They'll have the fuel necessary for driving toward the purpose.

A great example of this can be seen in one of the foundational values we've embraced as a church: "Excellence honors God and inspires people." This value is inspired by passages like Colossians 3:23 and Hebrews 10:24: "Whatever you do, work at it with all your heart, as working for the Lord, not for men." "And let us consider how we may spur one another on toward love and good deeds." I believe nothing deserves excellence more than the church of Jesus Christ.

Businesspeople are willing to do whatever it takes to do their business with excellence. Of course, they do it to make a few more dollars. While there's certainly nothing wrong with making a profit, at best, it's for temporary gain. Still, many of our churches, which are dealing with eternity, are willing to settle for mediocrity. This is wrong. If anything deserves excellence, it's the church of Jesus Christ. Because I believe this so strongly, this value is one of the seven primary values of our church. We talk about excellence all the time, and it has become a part of the fabric of our church. As a result, we're driven by it. In whatever we do, we seek to do it with the kind of excellence that will honor God and inspire people. The proof of this can be seen in the impact of our ministries.

> **Nothing deserves excellence more than the church of Jesus Christ.**

For example, every year we do a Christmas program with every ounce of excellence we can squeeze out of it. As a result, people are inspired. Close to thirty thousand people attend each year. Interestingly, a high percentage of the people who attend are not believers. Why would nonbelievers want to come to a church Christmas concert? The answer is simply that excellence inspires people. One year, I received an e-mail from a nonbeliever who had attended. This person frequented Broadway, but if asked to choose between Broadway and our Christmas presentation, this person would choose our church. Of course, God is honored whenever we do our best in His name. However, the significant number of spiritual decisions made at this presentation each year honors Him above anything we could do. This reveals that values really do drive us.

The question each leader and church must answer is, "Are we being driven by the right values?" If a church is going to transition, the appropriate values need to be spelled out and poured into the church.

Strategy

Our strategy *designs* us. Though most don't think in these terms, the choices and options for how a church will do ministry are vast. If they turn into any and every opportunity available to them, as some do, they'll never get anywhere. If they don't avail themselves of any of the opportunities and just stay parked where they've been for the last twenty-five years, they'll continue to miss the point. In order to balance these two extremes, a church needs to develop a strategy. It provides the road map for how to get to the vision, the preferred picture of the future.

When I was a child, my parents did something so impressive that I remember the experience to this day. We took a month-long family road trip from Michigan to the West Coast and back. Along the way, we saw almost everything worth seeing between the two. We visited the Grand Canyon, Las Vegas, and the Petrified and Redwood Forests. Then, we topped the vacation off with the Seattle World's Fair. It was an amazing trip. But it didn't just happen. Though my brothers and I simply had to get in and out of the car, my parents had to map out every detail. Of course, I had no clue at the time that they had mapped out the trip. From my young perspective, I thought it was magical. You get in the car, goof off with your brothers, sleep for a while, whine for a while, and then magically arrive at cool places. Of course, it doesn't work that way.

But this is how many churches go about ministry. They have no strategy for how to accomplish the vision and purpose that God has assigned. They just show up every week, find their favorite seats, enjoy some time with the spiritual family, sleep for a while, perhaps even whine a little. And somehow the church is supposed to magically arrive at the awesome destinations God desires for it. It doesn't happen this way. Someone has to map out a strategy.

In talking to a lot of church leaders, I have found that most of them do have a general idea of God's vision and purpose for the church. They know they're supposed to care about and reach lost people with the love and hope of Christ. They seem to have a fairly good understanding that church should be a place where broken people can experience God putting them back together again. Most seem to know that God wants them to help the less fortunate. Not many of them miss that the church should be a place where believers can grow spiritually and serve. They have a fairly clear understanding of the point.

However, it almost always gets a bit murky when I ask them how they're going to do it. I ask, "What's your strategy?" They have no clue. They unlock the doors of the church at the right time. They read the right Bible passages for the day. They say the right prayers. They sing the right songs. They make the right announcements. They keep the literature rack full. They give the right sermons on the right days. But more often than not, they have no idea how to become the church that God has called them to be. In other words, they're doing church like I did the trip to California. They're just getting in, taking a ride, and hoping they'll arrive at some cool destinations.

The bottom line is that a church without a strategy is a church that is not and cannot be working right. If a church doesn't know how to do it, they're not going to do it. This is where an old and overused cliché could help: "It's better to shoot at a target and miss than to shoot at nothing and hit it." For the church to successfully become the hope of the world, it must have and follow a strategy.

Developing a Ministry Charter

Of course, it's one thing to know you need a strategy to accomplish your vision. It's an entirely different story to actually create one. I can't even imagine what kind of vacation my family would have experienced if they had asked me, as a three-year-old, to map out our California trip. Of this I'm certain: we would have never gotten to California or any of the other cool places we visited. At best, my map would have been developed by throwing darts at the board.

Blood, Sweat, and Tears

It's vital to walk through some important principles for developing a ministry charter for a church. It's important to know that it's not necessarily easy, and it isn't something that happens quickly. It takes blood, sweat, and tears. But, in the end, it's worth it. If done well, it frees the church to be the church—the hope of the world.

When a church spells out its vision, purpose, values, and strategy, it is literally creating (or identifying) the genetic code through which the church will develop. If done well, it will provide a clear picture of what the church will look like when it's working right. For this reason, it's vital that the church takes great care when developing a charter. Though it's certainly wise and valuable to learn and pull from other churches, the finished product should be both fitting and unique to the individual church. Unfortunately, a lot of churches simply adopt another church's description without running it through the filter of their own setting, history, personalities, leader, and abilities. This doesn't usually work. They usually choose the description of a church that doesn't match their uniqueness. As a result, it can't produce the desired effects in their ministry no matter how hard they work it. The churches emulated most often are the large and successful ones. While this makes sense, the reality is that their success is usually related more to the unique gifting of the leader than to their ministry charter. Simply borrowing their vision, purpose, values, and strategy (as well stated as they may be) won't bring about the same results without a similar leader. This is why it's vital for each church to create an appropriate ministry description that matches its strengths and weaknesses.

Borrowing another church's ministry charter may not work, simply because that would be too easy. When there is no effort invested, there is no compelling reason to use it or to keep it. So when it doesn't work, which will be the case with any plan not fully engaged, the church will feel no loss in chucking it. This happens a lot, and it always hurts the church. I've seen it happen this way. Pastors will go to a conference and get inspired. This becomes the catalyst for how they want to do ministry at their churches. With very little effort or prayer, they take the ideas back to their churches and begin passionately preaching them. The churches get excited. Finally, the pastor is passionate about something! The problem that generally follows is that nothing happens. This is predictable because, while inspired by the ideas, the pastors have no plans for implementation. Of course, if they don't have a plan, they certainly can't follow it. So nothing changes in the church.

A couple of months or years later, the same pastors attend a different conference and the pattern repeats itself. This is the result of the cost that's being paid for the plan. When someone buys cheap paper plates and plastic silverware, she has no problem discarding it after one use. This doesn't happen with expensive china. The same is true in the church. When you have no real investment in a plan, it's easy to discard it when you've never used it or only used it a couple of times. But when you make some serious investments in developing a plan, you tend to invest yourself in making it work. It tends to be a better reflection of your unique strengths, circumstances, and passions. Continually changing courses will kill the church.

Shared Ownership

Churches need to take this process seriously. They need to make sure their ministry charters genuinely reflect God's unique will and calling for them. If this is to happen, then the development of the vision, purpose, values, and strategy cannot be a one-person job. Though I believe that the pastor should be a catalyst, he should not attempt to do it alone. If it's one person's ministry charter, what happens if or when that one person leaves the church? It needs to be developed through a process involving a group of uniquely gifted people who have a stake in the church. If this happens, the plan will be embraced and worked, even if God calls the pastor away. Shared ownership is powerful in moving a church forward.

Prayer

Prayer should be the foundation of this process. After all, it's God's church. If He's not inspiring the vision, purpose, values, and strategy, then the church is in trouble. I love James 1:5–7 as it applies to this: "If any of you lacks wisdom, he should ask God, who gives generously to all without finding fault, and it will be given to him." We all need wisdom. Therefore, we should all be asking Him for it—especially when we're in a process of determining His will for the church. If the church has any hope of becoming everything God desires it to be, we need to bathe the planning process in prayer.

Let Scripture Be the Guide

In spelling out the ministry charter, Scripture must be the guide. If they don't flow out of God's Word, the church needs to start over. This is the problem with many churches that aren't working right today: their ministry purpose and values have no basis or authority. Without the compelling authority of God's Word, they will not lead the church. Apart from God's truth, there is no hope to offer. A true church will never be motivated to embrace change if it can't be clearly established that the changes are in keeping with God's Word. The only legitimate vision, purpose, and values for a church are those lifted from the pages of the Word of God.

Different Churches, Different Strategies

While the strategy should complement and align with Scripture, unlike the vision, purpose, and values, the strategy isn't necessarily extracted from Scripture. Churches that declare they have a scriptural strategy are heading for trouble. This was a significant problem in our church when I first arrived. They had been told they were doing church the "Bible way." As a result, to change anything they were doing would be a sin. The problem was that it wasn't the "Bible way." It had been an effective way to do ministry in the mid-twentieth century for Southerners. It aligned with the purpose and values God has given the church, and in that time period it worked. But when it stopped working, it needed to be changed. A strategy is only meaningful if it leads to fulfilling God's purpose. When it doesn't accomplish this, it must be changed, or the church will fail to fulfill God's purpose. This is true compromise. Too many churches fall in love with the way they do ministry instead of with the reason they do ministry. This has to stop!

The strategy should never compromise the clearly expressed principles and values of God's Word. As long as this isn't happening, anything goes. The ultimate point of the strategy needs to be that it works at accomplishing the purpose of the church. If it does, it should be used. If it doesn't, it should be changed.

Though there is bound to be overlap among churches and though we can all learn from each other, each church should have its own strategy. While every church does have to fulfill the Great Commission, every church doesn't have to do it the same way. God didn't command a specific way to reach people. He didn't say a church had to knock on a stranger's door, start a bus ministry, sponsor crusades and revivals, or preach evangelistically on Sunday nights. He simply said we need to reach people. Though there's nothing necessarily wrong with any of the above strategies, there is nothing inherently right with them either. The only question is whether they are the best means of accomplishing what God has commanded your church to do. If yes, your church should do them. If no, your church shouldn't. The problem is that churches that do them tend to condemn those who don't. And because they believe they are scriptural strategies, they keep doing them even when they don't work. This is killing too many of our churches. So while the strategy should always complement and never compromise God's Word, the key issue is whether it works. If it doesn't, the church needs to develop a new strategy.

> **The only legitimate vision, purpose, and values for a church are those lifted from the pages of the Word of God.**

Make It Your Own

In developing your ministry charter, the church can and should research other biblically based churches. This will significantly help in writing an effective ministry charter. There is much to be learned from what God has done and is doing in other churches. As a church exposes itself to a wide range of different ministries, it will find some that have nothing in common and others that are very similar. By doing this, a church is opening itself to ideas through which the Holy Spirit can inspire. When a church never looks outside of its own world, it is very limited. Since God is bigger than any one church or denomination, I strongly believe that we get a bigger and better view of God and what He's doing in the church by looking outside our realm. Of course, each church needs to know and be committed to God's truth. This can't be compromised. But, in examining other churches, God will spark ideas that can help a church create a description that clearly expresses its particular vision, purpose, values, and strategy.

> **The ministry charter must ultimately identify the unique heartbeat of each individual church.**

Since no church today is the first church, no church has to start totally from scratch. Because most leaders and churches aren't called to be pioneers, they can follow trails tested and tried by others. But, as I mentioned earlier in this chapter, it needs to fit each individual church. The ministry charter must ultimately identify the unique heartbeat of each individual church.

Before I came to NorthRidge, my driving passion as a church leader was drawn from Matthew 16:18: "I will build my church, and the gates of Hades will not overcome it." As far back as I can remember in my ministry experience, I have been driven by the concept that the church is offensive, not defensive. As well, Acts 2 was significant to me. I loved the picture it painted of the church. I knew that it was a picture not of what the church once was but of what the church was supposed to be. It pictures a church as a hub, attracting different people from different places in different ways to the hope of Christ.

But I had no idea how to put this into a vision. In conjunction with my leadership team, we worked hard to put together our ministry charter. We examined many other churches. We were able to incorporate a lot of ideas that made sense to our setting and matched the rhythm of our hearts for the church. But even with all of this exposure, experience, and effort, we weren't able to land on a vision that hit the target for us.

One day, while on my knees with the Bible opened to Acts 2:41–47, the picture of what was happening in that passage leaped off the page. People were discovering Christ. Thousands of them discovered Him. People were developing in Christ. They were committing themselves to the apostles' teaching. People were experiencing Christ. This part was really important to me. The consequence of people discovering and developing in Christ was not a simple name change—from pagan to Christian. It changed everything. They began experiencing the power, promises, purpose, presence, and peace of God. This was it for me. All the pieces came together in that moment. Our vision is "to be a center for discovering, developing in, and experiencing Christ." This matches my passion and heart for ministry. And even more, it fits our church perfectly.

It Doesn't Happen Overnight

Our church's vision didn't happen overnight. It took a long journey with many people. We saturated ourselves with all God has revealed about His design for the church, and we made sure our vision faithfully pictured that design. We exposed ourselves to many other churches and their inspiring visions. Without taking the time to do this, I probably would have never landed on our vision. Finally, it fell in place as I was on my knees in the Bible and prayer. I believe this is the journey every church needs to take, if they're going to be impassioned and compelled to work.

Our purpose and values were inspired in much the same way. In fact, they came prior to the vision statement. Though some of our values are original, most of them have been our own reworking of biblical values beautifully and creatively expressed by other churches. However, in all of our research, exposure to other churches, and work, there was one very important value that we missed: the responsibility of the church to provide compassion and care for those broken, hurting, and less fortunate.

To be honest, I never even thought of creating a value to motivate this area of ministry. Fortunately, I had someone on my team who noticed the oversight. As I recall, he called and asked to see me about a problem, and I agreed to meet with him. When we met, he said that he was having a problem finding one of our church values that motivated and drove people to participate in our care and compassion ministries. So I went through our existing values with him. Though I tried to make a couple of them fit, in the end, I had to agree with him. We had missed the value of care.

As a result, I dove into Matthew 25 and other passages and developed a biblical and relevant value for care and compassion that would drive our church to invest in it. In fact, it has become a very significant and driving force in my leadership and our overall church ministry.

The lesson is that developing a ministry charter that genuinely defines, directs, drives, and designs a church, requires a long process and needs to remain malleable. As circumstances change, it will need to evolve in order to address those changes.

Don't Ask . . . Sell

If the process of developing the ministry charter included the appropriate influencers in the church, they should be committed to embracing, declaring, and supporting it. In order for the ministry charter to shape the behavior of the entire church, it must be effectively and passionately communicated to the people. Unfortunately, this is where many pastors and church leaders drop the ball.

I'm amazed at how many "leaders" ask their people to vote on whether they should fulfill God's purpose and values. God doesn't want the leader asking people to vote on whether they will do right; He wants the leader motivating people to do right. As the Bible illustrates, Jesus was respected because He taught with authority (Matthew 7:28–29). Pastors can teach with the same authority when they teach God's clearly revealed Word. In presenting God's vision, purpose, and values to the church, pastors need to sell it. And then, once sold, for integrity purposes, the pastors have two responsibilities.

> **In order for the ministry charter to shape the behavior of the entire church, it must be effectively and passionately communicated to the people.**

First, they need to make sure that everything in the ministry functions in accordance with the ministry charter. Every decision, program, expenditure, and hire needs to agree with and support the fulfillment of the mission charter. If the church doesn't live by the charter, the church will get off track and the people will know that it was just another flash-in-the-pan idea.

Second, the pastor needs to incorporate the church's purpose and values into their sermons as much as possible. People need to see how the values fit in to the living of their lives as believers. As well, it will allow for the values to become absorbed into the thinking of those who are part of the church. Typically, the only time many pastors mention vision, purpose, values, and strategy is when they're introducing it. This won't work. The ministry charter has to be continually seen and heard, or it won't become a reality. As well, there are pastors who only talk about these things once a year. This won't work either. After all, out of sight, out of mind. It also misses the new people. While I highly recommend an annual vision series, it shouldn't be the only time the church hears about these things. The church's vision needs to be constantly kept before the people in the context of teaching. In this way, it can and will become the driving force behind the ministry.

CHAPTER 9

Can You Hear Me Now?

Communication, Communication, Communication

When it comes to successfully transitioning a church, communication is essential. If a leader doesn't effectively communicate, the church will not embrace the leadership or vision.

As with all relationships, communication is the link between leaders and people. It provides the only bridge for genuinely understanding and connecting to one another. Without consistently good communication, there's no way for church leaders and people to stay on the same page or move in the same direction. This explains why so many churches aren't doing either. If a church leadership team developed the perfect ministry charter for their environment, as we talked about in the last chapter, it would be worthless and create no impact without consistent and clear communication.

Common Traps That Kill Communication

I learned this the hard way in my first ministry. My failure to understand the importance and difficulty of communication led to the failure of my ministry in that church. Though I tried, I never connected with the congregation in a way that got us on the same page and moving in the same direction. I thought we were together, but we couldn't have been further apart. I fell into the common traps that kill successful communication.

One-Way Communication

The first trap is *one-way communication*. I honestly thought people would listen intently to and accept every word I said because I was the pastor. Oops. I found out the hard way that it doesn't work this way. Though laughable now, I was infected with the common disease of naïveté. I also had a hugely overestimated opinion of my ability as a communicator. When these two combined, they became lethal to any hope I had of genuinely communicating with those people, and there were only eighteen of them when I started.

> **If a leader doesn't effectively communicate, the church will not embrace the leadership or vision.**

Many pastors sincerely believe that if they say something from the pulpit, it's done and they should never have to say it again. This is seen in how they lay out their vision in one talk and then never go back to it. Of course, this doesn't work, even in a personal conversation where both individuals know, accept, trust, and actually listen to each other. How could we expect it to work in an impersonal, one-way conversation from a person on a platform to many people at varying stages of attention, understanding, acceptance, and trust? Hope as we might, saying something once won't get it done. It didn't work for Jesus with the disciples, and it certainly won't work in the church. In order to expect people to understand and embrace a vision, we need to communicate it clearly and consistently.

Ambiguity

The second trap is *ambiguity*. Lack of clarity kills communication, yet it's a common malady. We don't say what we mean or mean what we say. In fact, we often say the opposite. I know it's happened to me in my marriage. I'll ask my wife, "Are you upset?" She'll say, "No." but she doesn't mean "no." She means "yes!" When we were newly married, she would often say, "Just do what you want." I honestly thought she was the most approving wife in the world. How did I get so lucky? On one occasion, I wanted to buy a motorcycle, though we really didn't have the money. There were a ton of higher-priorities items we needed. But after a short conversation, she said, "Just do what you want." Man, I loved that motorcycle . . . until I got home. That's when I found out that she didn't mean what she said. She meant, "If you buy that motorcycle, I'll kill you."

Ambiguity keeps people from genuinely communicating. I wasn't smart enough to have this one figured out during my first pastorate. When I was a candidate to be their pastor, I asked them some questions like, "Do you genuinely care about reaching lost people? Do you want to grow? Are you willing to change in order to reach lost people and grow as a church?" I was thrilled when they gave me all the right answers. They told me everything I wanted to hear. The problem was that sometimes people don't say what they mean. They say what they know the person wants to hear. Like with my wife and the motorcycle, my failure to understand this ruined any opportunity for me to succeed in connecting to, genuinely understanding, and leading these people.

Assumption

The third trap is *assumption*. This happens in communication all the time, especially in marriage. One guy found this out in a big way. He said, "I married Miss Right. Little did I know that her first name was 'Always.'" This is a common roadblock to good communication.

Though I had no clue at the time, those in leadership at my first church were not on the same page with me. I assumed they were. Like the guy with his wife, my assumption was wrong. As is usually the case, both sides were making invalid assumptions. They assumed I was going to lead the church to be everything *they* wanted the church to be. I assumed they wanted me to lead the church to be everything *God* wanted the church to be.

I discovered the problem at a board meeting. It was probably my third meeting. The board members informed me that they were taking away all of the pastoral authority I'd been given to lead the church. Since they liked my teaching and preaching, they just wanted me to stick to those. Because they didn't like my leadership, they would go ahead and lead. My jaw hit the table. I was caught by surprise. Of course, this is what happens when you are living in the illusion created by assumption. But I regrouped and started doing what I was called to do—leading. I asked them to get out their Bibles in order to do a study on the church and how it should be structured. No one reached for their Bibles, but the "leader" spoke up. He said (and I'm not kidding), "We've tried the Bible way, and it doesn't work here." This time my jaw got bruised it dropped so hard. I had assumed that these guys were on the same page with me about the Bible. I was wrong.

It went downhill from there. They pulled out their church constitution and claimed the right to control the pastor. It wasn't in the constitution, but they used their right to vote as the authority to demote me to their teaching and preaching puppet. I informed them that, as long as I was pastor, we'd be following the Bible, not the constitution, because only the Bible was inspired. Once again, their spokesman surprised me. He said, "How do you know the constitution isn't inspired? Godly men wrote it too." Well, I put my Bible away because now I knew I wouldn't need it.

Through this experience, I learned quickly that positive relationships and communication cannot exist when they are built on assumptions. Since that time, I have sought to avoid, to the best of my ability, communication based on assumption.

Dishonesty

The fourth common trap that kills communication is *dishonesty*. By making it one of the Ten Commandments, God clearly identified dishonesty as both a sin and something to be avoided. Along with that, it just makes sense that dishonesty would destroy "honest" communication. Yet dishonesty remains a problem. It would be easier to understand if it were limited to those who are clearly not Christ-followers. But it's not.

Unfortunately, dishonesty is prevalent in the church because the church will always have both genuine believers and counterfeit believers. Jesus made this clear in His story about the wheat and the weeds in Matthew 13:24–30. However, it's not all explained by this. People are dishonest when it's the only way they can get what they want. This is why the leaders in the first church I pastored were dishonest.

Because I wasn't the kind of pastor they wanted, they turned to dishonesty to get rid of me. Though loving and kind to my face, they went behind my back to round up the needed votes to fire me. The church was growing, people were coming to faith, and we were planning a big baptism service. But they wanted me out so badly that they were dishonest with me. When I found this out, I resigned in order to save all the new believers from the inevitable war.

I resigned on the morning that we were to baptize eighteen new believers. Following my resignation, one of the "spiritual leaders" closed in prayer. He *thanked* God for answering their prayers in such a clear and powerful way. They closed the service without reaching out to the new believers and attenders. The reason was simple: they didn't care about them, in spite of what they had told me during the interview. They have further revealed this by failing to reach out beyond their small circle for the past twenty years. They're still the same small handful of people they were when my wife and I first became a part of their ministry.

Sadly, my experience in that first church isn't unique. All of these common traps that kill communication are prevalent in churches. As always, they cause relational conflict and major problems. There is no way for a church to walk in harmony and unity in fulfilling God's purposes for the church when these common failures are preventing good communication. This is one of the many reasons that so many churches aren't working right. For the church to function effectively as the hope of the world, there must be communication, communication, communication.

The Difference Between Success and Failure

Through good communication, the leaders and people of a church can be—and stay—on the same page regardless of the issues they're facing. In fact, it is the difference between success and failure in a church.

We have to do everything in our power to eliminate the common traps that kill communication in our churches. As I proved in my first ministry, this isn't easily done, even in a smaller ministry. As a church grows and adds more people with even greater diversity, the task gets significantly more difficult. In the early days of our church, I was the primary source of communication. The congregation was small enough that I could personally relate to all staff, volunteers, and people. If there was a problem, I could address it. If there was a misunderstanding, I could clarify it. If there was a question, I could answer it. But as the church has grown, it's become impossible for me to personally communicate to everyone. Still, good communication is just as vital.

So in order to avoid the pitfalls and keep the church moving positively forward, we have created different systems and structures for communication at the same level of excellence as in smaller churches. For example, I now use the organization in order to maintain clear lines of communication. It begins with two teams: staff leadership team and elders. Through the leadership team, the communication flows to all of our church staff, volunteer leaders, and teachers, and then to all church volunteers. From there, it is passed to everyone in the church who is a part of a connection group of any kind. If there are any issues that arise, the communication comes back up through the same means. Without this, the church would slowly but surely stop working. After all, when you boil church ministry down, it's all about communication. For me, having experienced the pain and agony of a church with poor communication, this isn't an option. So we continue to make it a top-drawer priority.

> It's one thing to know *how* to communicate well. It's fully another to know *what* to communicate.

What Must Be Communicated

Of course, it's one thing to know *how* to communicate well. It's fully another to know *what* to communicate. As I have experienced the g-force of transition, I have discovered what must be communicated to successfully transition a church.

Personal Care

For a transition to get traction, the leader must get traction. This will never happen if the church doesn't know that the leader values them. Though it's a common cliché, it's vital for the leader to understand: "People don't care how much you know until they know how much you care." Because of this, the transition leader must show and communicate value for them.

When I first came to NorthRidge, I had no concept of this. Though I truly cared about the people, I assumed they would somehow automatically know it. They didn't. In fact, their perception was quite the opposite. After all, I was coming into a church spiraling downward so fast they were already making assessments as to how long before the doors would have to be closed . . . for good. So I believed that my first leadership priority was to do whatever it took to stop the bleeding. This motivated me to make some very significant changes in a short period of time. I thought that my honeymoon with the church would provide a short but necessary cover for these changes. As it turned out, I never experienced a honeymoon because of all the changes I was making.

Of course, these changes, which I'll discuss in more detail in the next chapter, affected a lot of people negatively. Since this was their first experience with my leadership, the perception was that I didn't care. Though there was nothing I could do about the negative impact of the changes I was making, I could have taken intentional steps to show publicly my value for the people. I was showing care and value to people, but it was happening out of the public eye. I made the mistake of assuming that the whole church knew. This allowed a perception to grow that their new pastor didn't care about them. As parents must do with their children, a pastor must publicly and personally communicate his love and compassion for the church family as much as possible. Of course, the actions must match the words, but actions aren't enough. I should have found ways to clearly demonstrate my care for the congregation from the very beginning. It took a long time to overcome this. When church leaders are seeking to lead change, they must show and communicate value to and for the people publicly as well as privately.

Burden

In order to lead people to embrace change, leaders must share and communicate the burden. Nehemiah is the poster boy for this truth. Jerusalem was in a mess because no one had a burden to fix it. People without a burden are content to do nothing. The people of Jerusalem were so content that they didn't even see the problem. Though dishonoring to God and an embarrassment before the world, the status quo was fine for them. People without a burden are generally people who are focused on themselves and looking for the easy, convenient, and comfortable route. Regrettably, this is the state of many of our churches.

Nehemiah showed up with a burden, and he passionately shared it with the people in Jerusalem. Everything changed. The people went from content and doing nothing to working sacrificially on the walls.

People in churches are generally good, sincere people. They've just lost their motivation, and their focus has turned inward. Yet this can all change as did the people in Nehemiah's day. They just need someone to remind them what the church is supposed to be. No one dreams of living a life of insignificance. Rather, they dream of making a difference, of being part of something bigger than themselves. When a leader shares that burden, it can wake people up to their dream. As a result, the unexpected can happen. Before Nehemiah showed up, no one could have imagined that the people of Jerusalem would become such a force for change. Yet in a moment, all this changed. They were motivated to become people of commitment and excellence. Someone just had to share the burden.

The church desperately needs leaders who will share the burden effectively. As with Jerusalem in that day, the problems in the church are not readily apparent. But the church is filled with people who dream of changing their world. They don't dream of living small, self-centered lives. God has put within them the desire and potential to bring hope to the world. Without knowing it, they're just waiting for someone to bring the dream to life by sharing the burden and showing the way.

Vision

Sharing a burden is powerful because vision flows out of burden. There is no vision without a burden. Though it's a tough truth to hear, when a leader or church is without a vision, the real problem is the lack of a burden. Burden drives a vision.

Nehemiah had never even been to Jerusalem, yet he got a vision for rebuilding it. Where did it come from? It flowed out of his burden. By looking outside of his own comfortable world, exposing himself to the great need in Jerusalem, and then seeing himself as a part of the problem and solution, Nehemiah developed a burden that drove everything else he would ever do in life. It ignited his vision for rebuilding and seeing God's glory return to Jerusalem. His burden drove him to change his entire life in order to accomplish God's purposes in this world. The church needs a vision driven by a burden. It needs a leader who will get and communicate a vision-producing burden today as Nehemiah did many yesterdays ago.

Sacrifice

The church was founded by and built on sacrifice. It began with the incomprehensible sacrifice of God for man. It became an insurmountable force in the world through the sacrifices of its early leaders. In Acts 7, Stephen became the first one to follow

Christ in sacrificing his life for the church. Throughout the generations, truth was carried forward on the back of sacrifice. Every sacrifice made for the cause of Christ flowed out of the burden to honor Him and share His hope. Paul said it best in 1 Corinthians 9:16: "When I preach the gospel, I cannot boast, for I am compelled to preach. Woe to me if I do not preach the gospel!" His many sacrifices to share God's truth, and ultimately the sacrifice of his life, flowed out of his burden.

The church desperately needs leaders who will share the burden effectively.

The reason some churches today are not willing to sacrifice their comfort, traditions, preferred music, style of ministry, clean buildings, or money is because they have no burden. It's not that they're bad people. They just need someone to share the burden with them. When these same people are captured by the burden that motivated Jesus, Stephen, and Paul, they, too, will begin sacrificing.

The Great Danger for the Church

Though vital, a burden is fragile. Just as it can be gained, it can be lost. While there are many potential causes for the loss of burden, the most significant are selfishness and success. Selfishness robs us of burden because it keeps us from seeing or caring about anyone or anything other than ourselves. Success robs us of burden because it eliminates need. Of course, need is the greatest motivator. It motivates a hungry person to work, an addicted person to seek help, and a lost person to accept guidance. In other words, it compels a person to surrender his pride and depend on someone else to survive. When a person goes through this, it almost always creates a heart for other people and their needs. Second Corinthians 1:3–4 reveals this principle: "Praise be to the God and

Father of our Lord Jesus Christ, the Father of compassion and the God of all comfort, who comforts us in all our troubles, so that we can comfort those in any trouble with the comfort we ourselves have received from God." However, when the need is eliminated, so is the motivation to care about anyone or anything other than ourselves.

In the Old Testament, Israel is the perfect example of this. When they were desperate, their hearts would eventually soften, and they would cry out to God for help. Of course, He would answer them and pour out His blessings into their lives. They would no longer be desperate. As a result, they would slowly but surely stop looking to and depending on God. Their hearts would once again turn inward and harden. And they would lose their passion and burden for anything other than themselves. Consuming self-interest is often the end result of success, and it eradicates burden for anyone or anything other than self. In return, this leads them back to emptiness, brokenness, and distorted values.

This same potential exists in the church. In the beginning, a church is often driven by burden. Their lives have been so impacted by God that they are driven to honor Him by helping others discover and experience Him in the same way. In order to accomplish this, they need God to show up. They have to trust Him for everything. Driven by this need, they fervently pray and passionately work. As a result, God blesses them. But then the cycle may begin. As they grow, they arrive at the place where they have the resources they need to survive. They have the critical mass of people necessary to build a building, hire a pastor, and pay the bills. Desperation for survival no longer motivates fervent prayer and passionate work. The tendency is to ease up. Rather than being driven to reach out to new people, they start turning inward and caring for the base. Though everything seems healthy, it's at this point they begin to die. They have lost the burden.

This is the great danger for the church. According to commonly accepted statistics, the average church in America is around one hundred people. This is just enough people to form the critical mass necessary to build a small building, pay the bills, and hire a pastor who will meet the needs of the church family. When they reach this stage, more often than not, they stop growing. They have everything they need and want. The problem is that the church doesn't exist for this purpose. In order for the church to continue fulfilling God's purpose, it must be driven by the desire to honor God and provide hope for hopeless people. It can't be driven by their selfish needs and desires. A church driven by a desire to honor God and provide hope for others can remain motivated forever. A church driven by selfishness will lose its motivation as soon as the needs and desires are met. If a church is going to maintain the burden necessary for renewing and keeping the church's health and effectiveness, it must be driven by the same heart for God and for others that drove Jesus to the cross.

Support from the People

If a church is going to change without compromise, there must be buy-in from the people. This means that the leader must sell the vision. Though many don't understand it, this is the leader's job. Yet more often than not, leaders blame their people for the problems in the church. I'm amazed at how many leaders rationalize the church's ineffectiveness and inability to change with the excuse that the people "don't want to do it," to which I say, "Of course they don't want to do it. Who wants to sacrifice?"

Think about Israel under Moses and Nehemiah. Israel didn't want to do it either. Moses and Nehemiah had to sell their visions to the people. They had to lead the people to buy in. This is the leader's job. They must get support from the people, or they aren't leading. People don't want change, but they do want the consequence of change. I've read that Tom Landry, the famous Dallas Cowboys coach, once said, "My job is to get men to do what they don't want to do in order to help them achieve everything they want to achieve." This is true for spiritual leaders as well.

Connect the Change to Values

If the church isn't doing what God has called them to do, the reason is simple: they're doing what comes naturally. It's the leader's job to inspire them to do something different. The way to do this is by communicating God's values. The leader must connect the reason for all the changes and the new direction for ministry to the values that the church already embraces. Though they may have lost focus on their values, they have them. The church wouldn't exist if they hadn't been driven by values that led people to make the necessary sacrifices. The leader needs to identify these values, dust them off, and clearly communicate them as the reason for the changes. In order to do this, the leader must become an expert on the church he leads.

> **The leader must connect the reason for all the changes and the new direction for ministry to the values that the church already embraces.**

This is exactly what I did to create support for change with the people in our church. I sought to discover the history of our church any way I could. There had been some material written about it. There were records from past meetings and events. But, by far, the most helpful means of discovery was talking to the people who had been part of the "good old days." As a result, I found that the overarching value of the church in the past had been the Great Commission. Almost everything they did in the past was driven by Jesus' value of "seeking to save what was lost." This church had been all about getting people saved. Their eyes would light up when they talked about the front of the church auditorium being filled with people who were coming to Christ.

Though they hadn't been reaching people for Christ for years and had mistakenly begun valuing the wrong things, fulfilling the Great Commission was still their great value and desire. As their new leader, my job was to show them how change without compromise would make it happen again. I had to connect the new way of ministry to that same value.

Connect Present Leadership to Past Leadership

In order to do this, I had to connect my leadership to that of the past leader. Though he had died fifteen years before I came to pastor, in many ways, he was still the pastor of the church. Though two other men had come and gone as pastor of the church during those fifteen years, the majority of people still referred to their predecessor. The church had a memorial library dedicated to this man, which housed a bust of his image, his glasses on an open Bible, and many other belongings. Though dead, he was still a significant presence and influence in the church. In truth, the church was still organized the way he had organized it.

If I was going to lead this ministry through change, it was important for me to connect what I was doing to what he had said. This proved to be a relatively easy assignment. Despite our differences, and there were many, our hearts beat for the same thing. We both were passionately committed to communicating God's truth to a lost and dying world. As a result, much of what he said applied directly to my ministry. For example, one of his well-known and documented quotes was "The message never changes, but methods must always change." This was both true and brilliant. And most important, it fully supported the premise of my leadership. I was claiming that we needed to change the way we were doing ministry without changing or compromising the message. Of course, the fact that I was saying it meant nothing to the church at the time. I was a new, young, and, in their minds, questionable leader. But this pastor, though dead, was beloved and respected. By connecting myself to his leadership and teaching, I was able to get more support for my leadership.

Connect the Past to the Future

Sometimes, in attempting to transition the church, leaders attack the past. In their minds, they feel attacking the past will help people disconnect from it and embrace the new. Though it sounds logical, it's not true and it doesn't work. In fact, it does the opposite. It disconnects the people from the new leader and new direction. They are proud of their heritage. If going forward means trashing their past, then more often than not, they won't go forward. The effective transition leader needs to connect the past to the future. By embracing and connecting with the church's past, the leader gives them a reason and confidence to connect with and embrace their vision of the future. They don't feel as if they're compromising or forsaking the past. Rather, they feel as if they're building on it. And they are.

In keeping with this, I introduced a phrase that would capture and help to effectively communicate this concept: "Great heritage, great future." Of course, everyone in the church bought the "great heritage" part. It was the reason they were still in the church. They loved their heritage. Because of all the difficulties the church was facing, few bought the "great future" part. However, it revealed clearly that I saw the future connected to and built on the past. This showed respect for the past that earned me a little more respect and trust in the present. There is great power in connecting the future direction of the church to the past direction and values. I always encourage leaders to avoid attacking yesterday, even if they disagree vehemently with some of what was done. Rather, leaders should embrace the strengths of yesterday's church and connect them to the new direction. This will allow the church to build onto the foundation of its great heritage an even greater future.

Connect Hearts

A leader creates support by finding where his heart meets the church's heart, and then building from there. In our story, some who were staunchly against the changes ultimately started fighting for the changes. Because they bought into the Great Commission, they ultimately embraced the transition. They wanted to see people get saved. As they started to see this happen, they stopped fighting against me and started fighting with me. These people are the true heroes of our church. They put aside self-interest and personal preferences in order to help our church fulfill God's purpose. Like Jesus, they left their comfort zones, and even some family and friends, to help people see God's light and experience His hope. Because of them, our church started working right again. Without them, it would have never happened.

We had a class of senior adults who gave me a plaque highlighting one million dollars given toward our church's new campus. This class sacrificed significantly to make the dream for "a great future" become a reality. Though the changes in our church cost them most everything they personally enjoyed in church, from the music to the style of preaching, they decided they were going to follow Jesus. He left heaven and came to earth for others. He said to the Father, "Not as I will, but as you will" (Matthew 26:39). They said the same thing. They're the heroes of our church. They're going to receive an unbelievable welcome and reward in heaven. Some of them already have. These kinds of people are in most every church. But unless the leader creates support through positive and effective communication, they will fight against the changes rather than for them.

Generate Positive Energy

In order to get a church to move toward and through change, the leader must generate positive energy. Though change is tough, people are generally willing to make the necessary sacrifices and effort if it makes life better; as long as it adds enthusiasm and excitement to their lives. This is seen when people take new jobs, buy new homes, and decide to have children. They believe the changes will add excitement and enthusiasm to their lives . . . make life better.

> **Because it deals in the eternal, the church is the one place on the planet worthy of excitement and enthusiasm.**

The same is true in the church. Most Christians are neither excited nor enthused about their church. This needs to change. Because it deals in the eternal, the church is the one place on the planet worthy of excitement and enthusiasm. While the world is suffering in the wake of death and destruction, the church is supposed to be experiencing and proclaiming the reality of the resurrection.

The message of the church is supposed to be that Jesus is alive. As a result, no matter how bad life gets, there is hope. This is something to get excited about. If people are going to embrace change, the leader must generate positive energy. People are attracted to and want to be around enthusiastic, excited, and encouraging leaders. If they expect to be followed, leaders have to smile. When they do, people will start smiling back.

When I first came to my present church, I was the first person to smile on the platform in a very long time. Everything had become so serious. The staff sat up on the platform during services, looking down at the people with somber faces. The result was predictable. The whole church was somber. This doesn't attract or inspire anyone. In order to inspire people, the leader must generate positive energy. The wave of change takes enthusiasm and excitement.

Those who lead in the church don't need to fake joy. They just need "faith" joy. No matter how bad life gets, Jesus is still alive and there is always hope. Church leaders need to start believing it, acting like it, and sharing it. Leaders may not feel joy. They may not be experiencing joy. In fact, their lives may be filled with nothing but depressing realities. However, by faith, they can have and share joy. If they don't, existing people will not follow and new people will not come. Why would they? Most people have enough depression in their lives without consistently putting themselves in a depressing environment.

If the church is going to change positively, the church needs to become a positive place. This starts with the pastor and other church leaders. In our setting, I became a positive force. Whether I was giving announcements or the message, I sought to be enthusiastic and excited. But it doesn't end with the pastor. We added staff and leaders who were positive forces in their areas of ministry. We transitioned our music from a somber style to a fresh, upbeat, and celebrative style. We started adding ministry programs that were positive. The reality is that enthusiasm builds more enthusiasm, excitement leads to more excitement, and joy spreads more joy. In order to bring positive change in a church, the people need to get excited about something.

Communicate to Every Person

Many pastors believe that communicating from the platform on the weekend is all they need to effectively lead the church. This is a fatal mistake.

Years ago, as a young pastor in another church, I communicated vision for a particular ministry from the platform for nearly six months. In my mind, I had cast vision brilliantly and consistently. In fact, I was excited about the potential impact of this particular ministry. Seldom had I started casting vision so early and consistently about an important ministry event. Three days before the event, we were having difficulty recruiting and training volunteers. The reason: they didn't understand it. I had talked about it from the platform until I was blue in the face, yet

There is nothing more difficult to get people embracing than change.

people genuinely didn't understand what it was about. This is when I realized that saying it from the pulpit wasn't enough. If I was going to genuinely get people to understand and embrace an issue, I needed to identify and communicate appropriately at every level in the church.

There is nothing more difficult to get people embracing than change. It requires great understanding. It requires communicating in a way and an environment where people are comfortable to ask questions and challenge the issues. This can't happen in an auditorium setting where the communication is all one-way.

For this reason, during the NorthRidge transition, I identified and sought to communicate relevantly and personally to and with every level within our church. I communicated separately with staff, leaders, and teachers. I made sure that I went into all the classes and groups to communicate with them about the issues of change and how they would or wouldn't be affected. At the same time, I spoke about these issues in our larger settings and services. At times, I even went into individual homes where a group had gathered together intentionally. Though this kind of communication is vital to all leadership, it is a matter of life and death in leading change.

Though I didn't convince everyone, I was able to define myself, show my heart, and lay out the vision rather than allowing it to filter through others. No one was able to spread mistruths about me convincingly. They couldn't say that I didn't love and care about God's Word. Because I had communicated at every level of the church, most people got to see and hear what I stood for first-hand. This protected me from malicious and destructive rumors. Too many leaders allow themselves to be defined by other people because they don't take the time to communicate at every level. They show up and communicate to the crowd, but that's it. This kind of communication, on its own, will not create the necessary understanding for change to be fully embraced or to get traction with the majority of people.

Instill the Values

Since values ultimately drive people, for a church to embrace change, the right values must be instilled into the soul of the church. This only happens by communicating, communicating, and communicating. In order for the values to become part of the soul of a church, they must be consistently connected to everything being done. They must be connected to what's being added, subtracted, and left the same. The leader needs to connect changes to the relevant value. If he can't connect an activity to a value, then he needs to either write a new value (as I did when we didn't have any driving value for our care and compassion ministries), or cancel the activity.

Answer the Questions

Finally, it's important to realize that, as a church is going through a season of change, there will be a multitude of questions that continually rise to the surface. Most of these questions will deal with "why." It's vital that the leader continually seek to answer these questions, even when he has been asked a hundred times already. As long as questions are being asked, the leader can know that people are on board enough to be asking questions.

Therefore, though it can be frustrating, it's vital to keep answering. Understanding is required for people to follow a leader through change. Understanding requires communication, communication, and more communication. As I said at the beginning of this chapter, communication provides the only bridge for genuinely understanding and connecting to each other. So, whatever you do, don't stop communicating.

CHAPTER 10

Know What's Killing You

Identifying the Essential Targets of Change

For years, I talked about going skydiving. Then a guy who did it regularly, as his hobby, started attending our church. When he heard me talking, he invited me to go with him. Up until that moment, I thought I had been serious. Though I didn't show it on the outside (I don't think), my insides froze upon his invitation. All of a sudden I knew the truth: I liked talking about jumping, but I really wasn't interested in actually doing it. If I had been, I would have done something about it already. I was in a quandary. But my fear of losing face proved to be stronger than my fear of jumping. We set the date, and the date arrived. Though I looked for a legitimate way out, I couldn't find one. So I was locked in. On the outside, I was exuding confidence. On the inside, I was questioning my sanity and looking carefully at my life insurance policy.

At this point, it was out of my control. The train was too far down the track, as they say. My son had decided to join me. How could I not jump with him counting on me? The creative arts team at our church had decided this would be a great illustration for one of my talks, so they scheduled to have it videotaped. I was hooked. As I got on the plane, I plastered a smile on my face and put both thumbs up in the air, but I felt like a lamb being led to the slaughter. I was nervous, and it intensified as the plane took off.

On the way up, the "professional" I was jumping with made sure that we were properly connected. Finally, we were at altitude.

The regular and experienced divers jumped first. I remembered watching in amazement. The guy from our church jumped out backward and did a flip. Then it was my turn. We inched to the door. "One, two, three," and my partner pushed me out the door. Though initially leaving the safety of the plane was scary, it was the last bit of fear I remember. From then on, it was pure exhilaration. The only way that I can describe the feeling is that every sense in my body was overloaded. There was absolutely no way to take in all the feelings. I literally had to focus consciously on one or two things; everything else was a blur. It was a wild ride. As someone who can process fairly quickly, I was amazed at how little I could take in of the experience. It just happened in a rush around me. Then, when the chute opened, it transformed the experience from a seemingly out-of-control frenzy to one of the most peaceful, quiet moments I've ever experienced. From beginning to end, it was an unbelievable event.

Though it may seem like an odd comparison, the experience of change can be a lot like my skydiving experience. Though it's easy for people to talk about, most are fearful about going through with it. They avoid it as long as possible. When change becomes a reality, they want to know as much as they can about the changes to feel comfortable with what's to come. This is why the previous chapter on communication is so important. Just as I experienced sensory overload during the jump, many people experience overload during change. People can only embrace so much change at once.

Limit the Changes

To effectively help people process change, the number of changes must be limited. Everything cannot be changed at once. The good news is that in any given church, no matter how bad things may be, there are usually only a couple of issues hurting and hindering the church significantly. For a successful transition, leaders must identify those key issues. They must identify the essential targets of change. They have to become an expert on their church. They must know its condition and isolate the causes. Then, they must identify the crucial areas in need of change.

> **Most church transitions experience difficulty because the leaders either change too many things at one time or change the wrong things.**

Most church transitions experience difficulty because the leaders either change too many things at one time or change the wrong things. Both of these mistakes are potentially harmful. If too many changes are made, the church can become overloaded, stop embracing the change, and retreat. If the wrong adjustments are made, the mistakes can hinder the positive results the church needs and expects from them. This will cause the church to question leadership and pull back from supporting future changes. It's vital that the right changes are made without overloading the people.

Kill What's Killing You

When I was a young leader, an experienced pastor gave me great advice; it has helped me through the years in determining what needs to be changed and what doesn't: "You've got to kill what's killing you, but you can let what isn't killing you die of natural causes." Simply, differentiate between those things that are actually hurting the church and those things that just aren't helping the church. If something's hurting the church, it must be removed. On the other hand, if something's not helping the church, it doesn't need to be aggressively eliminated. It can be left to die on its own. It's important for a leader to use the influence he's won on the right choices and changes. This will ensure that he gains more influence than he loses.

In our church, this was easy. The Sunday morning service was killing us. We couldn't reach new people because the service was irrelevant to everyone but insiders. More often than not, this is the problem in churches that aren't reaching people. Because of this, we say, "As the weekend goes, so goes the church." If the primary services of the church aren't relevant to outsiders, the church will not grow or reach people. In general, this is the place where change needs to begin.

We immediately began changing this service. It was the essential target of change. If we didn't change it, the church would not reach new people. So we changed everything about this service. We changed the style, music, design, elements, and look of the services. We also changed the people involved. We changed the services to relate and reach out to younger people. However, we didn't change all of the areas of our church that were relevant to our existing older people. Initially, we just changed the one Sunday morning service. We needed a place that could be relevant to new people, or soon we would be turning off the lights for the last time.

We didn't start reaching new people immediately, and our existing people didn't like the changes. Though I continued to explain the values to the church, there was tension in the ministry. On one occasion, though he fully believed in and supported the transition, our music pastor out of sheer desperation came to me and said, "These people don't like this music. Maybe we should go back to singing the music they like." Though it would have been easier, I said, "No. the music isn't for these people. It's for the people we're trying to reach." He agreed, but it didn't make it any easier. In fact, during that difficult season of change, he told me that leading worship was like going to the dentist—painful but necessary.

Another time, after he attempted to lead the church in worship, he walked by me on the platform and said, "I can't find the pulse of these people." I quipped, "Don't worry; they don't have a pulse." They were wonderful people but, at the time, they had no spiritual enthusiasm or excitement. The church was dead. We've had a lot of laughs over that quip through the years. To be honest, it was tough to make and stay true to these changes. The majority of people in the church couldn't identify with the changes and didn't like them. Some became belligerent and cruel. They would pick the most appropriate time to draw attention to themselves, and then they'd walk out. Though I'm sure they were doing it "in the name of Jesus," it wasn't encouraging those of us who were doing our best to serve Jesus in those days. However, as tough as these times were, they were necessary to open the church up to new people.

God affirmed the strategy beautifully in an awesome and obvious way shortly after making these changes. A couple in their early twenties visited our church at the recommendation of a family member who had heard me speak at an outside engagement. Though they knew nothing about the condition of the church, they came. Later, they told me the story. They decided to sit in the balcony. Having arrived a little early, they sat for a while and observed the church. Before the service had even started, they concluded the church wasn't for them. The church was filled with older people with whom they couldn't relate. Though they felt like leaving, out of respect, they stayed. When the church service began, they experienced the surprise of their lives. Though it had appeared the church wasn't for them before the service started, they were blown away by the service itself. The crowd wasn't what they were looking for, but the service was everything they were looking for and needed. They felt it had been designed just for them. They so connected with it that they decided to stay and make the church their home. They eventually became a part of the core of the church along with hundreds of others just like them who were reached because we changed the services to effectively communicate to them.

For a church to effectively transition, they have to know what's hindering their effectiveness, and they need to eliminate it. But they don't have to change everything. In fact, they shouldn't.

Provide for Existing People

This leads to the next vital principle in identifying essential targets of change. While the church makes the essential changes for reaching new people, at the same time they must continue to provide a place for existing people. This provides some stability for existing people in the midst of the significant change. Too many leaders and churches change everything at once. This leaves no safe place for the people who have always called the church home. It disrupts every part of their lives and leaves them no option but to leave or fight. It creates an adversarial relationship that doesn't have to be part of a transition. While it's true that the church must establish points of relevance for outsiders, it is not true that every point of relevance for insiders should be removed. The church should seek to provide relevant ministry opportunities for both existing people and new.

Church leaders sometimes make the mistake of seeing the existing members as the enemy. While some are negative and disruptive, church members are not enemies. They are people of God who have given of themselves through the years, often sacrificially, in order to start, build, and grow the church. Without them, the church and all of its resources wouldn't exist. Though they may have become part of the problem and may never accept the changes, in general, the church should attempt to provide a place for them. The goal in change isn't to get rid of the existing people. The goal is to get the existing people committed to being so like Jesus that they're willing to sacrifice what they love in order to reach those whom God loves.

In order to accomplish this in our setting, we changed the Sunday morning service but left the adult classes alone. If their classes never changed, it wouldn't keep the church from growing. Therefore, we encouraged them to continue doing what they loved doing in their classes. Nothing had to change. This allowed them a place to be shepherded and encouraged spiritually without hindering our ability to design services to reach new people. This allowed us to honor and keep them while we honored God by reaching out to those who so desperately needed His hope.

While the church makes the essential changes for reaching new people, at the same time they must continue to provide a place for existing people.

This arrangement also gave us leverage when complaints came in about our services. When they complained that we didn't sing hymns, we reminded them that they sing hymns every week in their class. When they expressed concern as to why their teachers weren't on the platform in the Sunday service anymore, we were able to tell them because they get to teach every week in their class. Though we changed a lot, none of the changes removed their ability to enjoy their preferred music and teaching. It proved a powerful means for removing the teeth of the complaints.

The lesson is simple but important. If the church continues providing a place for existing people as it targets new people, it will experience less loss and greater support. Think about it. If a leader takes all relevant ministries away from existing people, why would they support his or her leadership? They wouldn't. Besides, if we take an honest look into Scripture, the church isn't supposed to be exclusive to one generation or group. There should be different opportunities within the church where people can find a place and group that is relevant to them in both life and circumstance. Though existing people should have opportunities to connect with their cultural language and preferences, new people shouldn't be expected or encouraged to go into those environments. They should have opportunities that are more relevant to their cultural language and preferences. Ultimately, there needs to be connection and community opportunities for all the groups represented in a church.

Change the Base of Influence

No matter how well a leader and church balance the ministry, there will always be those who want more for themselves. In fact, there will always be those who genuinely believe that it is all about them. Though this is totally contrary to Christ and His ideals, these people often have a loud voice in the church and, at times, significant influence. After all, as mentioned in chapter 5, a church never gets to the wrong place because it has all of the right leaders. Therefore, the positive changes being made will have potential roadblocks and face strong challenges, even from existing leaders. The only way to effectively overcome these challenges and insure the changes is to make sure the primary influencers in a church understand, embrace, and are willing to fight for the values of Christ and His ideals for the church.

This calls for intentionally changing and/or expanding the base of influence. The leader must change who holds the influence and who people look up to in the church. This is especially true if those who hold the influence are standing in the way of fulfilling the Great Commission. Of course, this is a process that takes time and requires wisdom. James 1:5 must be the constant companion of a leader of transition: "If any of you lacks wisdom, he should ask God, who gives generously to all without finding fault, and it will be given to him." I believe this because of the mistakes I've made.

In my first pastoral ministry, I didn't seek God's wisdom as it related to the placement of leaders. I had the opportunity to begin influencing a change in leadership early on in the ministry. I didn't have the wisdom to know how vital this was. As a result, I stood by and supported the renewed appointment of a man to the board. He turned out to be the man who led the charge against my leadership; he was the one who thought the Bible way of doing church wouldn't work at that church. The sad reality is that I, for lack of insight into the importance of who held leadership influence, supported this man's return to office. It was an extremely valuable lesson learned the hard way. However, as I moved forward in ministry, it helped me to embrace the difficult choice of changing leaders over watching the wrong leaders destroy the work of the church.

Though I've certainly had my share of failures in this area, I've also made some successful moves as well. Though we did experience some hiccups, the way we went about changing and expanding the base of influence in our present ministry worked out positively.

Because I inherited staff and leaders who had been in the church for years, I decided if my leadership was going to gain traction, it was important for me to gradually reduce their influence. The only way to do this was to remove them from the platform in our services so they couldn't gain influence with the new people we reached. Though some people complained that these men were no longer being given the opportunity, I merely pointed out that they hadn't been released; they were still leading and teaching their classes. As well, I moved new people into positions of influence. Slowly, as these new leaders gained influence, it became possible for them to rise to levels of leadership in the church that made significant change possible. It must be done slowly, but it must be done.

Many leaders fail to understand the importance of this and, as a result, never genuinely become the leader of the church. They always have less influence. No matter how long they stay, they will never truly be able to lead. Though they're called "pastor," they remain the outsider. This was true of me when I first came to my present ministry. They called me the senior pastor, but I was the outsider. Though they gave me the positional authority to lead the staff, the staff had more influence than I did. The only way I became the true leader of this church was by slowly but intentionally changing the base of influence.

Winning Influence Requires Character and Competence

In order to change the base of influence, I had to win influence. Winning influence can only be accomplished by establishing character and competence. This takes time. But if a leader is authentic in character, it will be seen. My character was tested all the time. When I didn't know it, people were watching. Though I'm far from perfect, at least I admit it. Because people, over time, saw that I was authentic in character, they began giving me more and more influence in their lives. My competence as a leader was on the line with every decision I made. Many people were waiting for the changes to fail. By God's grace, though we did continue to decline during the first six years, it slowed as we began reaching new people. The more my leadership led the church to positively impact lives, the more influence I established.

There were also direct tests to my leadership. There were a couple of people who wanted to lead me. In order to put me in their box, they attempted to leverage me. In these cases, I had to bolster the courage to use my leadership with the church to remove them from places of influence. My leadership was being tested. If I didn't rise to the occasion, I would have never been able to develop the influence to move this ministry through the significant transition we've had the privilege of experiencing. Too many leaders buckle under the pressure of people challenging their leadership. When they blink, they lose the ability to lead.

> **Too many leaders buckle under the pressure of people challenging their leadership.**

As a result of proving my character and competence over time, the base of influence began changing toward me as the leader. As the result of this, in a short four years, the church voted to leave their old church building and campus in order to move seventeen miles west and build a new building and campus. This meant they chose to follow my leadership rather than to continue following the leadership of the pastor they had loved and followed for so many years. They chose to dismantle the Memorial Library. After four years of ministry, it was this vote that finally established me as the pastor of the church. If I hadn't intentionally changed and expanded the base of influence, this would have never happened. Though it took many sleepless nights, it was worth it.

Plant Seeds Today for Change Tomorrow

In order to lead change, the leader must always be thinking ahead. Change doesn't happen when you announce it. Change grows. Therefore, the leader must consistently plant seeds in the present for future change.

This must be done at every stage of leadership. Before I was called to my present ministry, I began planting seeds during the interview process for future change. Many leaders focus on getting the job. In so doing, they play to the music of the people interviewing. They win them over by agreeing with, or at least not challenging, their ideas. Though it may win them the job, it creates difficulty for leading in the future. They will be challenged by their own words. I made this mistake in my first ministry. I wanted the opportunity to pastor that church so much that I told them what they wanted to hear, and I ignored what I heard them say. I learned the hard way that this kind of behavior never ends well for a leader. I learned that if I compromise myself to get a position I really want, it will more than likely become my worst nightmare.

As a result, when interviewing for my present position, I planted seeds for many of the changes I would be making if they called me to be their pastor. I held back no punches. To be honest, though I really believed that God had called me, it was hard to believe that this particular leadership group would ever agree to make me the candidate. As I already mentioned, forty-two men had to affirm me as the candidate. But I wasn't going to limit my future leadership by playing to their ideas about ministry. I forthrightly told them what I would do. In this way, the seeds of change I had planted would already be growing when I arrived.

Once I became pastor, I planted seeds of change for years. Though not always possible, the general rule is that the bigger and more difficult the change, the further ahead the seed should be planted. Because of this, I started planting seeds for the idea of changing the church name almost a decade before I led the change. Our name was Temple Baptist Church. From the very beginning, I saw two significant challenges with the name. The first was the name "Temple." It was a confusing name. There were people who thought we were a Jewish Baptist church. This was confusing, to say the least. The second was the name "Baptist." Most people thought our name meant that we were part of a "Baptist denomination." We weren't. Though people think they know what the word "Baptist" means, most don't. In our particular area of the world, there are so many different kinds of "Baptist" churches and so much diversity within the realm of "Baptist" churches that it created significant confusion. If a person ever had a bad experience at any church with that name, he or she would likely never attend another one.

Because of these obvious problems, I started planting the seed for changing the name early in my ministry. In one of my Deacon Discipleship meetings, I challenged them with this scenario: "What if the name of our church, Temple Baptist, ever got in the way of or became an obstacle for us in introducing people to the truth about Jesus Christ? What would we do as a church?" Of course, most of them reacted immediately with an absolute, "We're not changing our name!" It was the answer I expected, but I continued to challenge them on the concept. "What if the name of our church became an obstacle for people to find Jesus? What's the most important name to you, Temple Baptist or Jesus?" Interestingly, a couple of them actually said something like "Temple Baptist is Jesus to me." Obviously, I got what I wanted. The real problems started surfacing. Some of the leaders had fallen in love with and begun valuing their church and its culture more than they did Jesus Himself. No wonder the church was hurting. A couple of the leaders, though they certainly weren't in favor of changing the name at the time, finally acknowledged that they would change the name of the church before they would accept diminishing the name of Jesus. This was nearly ten years before we actually changed the name.

Successful change takes time to grow. In those early years, I was only planting seeds. This wasn't a change that I would have even considered unless and until the church was healthy and growing. If an unhealthy church changes its name, it doesn't make them healthy. They still won't grow. In my opinion, a church might as well let the old name keep all the old baggage. Don't bury the name until you can bury all the negative baggage with it. When the church is healthy, then you can change the name. But in order to lead successful change, a leader must plant seeds consistently.

When we changed our name, we were already a healthy, growing, and vibrant church. We only changed our name because it had become a significant hindrance in reaching the people we were targeting who had been hurt by and/or rejected religion. We found that people who had no confusion about a name like "Temple Baptist" would come to our church with no problem. But people who had issues with religion wouldn't come. It kept us from reaching them. We decided that reaching these people with the name of Jesus was more important than the name Temple Baptist. So we changed the name. Because the seed had been planted for so long and our motivation was clearly one of purpose, to the best of my knowledge, we only lost a couple of people when we changed our name. Change doesn't have to be destructive if it's led in a positive and thoughtful way. In order to do this, we must, with God's wisdom, clearly identify the essential targets of change and appropriately make the changes.

Painting the target has been the focus of the last three chapters. Unless we spell out our ministry charter; communicate consistently, clearly, and competently; and identify the critical areas for change; we won't have any potential for successfully moving our churches into and through the process for changing without compromise. However, once we've painted the target, it's time to pull the trigger.

PART 4

go for it

CHAPTER 11

Make It Fresh

Creating Fresh Opportunities for Momentum

The thought horrified me: *This is the best these people ever experience of Jesus.* I was on vacation with my family in another state, and we had decided to attend a church near where we were staying. The name, size, and location don't matter. What matters is how it made me feel. I'm a pastor who loves the church, and I would have rather been almost anywhere else. I actually regretted the decision to go to church. My family, reluctant about the decision before going, was in agony. I hated it. Not the people. Not the church. But what it meant. This was the best these people ever experienced of Jesus. And to my dismay, they were satisfied with it. Though this certainly bothered me, I was hopeful that most of them were true believers. At least they would experience the fullness of God and His presence one day in heaven, I reasoned. What I really hated was that a lost person may accidentally walk into this church, or, even worse, be invited. If my reaction as a believer was so negative, what would an unbeliever's reaction be? It saddened and angered me that this was perhaps the best picture of Jesus they may ever see.

While the people in that church had the best of intentions, in my opinion, they painted a distorted picture of God that morning. It wasn't an issue of talent, though I'm sure it wasn't the best they had to offer. It wasn't an issue of technology. It was an issue of staleness. It was clear that they were just repeating what they did every week. There was obviously little to no effort put into it. The service and message appeared to have been thrown together just before it started, because it was time for another service, not because they had something important to say. As a result, there was no passion or enthusiasm and no interesting content. They were just going through the motions. Their presentation of God was tired, routine, passionless, and boring . . . very boring. This isn't God. This isn't even close to God. But this is a common picture being painted by churches all over the world. No wonder lost people are having a hard time believing in the God of the Bible. No wonder so many believers are battling with the concept of attending church. When not attending church is more inspiring spiritually than attending, there's a problem.

This experience, and many others since, inspired me to do whatever I could to help churches to change without compromise. I passionately desire for the church to live up to its billing as the hope of the world. But it will never come close until it starts painting a better picture of God. For this to happen, the church must create new and fresh opportunities to experience God and for gaining momentum into people's lives.

Stated simply, new, different, creative, exciting things need to start happening in the church. As long as these kinds of things aren't happening in the church, people will believe these things don't happen with God. As a result, they will look for a place where things are happening. The church needs to create moments in which people can experience God as fresh, not tired; exciting, not boring; and alive, not dead.

Experiencing moments like this is life-defining for me. All believers need opportunities like this. If the church doesn't create opportunities for these kinds of moments, people will conclude that either God is dead, or He just doesn't attend church anymore.

Since both are absolutely wrong, the church needs to start presenting a more accurate picture of God.

The Most Boring Way to Spend an Hour

Regrettably, churches today are generally known for their predictability. People know what's going to happen before they get there because the same thing happens every time they show up. As a result, many consider church to be one of the most boring ways to spend an hour. No wonder it's so hard for believers to invite people to church—even for those who passionately desire to invite them.

> **The church needs to create moments in which people can experience God as fresh, not tired; exciting, not boring; and alive, not dead.**

I remember hearing about one such church. I was told that one Sunday morning the pastor of the church noticed a little boy standing in their foyer of the church. The boy was staring up at a large plaque on the wall. Small American flags were mounted on either side of it. The boy had been staring at the plaque for some time. So the pastor walked up to him, put his arm around his shoulders, and said, "Good morning, young man."

"Good morning, Pastor." The boy was still focused on that plaque with those little flags. "Pastor, what is that plaque?"

"Well, son, it's a memorial to all the young men and women who died in the service." Soberly, they stood together, staring at the large plaque.

Finally, in a voice barely audible and trembling with fear, the boy asked, "Which service, Pastor? Morning or evening?"

What's really sad is that, more than likely, you got that joke before you read the punch line. The reason it makes people laugh is because it highlights a reality.

Debates rage as to why fewer people are going to church. One answer to that question is obvious: fewer people are attending because churches have become tired and predictable. They're offering nothing new or creative. They just keep repeating the same things over and over and over again. Some churches think it's more spiritual to sing all nine verses of an already boring hymn. For most people, this is underwhelming. It doesn't quite live up to the concept of a Savior who walked on water, raised the dead, and held the attention of crowds for days.

When you read the Gospels, it's obvious that no one ever knew what Jesus was going to do next, not even His closest friends and followers. He kept surprising people, and it ticked off the Pharisees. Like so many Christians and churches that seem to walk in their footsteps, they were appalled that Jesus kept breaking routine. But the Bible makes it clear that Jesus came to reveal God to us (John 14:8–9). Along with many other characteristics, He revealed a compelling, powerful, relevant, passionate, unpredictable, exciting, and personal God.

The Right Picture of God

Churches have been given the assignment to reveal God to the world. Yet when the church is old and tired, irrelevant and boring, powerless and predictable, people conclude that God is these things. When the church becomes stale, it paints the wrong picture of God. God is none of these things. He is everything Jesus revealed Him to be. Sadly, more often than not, He is little of what the church reveals Him to be.

The world needs churches that allow the real God to stand up and stand out. They need to see God for who He really is. He is always fresh and creative. If His church is going to represent Him properly, the church must also be fresh and creative. The church cannot keep using the same service order that's been used for decades. It's not as if Jesus Himself used it and commanded the church to do likewise.

The Church Should Surprise People

The church today needs to surprise people. At our church, one of the goals is for people to leave shaking their heads, saying, "You never know what you're going to experience at NorthRidge." When church is creative, it helps to keep faith and the desire for God alive. I've talked to some leaders who worry that their people will get upset if they change the order of things. Welcome to Jesus' world. However, it's important to remember that the people who got mad at Jesus were the people who had settled for the wrong picture of God. It's obvious that Jesus preferred their anger to allowing their polluted view of God

> **Fewer people are attending because churches have become tired and predictable.**

to stand. Likewise, though it certainly creates some discomfort, I would rather my ministry elicit anger than no emotion at all. Church isn't supposed to be a place without challenge. It's supposed to be a place that wakes the dead. Church needs to reveal that God is still alive and working. If people get mad about that truth, so be it. The church needs to be creative and innovative.

I believe the church in general has long lost this concept. Most Christians have been tainted by this misunderstanding. Being fresh and creative is not merely a good idea for helping the church to grow; it is our God-given assignment. As it was Jesus' job, so it is also for the church.

The Creative Centers of the World

The church represents God, the Creator. The only thing the world will ever know about God will come from the view they get from

God's people . . . His church. In light of this, shouldn't His churches be known as the creative centers of the world? They represent the Innovator and Creator of the world. As He clearly claims, He is always fresh, always new, and always writing a new song (Isaiah 42:9; 43:19). While it's true that God's character never changes, it's not true that He never changes what He does. He is fresh and creative, and He wants His people to be the same: "Sing to him a new song; play skillfully, and shout for joy" (Psalm 33:3). "He put a new song in my mouth, a hymn of praise to our God. Many will see and fear and put their trust in the Lord" (Psalm 40:3). As this passage says, when God's people reveal God for who He is, people will turn to Him.

> **Church isn't supposed to be a place without challenge. It's supposed to be a place that wakes the dead.**

Churches should be known as centers of innovation. Places of soaring imagination. After all, human beings are made in the image of God; they have been given the ability to imagine, innovate, and create. But the curse of sin has dummied it down and perverted these abilities.

However, Christians have been freed from sin's curse. They have been restored to their original design. They should exemplify the beauty and wonder of God's creativity. The church should always be creative, relevant, alive, and infusing the world with meaning, passion, and hope. Instead, many churches continue to follow an old and stale liturgy. Though it was creative and stirring centuries ago, for most it is no longer relevant. This is in keeping with the Pharisees, but not with Jesus. This robs the church today of God's presence and life, and it teaches the world that God lived in history but not today. It's an aberrant message. It's mistakenly putting a cover of irrelevance over the relevant light of God's love and hope.

God Is Only Experienced in the Present

The church needs to begin creating new and fresh opportunities for people to see, understand, and experience God. In so doing, it will create new momentum in the church. In order to do this, the church needs to evaluate itself for staleness. It needs to stop comparing itself with the historical church. Yes, God did great things in the past. But He did those great things because those people were living in the moment. They were designing new and creative opportunities for people to see, understand, and experience God's truth, love, and hope. If the church today is going to experience similar great things, it can't keep living in the past. It can't simply copy what yesterday's church did. Those churches were in different times, cultures, populations. The church needs to experience God in fresh ways—in the now. God is still doing new things. He's the same God, but He isn't always experienced in the same ways. The key to keeping a relationship with God alive, growing, and exciting is knowing and experiencing Him in new ways. The church needs to practice this.

At the time of this writing, my wife, Roxann, and I are heading toward our thirty-first wedding anniversary. Given how relationally ignorant I was as a younger man, this is quite a feat. Let me introduce you to my shallowness. We were engaged and soon to be married, but I was wrestling with the concept of "forever." It wasn't that I questioned my love for or commitment to her. Those were rock solid. But I was wrestling with what a relationship that lasted forever was like. After all, I had never experienced forever. So, wanting to share my thoughts and benefit from her relational strengths, I asked her the question that we have laughed about for years. It went something like this: "Roxann, I love you with my life, and I couldn't be happier that we're getting married. I just have one nagging question. What are we going to talk about for the rest of our lives?" This would be funny if I hadn't been serious.

I honestly had no clue. At that point, I only had about a half hour of worthy material. Looking back, I'm surprised she didn't cancel the wedding. Instead, she gave the perfect answer. She said, "I think we'll talk about whatever happens each day." Wow, what a thought. She understood what I didn't. Relationships happen in the present. Good relationships are built on daily experiences. As a result of all the new experiences, the relationship changes and grows. The newness of each day keeps the relationship alive and exciting. Couples who don't continue to experience each other in new ways lose the joy and excitement of the relationship.

> **The church needs to experience God in fresh ways—in the now. God is still doing new things.**

Unfortunately, many churches are no longer experiencing God in authentic and creative ways. They are limited to their memories of what God once did. They have locked God inside a box. They've turned the church into a museum to display artifacts of a God who once interacted with mankind. For this reason, they keep talking about the same things, in the same ways. All of their stories about God are past tense. They are having no new experiences with God, as if God is dead. In fact, this is the idea the world is getting from many churches these days.

On the contrary, our relationship with God should be defined by how He's revealing Himself to us today. The God of Acts 2, the God who showed up in new, exciting, and startling ways, is present today. Acts 2 isn't a picture of what God was like and what God once did. It's the picture of what God is like and what He still wants to do. He wants to reveal Himself to us in novel and surprising ways. God wants His people and the world to experience Him anew. When this happens, the church will no longer be talking about a predictable, tired, dusty God. They will be talking about Him in passionate and exciting ways.

The obvious problem is that many churches are not genuinely experiencing the living God in fresh ways these days. If they were, it would be evident in the way they presented Him. Though they may have had an experience with God in the past, they haven't for some time. As a result, they keep focusing on their past experience. Even worse, there are many people in churches who have never personally experienced God. They are just repeating stories about God from other people's past experiences. Of course, we can benefit a great deal from people's stories. The Bible often reveals the truth about God through life story. However, a believer's relationship and experience with God must go beyond another person's story or past experience. If believers aren't experiencing God in real and personal ways, the church will only be able to talk about God in the third person. This will render the church powerless in genuinely introducing people to God. If a church is living off past experiences with God, it will be ineffective at connecting people with God today. God can't be found in the past. He can only be found in the present. It's time the church starts talking about the God it knows today. Telling present-tense stories of God and His work, while remaining true to His Word, creates an exciting and relevant connection for people. If the church isn't introducing new and creative elements into its ministry, it's clear that they aren't experiencing or communicating the reality of God in fresh ways.

Some Have Locked God in the Past

Think about what happened to Isaiah in the Old Testament. Though he was a prophet, he wasn't experiencing God's reality in his everyday life. He had seemingly locked God in the past. This allowed him to preach God's truth and judgment without taking stock of his own life. Until, that is, God clearly revealed Himself in Isaiah 6. Suddenly, he was personally standing in God's presence.

His attitude changed. Rather than pointing his fingers at others while remaining unaffected, he fell on his face before God. His personal experience with God changed his life and ministry.

The same phenomenon happened in the New Testament with Paul. He was living for and worshipping a God who lived in history. He knew nothing of a personal or living relationship with God. His love for God was academic. He loved God the way a person loves a beautiful museum piece. Then God showed up. When Paul personally experienced the reality of God, it changed everything. God wasn't something to talk about; He was someone to know. God wasn't about routine and tradition; He was about singing a new song and truth. He transformed Paul's life and ministry. When people genuinely meet and experience God, they are never the same. This is what churches should be doing. When they do, lives are changed. When they don't, lives don't change, the church grows stale, and God appears irrelevant.

When the church locks God in the past, He seems no different to people than any other historical figure. It may be interesting to study the lives and works of Washington, Jefferson, and Lincoln. In fact, it is so interesting to some that they devote their lives to studying and writing about them. But their work doesn't transform lives or fill the world with hope. One of the reasons so many people are rejecting God is that they have no interest in or use for one more historical figure. But, if they could personally experience His relevance in their lives, they would change their tune. It's happened to me, and it's happening in our church. It's supposed to be happening in every believer's life and in all churches.

The church needs to help people understand that, unlike Washington and Lincoln, Jesus' tomb is empty. Unlike historical figures who lived and then died, Jesus is alive and working today. It takes more than just words to reveal this to the world. Since the church claims to be Jesus' work, it needs to reflect Him. Because He is not old, tired, powerless, or irrelevant, the church needs to provide fresh opportunities for learning about, understanding, and experiencing Him in the present. When this happens in a church, it changes everything—especially people's lives. And, as lives begin changing, people start talking. It creates a buzz throughout the community. As a result, people start coming to check out what all the talk is about. Along the way, many of them experience God and their lives change. In no time, the church is working right and providing genuine hope in a hopeless world.

Predictably Unpredictable

As I wrote earlier, one of the things we strive for in our services is for people to leave saying, "You never know what you're going to experience at NorthRidge." When someone comes or invites someone, we want that person to know that the service will be done with excellence, relevant to his or her life, and true to God's Word. But we don't want that visitor to know or be able to predict what will happen. This keeps the

> It's time the church starts talking about the God it knows today.

church from becoming dull and stale. It keeps providing new and unique ways to learn about and personally experience God. This is important to us, and we believe it should be important to all churches.

One of my favorite movies is *Groundhog Day* with Bill Murray. In the movie, Murray's obnoxious character gets trapped in the same day. He's forced to live Groundhog Day over and over and over. He's trapped in the same day, at the same place, and with the same people and opportunities. At the beginning of this experience, he gets excited about the opportunities of life without accountability. Thinking this will give him fulfillment, he starts doing anything he wants. Rather than fulfillment, it leads to despair. Though most people believe the opposite, this kind of self-directed and pleasure-obsessed life doesn't produce happiness or meaning. As a result of his despair, he kills himself in almost every conceivable way. But he keeps waking up on the same day, at the same time, and in the same place. He's locked in a moment of time, and it's miserable for him.

Finally, he decides that he's going to make the best of this one day. He does everything in his power to make Groundhog Day the perfect day for everyone living in this town. He uses the day to help fix every problem, save every person, and bring joy to the lives of as many as possible. In so doing, he finds the key for getting out of that day. He knows that he has finally woken to a brand-new day when something different happens. When asked about it, he says, "Anything different is good."

This is what people are begging for from the church: "anything different." They want to see that God is not trapped in a time or culture irrelevant to their lives. They want to know that He's as real for them in the twenty-first century as He was to those in the first century. For this reason, churches need to do whatever it takes to create new and exciting opportunities for people to learn about and experience God. It will create new momentum in the church. Of course, once a church is positively reflecting God, it's important to find ways to get new people to experience it.

Special Events

When our church was smaller and at the beginning stages of our transition, we found it was difficult to get people to come to a church service as their first step into our ministry. So we created fresh opportunities through other events.

We called a local school district and offered to host their graduation. Our thought was that people have to go to a graduation. If it was in our church building, it would give us the opportunity to build relationships with and serve them. If we did our job well, perhaps it would plant a seed for them to try our church. We are a polling place for our community. When people come to vote, we serve coffee. We run a video showing highlights of our church services and ministries. We have relevant church literature placed near the voting lines along with easy-access computer kiosks. We also have our auditorium doors wide open for people to walk around and view the building. Most important, we have people greeting and helping. After all, people are the church. Though people think they're coming to vote, we believe they're coming to find Jesus. Even if they aren't, we know they need Him. We have also hosted appropriate concerts. We do whatever works in creating innovative opportunities to introduce people to the God of hope that they so desperately need.

> This is what people are begging for from the church: "anything different."

Churches must be creative in their own settings. The goal is to expose as many people as possible to the church. Since people are the church, whatever a church does should involve their people. This presupposes that the people will be positive reflections for the church and the Lord. The goal is to plant a seed that compels as many people as possible to come back to church. If this is going to happen in any given church setting, there are two important principles that must be embraced and implemented.

First, each church must build off their unique strengths. They can't just copy other churches, unless they have similar strengths. For example, we had an auditorium large enough to house a high school graduation. If a church doesn't have the right-sized auditorium for this kind of event, it would be ridiculous to copy this idea. Each church must be innovative and imaginative within the confines of their God-given uniqueness.

Second, the church must embrace and implement the excellence factor. As one of our key values states, "excellence honors God and inspires people." If the church is going to appropriately reflect God and inspire people, it needs to be committed to excellence. Mediocrity does not reflect God and inspires no one. Excellence both honors God and inspires people. In order to create fresh momentum, the church must remember the excellence factor.

Inspired by Guest Services

One of the ministries at our church that significantly inspires me is our volunteer Guest Services team. When people come to our church, they know they are expected, wanted, prayed for, and planned for. I frequently hear how Guest Services went above and beyond in caring for people. The most important touch people get is the first one. The reason is simple: the first touch establishes the perception people have of our church, so we've developed a top-notch Guest Services parking team. They're amazing. And they are committed to serving with excellence that honors God and inspires people.

These wonderful people make my job easy. By the time people get into the service, they already love the church. It takes the pressure off me. They'll continue coming to our church in spite of me in order to be a part of a group of people like they find at NorthRidge. Our desire is for people to leave our church with this thought: *If God is the reason these people are so caring, happy, and helpful, then I want to get to know Him.*

It's important to notice that excellence doesn't always cost money, but it does require people—volunteers. Excellence is about doing one's best. As Colossians 3:23 says, "Whatever you do, work at it with all your heart, as working for the Lord, not for men."

The church should never put up with or settle for leftovers. They should always give their best. Either way, people will know.

Excellence Creates Enthusiastic Supporters

When we began creating fresh momentum as a church, we had little to no extra budget. But we had people, and people are the church. If people do everything with excellence, then the church is excellent. Excellence creates enthusiastic, excited, and loyal supporters. Though it started with us presenting God in new and creative ways, the momentum in our church today is the result of those who attend. As a result of what God has done in their lives through our church, they are now passionate about sharing it with others. As a result, new people are attending the church all the time. Of course, when they do, it's vital that they experience God as alive, personal, and real. If they don't, they will leave with the wrong picture of God.

> **Any church can change if they decide to reveal God for who He is.**

When I first came to our church, no one was coming to faith. No one was getting baptized. We were losing people every day. We had momentum, but it was in reverse. Then we started creating new opportunities for fresh experiences and momentum. Since I wasn't all that creative, I found people who were creative and got them involved. Together, we creatively built off our strengths, though we didn't have many. But we did what we could with excellence. As a result, people started removing God from their history book and allowing Him into their everyday lives. And, as it did with Isaiah and Paul, it changed everything.

As our people and church started changing, I celebrated them. There's nothing more motivating to people than being celebrated. Celebration adds excitement to life. According to Luke 15:7, God celebrates when lives start changing: "I tell you that in the same way there will be more rejoicing in heaven over one sinner who repents than over ninety-nine righteous persons who do not need to repent." Though there wasn't much to celebrate at first, I found anything that I could. People who celebrate are happier than people who don't. After a while, there was more and more to celebrate, and the celebrations began happening spontaneously. It was awesome. What a difference joy made in a church where depression had ruled for so long. Though it wasn't easy, it happened. It happened because we didn't settle for the God of a museum. We opted for the God of today. And as He promised in Matthew 16:18, He has built His church.

As I look back on my visit to that church while on vacation, I am saddened that experiences like that are the best some people ever see of Jesus. However, I'm excited that it doesn't have to stay that way. Any church can change if they decide to reveal God for who He is, the God of creation. My prayer is that every church that calls on God's name will commit to faithfully reflecting His image. My prayer is that you will commit yourself to making sure it happens in your life and church.

CHAPTER 12

There Will Be Casualties

Accepting Short-Term Losses
for Long-Term Gains

There is one question lurking in the shadows of every church contemplating transition: "How does a church transition without losing people?" It *doesn't*. This, more than anything else, prevents churches from doing what they know they need to do in order to fulfill God's purpose. Imagine that. For many churches, fear of losing people is a greater fear than failing God. It ought not to be.

The church is called to pattern itself after and represent Christ. Though Jesus loved people more than any church ever will, He experienced significant losses in order to fulfill the Father's purposes. Multitudes followed His ministry and heard His teaching. On several occasions, His pointed teaching prompted a mass exodus from the multitudes who had been following Him. Even more startling, there were only 120 faithful followers in the upper room after His resurrection and ascension. In His pursuit of God's will, He lost multitudes of followers. But because of His faithfulness in the face of loss, Jesus ultimately gained significantly more than He lost. The same will be true of the church that faithfully pursues God's will at any cost.

If a church is going to successfully change without compromise, it must be willing to accept short-term loss for long-term gain. This was certainly true with our transition at NorthRidge.

One of my proudest moments as a leader came during an exciting but difficult time. The church leaders and I were meeting to make the final decision to recommend the sale of our old church building. It was exciting because it was finally happening. We had purchased new property several years before, but we were waiting on God for the timing to move. We all agreed that the timing was right. However, this didn't mean that everyone in the church would respond positively. We were walking into a difficult season. As each leader affirmed the decision, they shared some of their feelings. What one of the leaders said blew my socks off. This man had been a member of the church for nearly four decades. During the early years of my leadership, he had wrestled with some of the changes. In this moment, he talked about his history with the church and how meaningful it had been in his life. Then, to the best of my recollection, he said, "I'm for this decision. Though I'm going to lose some of my dearest friends in this move, I will gain new friends. They will be people whose lives are forever changed as a result of our decision today. My personal losses can't be compared to the eternal gains." This was a proud moment for me. He got it. And I'm proud to say that he still has it, along with many new friends.

Playing to the Right Audience

Many leaders have a hard time making a decision like this because they're playing to the wrong audience. They're playing to the people who pay them instead of to the God who made them. They're playing to insiders rather than outsiders. Though this certainly feels good in the moment, it always leads to missing the point and losing the pleasure of God.

To successfully transition a church, the leader has to play to the right audience—the audience of One. This is the example that Jesus established for us: "I have brought you glory on earth by completing the work you gave me to do" (John 17:4). Paul modeled this as well in Galatians 1:10: "Am I now trying to win the approval of men, or of God? Or am I trying to please men? If I were still trying to please men, I would not be a servant of Christ." Paul followed the example of Jesus in making God's approval His only desire. I love the way he said it in Acts 20:24: "But my life is worth nothing unless I use it for doing the work assigned me by the Lord Jesus—the work of telling others the Good News about God's wonderful kindness and love" (NLT). This is the work that God has assigned the church. As with Paul and Jesus, fulfilling the assignment will require accepting some short-term losses for God's desired long-term gains. In order to accomplish this, the church, like Jesus and Paul, must long for God's pleasure more than anything else.

> If a church refuses to change, it will lose its opportunity to experience God's pleasure and the joy of seeing new people find hope.

Three Practical Realities

Though I won't diminish the difficulties and losses that come with making decisions for the long term, it's important to know that it's not all bad news. There are positive short-term benefits as well. While it's true that you can't transition a church without accepting short-term losses for long-term gains, there are three practical realties that shine a different light on this issue. If understood, they can make the right decision significantly easier for the church.

If the Church Doesn't Change, It Will Lose People

If a dying church doesn't change, it will lose the people whose hearts beat for the church to be the hope of the world. It will lose the people who desire, more than their own comfort, God's pleasure. It will lose the people who are living not for themselves but for others. In other words, they will lose the people who look like Jesus. These are not the people a church can afford losing. But it's the cost of living for the short term.

Our church lost two-thirds of its people in the ten years before I arrived. Though not true of all of them, many of these were people who wouldn't settle for anything less than a church determined to fulfill God's purposes and live for His pleasure. Losing them was a significant loss to the church. However, this kind of person generally leaves quietly and respectfully. They don't make a scene, create tension, or stir up conflict. With grace and dignity, they just move on to a setting where they feel God is being honored. But the impact of their loss is incalculable.

If the Church Doesn't Change, It Loses the Opportunity to Reach People

If a church is playing to insiders, they will never be able to reach outsiders. By putting all of their energy into playing defense, they eliminate the possibility of fielding a workable offense. This means they will be left to mourn their mounting losses rather than to celebrate their gains. The cost to the church is monumental. It guarantees as dark a future as the present.

Imagine the difference between a crowd gathering at a funeral home and one at a hospital nursery. No one wants to be at the funeral home. It's a place to be avoided. It represents loss, sadness, and death. People only go out of love and respect. Most desire to leave as soon as possible and not return. Yet people love visiting the hospital nursery. It represents gain, joy, and life. What a difference. It's a blast to be around a family who has just experienced the birth of a healthy child. It's invigorating. Generally, the hospital attendants have to kick people out so baby and mother can rest. Visitors are not in a hurry to leave, and they are eager to come back.

This is an accurate picture of the difference between a stale, declining, and dying church and a fresh, growing, and thriving church. Though it's tough to make decisions that will create short-term loss, in my estimation, it's even tougher to continue to be a part of a negative church. How many times can a person suffer the pain of loss with no hope of experiencing the joy of gain? The answer is different for everyone because of the different levels of tolerance. But it explains why so many good and godly people are leaving churches they love. It explains why so many good pastors are leaving their churches. Unless a church changes, it is locking itself into perpetual loss with no ability to make new gains. This isn't what God intends for the church, and it isn't necessary. But if a church refuses to change, it will lose its opportunity to experience God's pleasure and the joy of seeing new people find hope. It will fail to fulfill the God-given assignment. Eventually, they may have to set up a gravestone for their church.

If the Church Does Change, It Will Lose the Right People

When a church transitions to become the hope of the world, it often loses the right people. I don't necessarily mean bad or ungodly people—though to be honest, this is sometimes the case. Rather, I mean those people who, for whatever reason, will never be part of the church moving forward. They will always be dragging an anchor in the water. They will never fully embrace the values of the church as it seeks to follow Christ in relating to and speaking the language of its culture. By changing, the church will lose the people who create the greatest amount of tension, stir up unnecessary conflict, and keep the church fighting each other instead of the real enemy.

These kinds of people generally don't leave well. They tend to leave as much damage in their wake as possible. As well, they generally don't settle for leaving alone. They attempt to get as many as possible to leave with them. It seems to legitimatize their decision. Of course, they rationalize their negative behavior as standing up for God and right. The Pharisees did the same thing as they stood around the cross. This would all make sense and even have some justification if the church was compromising God's truth. But when this isn't the case, there is no excuse for this kind of behavior.

No Loss Feels Good or Right

Though this may make sense while reading about it in a book, in real life, no loss feels good or right. At one point in our transition, we had a class of sixty people leave our church. This was a significant loss at the time, and to be honest, it was agonizing and scary. Though they were the right people to leave, on the surface it was tragic and difficult to explain. Most of them were in their thirties. Supposedly, we were making all of our changes to reach younger people, so when almost the entire core of younger adults walked out, it was tough for most people to understand.

While reeling and doubting myself, I had to aggressively help the church understand how and why this could happen. As I shared with the church, age has nothing to do with mind-set. These younger adults were just as entrenched and committed to tradition as some of our senior adults. Though most were wonderful people, they had fallen into the trap of valuing cultural and traditional forms more than fulfilling the mission of the church. As often happens, the catalyst for their mass exodus was an outside influence. They were passing around and reading a book by a nationally renowned pastor and author who was attacking churches that were seeking to be relevant culturally. He claimed that a church couldn't embrace truth and be culturally relevant at the same time. He was dead wrong, but this group bought it. In protest of the changes, they left the church.

Though I knew they would never embrace our values and that their leaving was ultimately good for the church, it didn't soften the blow. Most of these people were givers and involved in various ministries of the church. When they left, it created a lot of concerns, doubts, and questions. But I didn't flinch. We were doing right. I knew we had to accept short-term losses for long-term gains, although, that was turning out to be easier said than experienced. While I have no regrets, I do have scars. But with all that God is doing today, I wear them proudly.

> **Though I have no regrets, I do have scars. But with all that God is doing today, I wear them proudly.**

It is the fear of circumstances like this one that keeps many churches from making changes and causes others to pull back from them. They would rather have the peace that comes with the wrong people leaving than the conflict that comes with the right people leaving. The problem is that the peace is always an illusion, and, at best, short-term. Ultimately, this decision will rob the church of its future.

Good and Spiritual People Can Disagree

One concept that challenges many churches is the fact that seemingly good, faithful, and godly people are against the changes. Though this is difficult to understand, with some people more than others, it must be accepted. There are a couple of explanations that have really helped me in coming to grips with this issue.

The simple fact is that genuinely good and spiritual people can disagree. In fact, God can use disagreements to separate them and move them in different directions for greater impact in the world. The best example of this truth is seen with Paul and Barnabas in Acts 15:36–41. Though they were both godly men, they had such a sharp disagreement that they split up their mission team. God ended up using this disagreement to double the impact.

The truth is that not all godly people are called to minister in the same way. In calling His children to different areas or people, God has also wired them to work in different ways. Their differences can create tension and conflict. Though it can be confusing and difficult to understand at times, when it happens, they must simply accept it and keep doing right. Though it took me a while to get this, the important lesson is that people who leave aren't necessarily unspiritual or wrong. It may be that they're just different.

People React Differently When God Shows Up

However, there are times when seemingly good and spiritual people are flat-out wrong. As is natural for people, over time they can confuse their preferred culture with Christianity. As a result, their Christianity becomes more about religion than relationship. It becomes identified by form rather than heart. When someone begins changing the forms, it sparks serious conflict. This was the problem with the Pharisees. When Jesus started changing their valued cultural and traditional forms, they went nuts.

The same happens today. Nothing upsets religious people's lives more than God showing up. They tend to have their lives in perfect order. They know when to stand up and sit down. They're comfortable in the system. It doesn't require much thinking or energy. When God shows up, as happened in the New Testament with Jesus, they hate it. The church today has to be careful about playing to the desires of those who appear to be spiritual but have fallen prey to the lure and ease of religion. Remember, genuinely spiritual people become like Christ. Jesus never served Himself at the expense of reaching out to others with God's love. In fact, as we've seen, He made it clear that, while lost people do this, it should never be this way with His followers (Matthew 20:26).

There is one possibility for explaining the challenge. In the parable of the weeds in Matthew 13:24–30, Jesus made it clear that there would always be a mixture of genuinely redeemed people and those who only appear to be redeemed. This is another explanation for why seemingly good and faithful people are against the changes. Though they may be wonderful people, they don't have the heart of Christ. Knowingly or unknowingly, they are masking a self-centered and unredeemed heart with good and faithful behavior. Of course, they have a problem with the church changing from a place that served their interests to one that sought to love, serve, and reach outsiders as Christ did.

Loving People Without Needing Them

Since it isn't possible to see into the hearts of people, it's impossible to know which reason applies in any situation. But it doesn't matter. If a church is going to fulfill its purpose, it must strive to love all people regardless of the condition of their hearts. At the same time, the church cannot allow those who disagree to dictate direction. I have found only one way to manage the tension of these two realities. Though I shared this earlier in the book, it bears repeating here. The leader and church must love people without needing them. It's vital that pastors love people regardless of their response to that love. However, it's just as vital that they don't allow themselves to need people.

Too many pastors and churches love people because they need them. They need their support, encouragement, and approval. When this happens, it makes it impossible to lead them. Because they need the people, they are not capable of making choices that could cause them to lose the people. These leaders and churches are serving their own personal needs rather than God's purposes. It will never work. Transitioning a church demands accepting short-term losses for long-term gains.

Though it is difficult and demanding to go through seasons of loss, it's important for the church. In fact, I wholeheartedly believe our church's health and growth today stem as much from those who left our ministry as from those who stayed. Simply put, as a result of the changes we made, the right people stayed and the right people left. I had a great confirmation of this. A relatively young man who had left our church years earlier decided to return. When he told me the reason, it cracked me up. He said, "My parents recently left the church because it was becoming too culturally relevant. I immediately decided to come. I knew if my parents hated it, I'd love it. I was right." In his mind, the right people left.

> **There is always risk in changing a church. But the risk is worth it because the church is worth it.**

Sadly, many churches are experiencing the opposite circumstance. They are neither healthy nor growing because the negative people have stayed and the positive people have left. These churches need to reverse this trend. Positively motivated and appropriately led change will do this naturally. It always does.

However, when this trend has gone to the extreme, leaving only negative people, as in my first ministry, it can lead to an unsuccessful transition even when it is led well. In this case, the leader should accept the short-term loss of a ministry and begin looking for the long-term opportunity to move forward in another environment. It's important to remember that there is always risk in changing a church. But the risk is worth it because the church is worth it.

Surprising Lessons

Through our experiences with the losses and gains of transition, we learned some surprising lessons that are fairly common in transition. In order to avoid the mistakes that can easily occur in the face of change, any church transitioning should be aware of and ready for them.

People Come Only for the Transition

The first one surprised me in the early days of our transition. As a church continues to transition, it will lose people who were only reached because they had begun transitioning. We would have never reached these people if we hadn't been willing to engage the difficulties and losses of change, yet they eventually left because we continued to change. We gained and lost them for the same reason. Though it was confusing at first, the reason is obvious: they liked the church as it was when they arrived. As it continued changing, it moved past them. This is a common and natural occurrence. When it happens, there isn't anything wrong, so the church attenders shouldn't allow it to upset or confuse them. Once again, the church must love people without needing them.

In the past few years, we've been making another huge transition in our music. Because I inherited a church that missed two generations due to their refusal to change, I am determined to utilize my leadership influence to ensure that our church remains relevant to today's culture, even though that culture is very different from the one I grew up with and feel most comfortable in. My job is not to lead the church to be everything I want or would enjoy it to be. My job is to take God's truth into the world I've been called to reach. This is every church's job.

As a result of our continued transitions, we have once again experienced the loss of people. However, we have impacted significantly more lives and are growing more rapidly than at any time in our past. The truth remains the truth. We are growing as much because of those we've lost as we are because of those we've kept.

People Bring Their Own Agendas

Our second lesson deals with a very serious issue. As a church begins to grow, some of the new people, especially those from other churches, bring their own agendas. Because so many churches are stale and boring, as a church starts making changes that create fresh excitement, people will come from other churches. Though this shouldn't be the goal, it's natural. Excitement draws people. When this happens, it's vital for the leader and church to understand that new people come with an agenda. This is where it's important to love them without needing them. Otherwise, the leader will begin compromising his agenda in order to accommodate and keep these people. This will kill transition. The leader and church must stand strong.

The number one agenda that people brought into our church was a social or political agenda. It was amazing how big the push was toward this from those coming into our church from the outside. We had clearly established that our agenda was spiritual. Though there are some worthy social and political goals in the world, there are other organizations working toward accomplishing them. We never believed it should be the church. The church, in our view, should be committed to reaching people for Christ. If we identified with a political view, we would eliminate our ability to reach half the population. We believe that introducing people to the One who could change their hearts was far more effective in changing the world's values than a petition or political election.

While as individual Christians we would be good citizens by voting our moral conscience, we wouldn't allow the church to become a political center. We felt this position best helped to represent Christ. He, too, lived in a morally bankrupt world. There were many religious zealots fighting those social and political causes. However, Jesus wasn't one of them. He fought for the hearts of people. In so doing, He could change the world from the inside out. We genuinely desired to follow Him on principle. In so doing, we determined that we would never shy away from teaching His moral and ethical values on any social issue; we just wouldn't allow it to be turned into or seen as a political issue in our church.

This wasn't a popular philosophy among many of the already churched believers who made their way into our environment. It was and has remained a hot topic for some people. We have said good-bye to many wonderful people who just couldn't buy into our view. However, we have reached thousands of people who may have never been reached with a political petition being signed in our lobby every week. Though every church must make its own choice on issues like this, they then need to stand against the outside influences that will seek to come in and change their agendas.

Choose Friends and Leaders Carefully

Finally, I learned that some of the people who seemed to love me the most ended up hurting the church or me the most. Once again, I found that I had to love people without needing them. In my early days, I loved for people to tell me how great I was in contrast to their last pastor. It gave me great short-term gain. However, it usually worked out to be long-term loss. Most people attempting to ingratiate themselves to me at the expense of their last pastor wanted something from me. When they didn't get it, they stirred up trouble in our church and then went to other churches, doing the same thing at my expense. The lesson here is simple: every leader needs to be careful about people who want to be their best friends. They usually have a reason. I have found the best friends for me are those who didn't aggressively seek my friendship.

This lesson also has application to people seeking leadership. Just as with those seeking my friendship, I have become extremely skeptical of people who come in and aggressively pursue leadership. In our setting, we are very patient in the selection of leadership. It's important to us that they're embracing the vision and values of the church rather than seeking to change them. Generally, only time will tell. People with their own agenda are generally impatient. When they don't get what they want quickly, their inclination is to stir up a little trouble and leave. Since a healthy leadership team is so important to a healthy church, it is always worth the wait.

In any transition, there will be losses. This is an unavoidable reality. In the end, the positive gains outweigh the losses. If you genuinely desire to lead the church successfully through change without compromise, you must be willing to accept short-term loss for long-term gain.

I have found that there's only one way to positively navigate the turbulent times of loss. Like Jesus and Paul, you must make the commitment to and continually focus on playing to the audience of One. During a season of tough decisions in my ministry, I wrote this note to myself on an index card and taped it at eye level in my study office: "If everyone applauds me but God, I'm a failure. If no one applauds me but God, I'm a success. Whose applause am I living for?" If you're going to live faithfully and effectively for God and lead the church in this world, you must make sure that you're playing to the right audience.

CHAPTER 13

Double Your Investment

Hard Work and Huge Faith

Generally, we are not balanced in our lives and investments; we tend to be on one extreme or the other. I've often compared this reality to the swinging of a pendulum. When a pendulum is in motion, it swings from one extreme to another while passing quickly past the balanced middle. We tend to live our lives the same way—to the extremes. There are those who work constantly, while inadequately investing in the other areas of their lives. While on the other side, there are those who relax or play constantly, leaving work for others. For the few who have been handed financial security, this can work. However, for the majority, this leads to financial calamity. Living to the extremes, to the neglect of other important areas of life, isn't generally the way to success or fulfillment. Genuine success and happiness require a balanced investment in the essential values and priorities of life.

So it is with ministry. The Bible makes it clear that there are two essential values and priorities that must be invested by anyone desiring success and fulfillment in their spiritual lives and/or ministry. Those two essentials are hard work and huge faith.

The balance between these two essentials is clearly evident in every biblical success story and clearly missing in every failure. When you look at the lives of Moses, Joshua, Samuel, David,

Nehemiah, Jesus, and Paul, it is clear that they worked extremely hard while at the same time walking by faith. On the other side, when you look at the lives of King Saul, all of the failed kings of the Old Testament, and Judas (the failed disciple of Jesus), they all worked hard but failed to walk by faith.

I Will Build My Church

Though this reality is obvious in Scripture, I missed it for years. To be honest, most do. I missed it, as many of the failures in the Bible, on the hard work side. The pendulum of my life swung to work. I worked hard in ministry. However, more often than not, I worked as if I could build the church on my own. Though my words about trusting and needing God were correct, my life didn't support the words. I didn't have time or, in my mind, the need to bathe my work in prayer or to seek God's face about the work I should be doing. I just went after it.

In the opening days of my ministry at NorthRidge, I was interviewed by the primary newspaper in our area. They made a huge error. In the interview, I shared that my approach to ministry was offensive rather than defensive. As biblical support of the legitimacy of this, I quoted Matthew 16:18: "I will build my church, and the gates of Hades will not overcome it." Of course, I clearly attributed those words to Jesus as I applied them to my approach to ministry. Well, the newspaper ran it this way: "Powell said, 'I will build my church.'" I was aghast. Everyone in the church was going to read this article. I was still an unknown commodity as the pastor of the church. This was all I needed. They would think that I was full of myself. So the next Sunday, I stood up and corrected the paper. I reminded them to not believe everything they read.

In retrospect, as horrible as it sounds, it really was an accurate depiction of how I went about ministry. I worked hard without balancing it with huge faith. And, as could have been predicted, I blew it. I was failing spectacularly. Though I was doing many of the right things for transitioning the church, nothing was working. After nearly two years of hard work and no positive signs of improvement, I came to the realization that much of what I had done in ministry was based upon self-effort and self-dependence. I was trying to build the church on my own. Though I would have never formed the words in my mouth, I was acting as if it were my church to build . . . as if my leadership were enough to enable it to prevail against the gates of hell. Obviously, I was wrong.

I Finally Heard Jesus Knocking

As a result, I began the long and difficult process of swinging the pendulum of my life and ministry back to a balance position. There weren't that many obvious outward changes. I was still working hard. However, inwardly, there were many significant changes. I began seeking the Lord as a priority of my daily journey. Before making decisions or investments, I would make sure that I was pursuing His wisdom and presence. The concept of Zechariah 4:6 became a conscious focus of my ministry effort: "'Not by might nor by power, but by my Spirit,' says the LORD Almighty." Simply put, I finally heard Jesus knocking, as Revelation 3:20 talks about, and I began opening the door. It changed everything. As I began opening the door of my life and ministry to God, He began pouring out His wisdom, guidance, and power. The church started responding, and we started to see lives being transformed.

Out of this experience, I started a prayer ministry. I realized I couldn't do ministry without the prayer and support of others. Though the results of combining huge faith with my hard work shouldn't have surprised me, it did. God started showing up in ways that I couldn't comprehend. For the first time, Ephesians 3:20 started becoming the reality of my leadership experience: "[God] is able to do immeasurably more than all we ask or imagine, according to his power that is at work within us."

Some Swing to the Other Extreme

Though I missed this concept on the hard work side, many in ministry seem to allow the pendulum to swing to the other extreme. They emphasize huge faith without hard work. They just believe God will make all the right stuff happen in their lives and ministries without the need to expend effort. Though certainly more spiritual in appearance, it is just as imbalanced and ineffective as the mistake I made.

This reminds me of Joshua's experience with God during one of the minor glitches in his leadership life, found in Joshua 7. After experiencing an unbelievable victory over Jericho, Joshua led Israel to attack the town of Ai. They were routed. It appeared that they did all the right things militarily, yet they went down to a significant defeat. The reason was simple. Though working hard, their faith had been undercut by sin. Therefore, God wasn't empowering or protecting them. As always, this leads to failure.

The first thing Joshua did was get down on his knees and start asking God to help. In a surprising turn of events, God told him to get off his knees and stop praying. Since Joshua knew what was right to do, he didn't need to pray anymore. He needed to do the necessary work to fix the problem. In other words, God was saying that Joshua's faith was fine. It was time for him to do the work required to fix the problem. I believe God is saying the same thing to many pastors, leaders, and churches today.

Years ago, I found a passage of Scripture that perfectly describes the requirements for leading a church through change: "The horse is made ready for the day of battle, but victory rests with the LORD" (Proverbs 21:31). Preparing a horse for battle is a description of hard work. But, as this proverb makes so brilliantly clear, hard work doesn't secure success. Success rests with the Lord. In simple words, it demands faith. Though it's true in all of life, it is doubly true in successfully transitioning a church. Change demands both hard work and huge faith.

Hard Work

There is a commonly accepted fallacy that church work is easy. I'll never forget the time I was approached by a man who hated his career. He was the owner of a landscape company. It was hard work, and in his circumstance, it came with little reward. He couldn't get people to pay him. As a result, he was considering changing vocations. When I asked him what he'd like to do, he said, "What you do looks nice." I had to

> **Change demands both hard work and huge faith.**

work very hard in that moment to keep from laughing. But this seems to be a common thought. Many have the idea that success and work is harder in the marketplace. Of course, they're wrong.

Don't misunderstand. I'm not saying that everyone in ministry works hard. They don't. But the same is true in the marketplace. I believe more people work hard in ministry than in the marketplace.

Pastors Need to Share Their Lives

The truth that ministry is hard work isn't common knowledge. One of the reasons is that so few pastors share their lives in a way people would know. Even when they're at the end of their rope investing in others and attempting to manage the affairs of the church, they carry themselves with grace. They're the ones reaching out with care and compassion to help others. Very seldom is the role reversed. As a result, most people never see them frazzled or frantic. They only see them living and responding with grace. Though it's a high compliment, it doesn't reveal how tough their work is.

This was illustrated for me in living color shortly after arriving at NorthRidge. A young man who had been in the church for years asked to have lunch with me. Since I was seeking to build relationships in the church and gain a greater understanding of the history, I gladly agreed. After all of the normal conversation, he finally got up the nerve to bring our discussion around to the reason for the lunch. He wanted to know what I did as a pastor. Since all of my predecessors had been older, this young man wouldn't have dared ask them such a question. And I'm sure that those pastors felt that everyone in the church knew what they did and how hard they worked. They were wrong. This young man had no clue as to what a pastor did on a daily basis. He, as so many in the church, only saw the pastor on the platform, giving a talk. He had no idea how a pastor went about preparing a talk, and he didn't have a clue of anything else a pastor did. This was an eye-opener for me. If people were going to know about the work involved in ministry, I was going to have to let them in close enough to see and experience it.

Pastors Need to Share the Ministry

Most pastors also don't share the work of ministry well. Though God makes it clear in Ephesians 4:11–12 that their job is to train others for ministry, most pastors do a significant portion of the ministry themselves. This is another reason the church isn't working right. It was never meant to be a one-person show. Romans 12 and 1 Corinthians 12 are clear on this. The church, like a body, can only function if all the various parts are working right. In most churches, they're not. More often than not, pastors are carrying most of the load themselves. This paralyzes the church body. If pastors would do a better job of sharing the work of ministry, the church would walk with less of a limp and more people would understand how much work is involved.

However, as in any worthwhile endeavor, the building of an effective church ministry requires dedicated and consistent hard work. If hard work isn't being invested, the church will not be effective. In my case, it took everything I had to give and more. I had to eliminate every extracurricular activity. I let go of everything in order to focus on my two primary commitments and values: family and ministry. Though I wouldn't have minded pursuing some other interests, my passion and values for family and church drove me to focus exclusively on them. I wanted to be successful in those things that would matter for eternity. I don't regret my decision.

> If pastors would do a better job of sharing the work of ministry, the church would walk with less of a limp and more people would understand how much work is involved.

Yet during those hard-charging years, I also needed to honor the principle of rest. When I didn't, I got myself in trouble physically and emotionally. When this happened, it didn't serve the interests of my family or church. However, rest didn't demand a huge portfolio of hobbies and recreation. It just demanded appropriate time for relaxation and renewal. In the Old Testament economy, God established it as one day a week—the Sabbath. While many are hurting themselves and the church by ignoring the Sabbath principle, others are using it to justify a life of ease. As always, balance is the key.

If you are a leader who genuinely cares about and wants to effectively lead the church, it will demand hard work and sacrificing other desirable investments of life. As Jesus said in Luke 14:33, "In the same way, any of you who does not give up everything he has cannot be my disciple." The good news is that the results will be worth it. Paul makes this clear in my life verse: "Therefore, my dear brothers, stand firm. Let nothing move you. Always give yourselves fully to the work of the Lord, because you know that your labor in the Lord is not in vain" (1 Corinthians 15:58).

Huge Faith

However, as I've pointed out, hard work isn't enough. Success in spiritual life and ministry also demands huge faith. This truth is clearly seen throughout Scripture. Moses worked hard and accomplished great things. However, it wasn't his work that ultimately made the difference. As hard as he worked, he couldn't convince Pharaoh to let God's people go. God did that by sending the plagues. As hard as he worked at leading God's people out of Egypt, it would have all ended in failure without God parting the sea. Hard work is never enough.

Abraham also provides a beautiful picture of this truth. Abraham worked hard and sacrificed much in following God. He obeyed God in ways that leave us shaking our heads. How could an eighty-year-old man just pull up stakes and head off into the unknown? How could he honestly trust God for a child in light of the impossible realities of his wife's barrenness and their age? She was ninety. He was one hundred. When he received that child, he then found the inner fortitude to willingly offer him as a sacrifice to the God who had promised and faithfully given the boy. Though it's simple for us to read, I can't imagine the difficulty of actually doing these things. Yet he did. And the Bible makes it clear how he managed it: "Yet he did not waver through unbelief regarding the promise of God, but was strengthened in his faith and gave glory to God, being fully persuaded that God had power to do what he had promised" (Romans 4:20–21). Abraham was able to do these unbelievable things because of his huge faith. It's for this reason that he is known as "the father of faith."

Unleashing the Church Demands Faith

When you and I, like Abraham, become fully persuaded that God has the power to do what He promised, we unleash the church. After all, He has clearly told us what He wants to do through us. He wants to build the church. He wants to do immeasurably more than we can ask or imagine. However, in order to experience the reality of these promises in our lives, we must exercise huge faith. As Hebrews 11:6 says, "Without faith it is impossible to please God, because anyone who comes to him must believe that he exists and that he rewards those who earnestly seek him." James 1:5–8 makes the same truth crystal clear: "If any of you lacks wisdom, he should ask God, who gives generously to all without finding fault, and it will be given to him. But when he asks, he must believe and not doubt, because he who doubts is like a wave of the sea, blown and tossed by the wind. That man should not think he will receive anything from the Lord; he is a double-minded man, unstable in all he does."

As a young man who wanted to be successful, I was extremely unstable. The reason is simple: I worked hard but had little faith. As my journey continued, I realized I was destined to instability and failure unless I began working in faith. I finally began waking up to the fact that, no matter how hard I worked, I ultimately had no control. As I realized this truth and started looking in faith to the One who is in control, I began experiencing very different results in the wake of the same kinds of effort.

Couldn't Have Made It More Obvious

There are so many experiences that come to mind in this regard and continually reaffirm the importance of working hard while believing completely. For approximately the first four years of my ministry at NorthRidge, I continued to talk about the possibility of relocation within seven to ten years. Though four years went by, I continued to say seven to ten years. The reason for this was simple. I knew that the entire future of my leadership and the church would ride on the success or failure of my leadership in the timing of relocation. If I led out too early, it would go down in defeat. If I waited too long, the church's losses and natural attrition could undercut our ability. Because of the importance of this defining leadership issue, I made a deal with God. If He would make the right moment obvious, I would put every ounce of my leadership toward making it happen. I just needed to know the right timing. I needed His wisdom. And in light of James 1:5–8, I believed He would honor this request.

> **Changing the church requires changing the hearts of people.**

Somewhere along the way, God gave me the name of the only church in the area that could afford and use our existing facility. This was an important issue. Selling that facility would be essential for funding the beginning stages of building a new facility. Though I had never met this pastor and knew little about him, I believed with all my heart that he was the solution to our issue. However, I didn't want to make a timing mistake. Therefore, as a part of my quest for God's wisdom, I asked Him to bring this man to me when the timing was right. Though I didn't think about it often, every once in a while I'd remember the issue and, in faith, place it at God's feet. I was determined to not move until God made it clear that it was time.

Unexpectedly, my assistant handed me a message that this man had called me. Upon returning the call, he asked for a meeting as soon as possible. We set it up for the next day. My assistant politely showed him to my office. We introduced ourselves to each other. And then, it happened. Nervously, he blurted out these words: "God told me to tell you to sell me your church building." Well, I knew I had my answer. It was time for me to lead. Though I knew what the end result would be, it was my responsibility to make sure that the sale price was fair. Therefore, I told him that we were definitely interested. However, if God had genuinely told him to buy our building, God would surely have given him the right price. So I asked what they were offering. The next day, they proffered an offer that was on target. As a result, I knew the timing was right. God couldn't have made it more obvious. Now it was time for me to do the hard work of leading. Though scary, it was easy in light of what faith had produced.

Only God Can Build His Church

Accomplishing anything of eternal significance requires a double investment—hard work and huge faith. This is especially true when building the church. After all, changing the church requires changing the hearts of people. No one can do this but God. Therefore, make sure that, while you work hard and smart, you also continue to walk by faith. Jesus made this perfectly clear in Matthew 17:20: "If you have faith as small as a mustard seed, you can say to this mountain, 'Move from here to there' and it will move. Nothing will be impossible for you."

Everything I'm experiencing today in ministry stems from grace. I'm not saying my gifts and my leadership haven't been a part of the equation. But I am saying that no matter how hard I work, only God can build His church. The same is true for you. As Proverbs 21:31 says, "The horse is made ready for the day of battle, but victory rests with the LORD."

CHAPTER 14

Straight Ahead

Staying the Course

Though last, this principle is certainly not least. If you are going to change your church without compromising the truth, you must stay the course. You've got to hold that ship's wheel. And it's not easy. The storms will get violent and rage and beat against you. People will try every conceivable way to convince you to turn the wheel back or in another direction. And if you don't, they will try and pry your hands off the wheel any way they can. I've experienced this time and again.

Of course, this shouldn't be news to those of us in ministry, and it only makes sense. God has clearly warned us about spiritual warfare. Paul, who knew about it as well as anyone, devoted the entire sixth chapter of his letter to the church at Ephesus to this issue. Satan will seek to undermine and attack any effort to move the church toward greater effectiveness. He will leverage the same forces against those leading the church to clearly reflect Christ in this world, as he did against Christ Himself. Jesus made this clear in John 15:18–21:

> If the world hates you, keep in mind that it hated me first. If you belonged to the world, it would love you as its own. As it is, you do not belong to the world, but I have chosen you out of the world. That is why the world hates you. Remember the words I spoke to you: "No servant is greater than his master."

> If they persecuted me, they will persecute you also. If they obeyed my teaching, they will obey yours also. They will treat you this way because of my name, for they do not know the One who sent me.

Following God Doesn't Guarantee Smooth Sailing

Unfortunately, believers often interpret God's involvement in their lives by the accompanying circumstances. If the circumstances are good, God must be involved. If not, then God is somehow missing. This is very bad theology. In holding to this thinking, they have to ignore the reality of almost every godly Bible character's life. Joseph is the perfect example. He is one of the more godly men in the Old Testament, yet he suffered tragic circumstance after tragic circumstance. His brothers hated his guts and sold him into slavery. His master in Egypt threw him into prison for something he didn't do. He was forgotten by everyone for years. But God was with him the entire time. In fact, God used these tragic circumstances to bring about the ultimate good. Joseph became prime minister of Egypt and was used by God to save and secure his family and all of God's people.

This common experience is often missed by pastors, leaders, and churches. If we're going to successfully lead our churches to effectiveness, we can't allow ourselves to miss this reality. As well, we must continually keep it in front of our people in order to keep them from doubting that God is working when tough times arise.

One experience in particular leaps out at me. We had been preparing our congregation for a major relocation. We had purchased property a couple of years before. As I explained in the previous chapter, God had made His timing perfectly clear. It was time to move. By God's grace, we secured a majority vote to sell the building and begin the process of building on our new campus. And then, it happened. We were stopped dead in our tracks.

Though we had done due diligence in seeking the favor of township officials before purchasing the property, as often happens in local politics, many of the officials had been replaced by the time we were ready to move forward. The new officials didn't feel the same way about our project as the former ones had. Our petition to build on our new property was unanimously rejected by the planning commission. It was devastating. We had worked hard and long to make sure that everything was done legally and properly, but we were shut down.

> **Satan will seek to undermine and attack any effort to move the church toward greater effectiveness.**

Many in the church began questioning whether God was in the move. If He was in the move, wouldn't everything be going smoothly? It was my job to help them see our experience through the lens of Scripture. In order to do this effectively, I had to keep a firm footing on the truth myself. I began teaching the church the truth about difficulties. Troubles aren't necessarily a sign that God isn't working. On the contrary, they are a common and expected part of living for and serving God.

I developed a series of talks entitled "Warfare Precedes Blessing," and I guided our church through the lives of godly men like Joseph, Abraham, Moses, Jesus, and Paul. Every single one of them encountered significant resistance to living and accomplishing God's will. I especially highlighted Paul. God's will for him was to start churches and win people to Christ, yet he encountered nothing but difficulty in completing his assignment. In fact, his words describe it better than I ever could. In 2 Corinthians 11:23–28, he told the story.

I have worked much harder, been in prison more frequently, been flogged more severely, and been exposed to death again and again. Five times I received from the Jews the forty lashes minus one. Three times I was beaten with rods, once I was stoned, three times I was shipwrecked, I spent a night and a day in the open sea, I have been constantly on the move. I have been in danger from rivers, in danger from bandits, in danger from my own countrymen, in danger from Gentiles; in danger in the city, in danger in the country, in danger at sea; and in danger from false brothers. I have labored and toiled and have often gone without sleep; I have known hunger and thirst and have often gone without food; I have been cold and naked. Besides everything else, I face daily the pressure of my concern for all the churches.

In 2 Corinthians 4:16–18, Paul shared important advice about how he faced these kinds of circumstances: "Therefore we do not lose heart. Though outwardly we are wasting away, yet inwardly we are being renewed day by day. For our light and momentary troubles are achieving for us an eternal glory that far outweighs them all. So we fix our eyes not on what is seen, but on what is unseen. For what is seen is temporary, but what is unseen is eternal."

Though I don't relish it, anyone who seeks to lead God's church and people will experience setbacks and difficulties. It's not a sign that God isn't with them or working; it's just a reality of the spiritual life. Warfare really does precede blessing. It also follows blessing. As I made our leaders and congregation aware of this truth, I compared our situation to Paul's. He was called to preach Christ, but as a Roman citizen, he was being prevented from exercising his rights. Therefore, he appealed to Caesar (Acts 25:11). Since this is exactly what was happening to us, I led the congregation to follow Paul in appealing to our Caesar. We took the township to court. In keeping with Paul's example, we didn't do this angrily or to extract revenge. We did it in order to pursue our rights under the law. In fact, we determined to use this as a God-given opportunity to share Christ in all of the settings this circumstance would afford us.

Our prayer and goal came from Paul's words in Philippians 1:12: "Now I want you to know, brothers, that what has happened to me has really served to advance the gospel." This is exactly what happened. We built positive relationships with some of the officials in our new township. In fact, as an ultimate result, many people who had at one time stood against us became part of the church. It was an amazing experience. In the end, the unanimous rejection changed to a unanimous acceptance. Though it wasn't easy, God was definitely in it. And it has proved to be worth all the effort and sacrifice.

Stay Long Enough for the Blessing

In order to successfully transition a church to effectiveness, you must stay the course. Too often, pastors leave the church just when they're starting to gain the influence required to lead. This is sad. They deal with the warfare, but they don't stay long enough for the blessing. There is nothing more tragic than a leader or church giving up just before God gives the breakthrough. Imagine if Joseph had given up on God before the blessing. Imagine the same for David as he was waiting to be king; Abraham waiting for a son; Noah waiting for a flood; Hannah waiting for a son; the disciples waiting for the promised Holy Spirit. It would have been tragic. A tragedy of the same magnitude happens every time one of God's children gives up in the face of difficulties. In so doing, they're missing what they're looking for . . . God's blessing.

Now, don't get me wrong. God does call pastors and people to leave their churches. Paul is an example of a man legitimately called to many different settings. But he wasn't running away; he was genuinely called to move on. Therefore, if you are contemplating a move, you need to make sure that God is directing your move. Make sure your motivations are right. If there is any question, stay the course. God does not call people to leave a transition in the middle of the storm. When it happens, it's an excuse to get out of the fire. The reality is that God would have called you to leave before the transition if He were the One calling.

When It's Done, It's Not Done

As part of staying the course in ministry, I had to learn a very important lesson. Transition is never done. Every new day brings another new challenge. We'll need God as much tomorrow as we needed Him today. When it's done, it's not done. In fact, I've developed four thoughts to help me remember this important truth.

Just Because I've Said It Doesn't Mean They've Got It

I've been guilty of this common mistake. Pastors and leaders will often work hard at developing and effectively presenting a vision talk. When done, they tend to give a sigh of relief and move on to other things. This is a huge mistake. Leader, you need to get hold of this reality. Just because you've said it, doesn't mean your people understood it. It takes years for them to get it; it requires saying it again and again. In order to turn a vision into reality, the leader must stay the course.

Just Because They've Got It Doesn't Mean They Embrace It

I have discovered this big-time in ministry, especially with church leaders. This is a common reality in working with church boards. Pastors will work on casting a vision with boards for a very, very long time. Finally, the board gets it, and then the board votes no. It's amazing how often this happens. When leading people, the leader must understand that just because they've got it, doesn't mean they embrace it. It's not enough for people to get it. They must believe it to the core of their being. They must become personally passionate about it. They must embrace it as their own. If they don't, they will continue to stand in the way rather than in support.

Of course, it's important to acknowledge that some people will never embrace the transition. This is why we need to be working toward transitioning the right people into leadership and the wrong people out.

Just Because They Embrace It Doesn't Mean They'll Work for It

For those of you who are pastors, I need to remind you that, while it's great to have people supporting you from the sidelines, your real need is to get people on the field with you. If you don't, no matter how hard you work, the church will not transition. It's vital that you get people working with you.

For those of you who aren't pastors, I want to give a special encouragement to you. I have often experienced the reality of this issue in my leadership ministry. I've often had people claim to fully embrace my vision only to stand on the sidelines, cheering, while I'm on the field, getting killed. Though having them cheer is better than having them shoot at me, I really need them to join me in the adventure. I want to encourage you to get in the game. Though it's fun to watch, it's more fun to play. Your pastor, church, and those without Christ desperately need you. You can make a difference if you will get in the game.

> In order to successfully transition a church to effectiveness, you must stay the course.

Just Because They're Working It Doesn't Mean They Will Keep to the Plan

The minute a leader feels as though his work is done, someone will veer off track. The leader's job is never done. If you're a leader, don't allow this to happen to you. Keep your eye on the ball. It's your job to keep people seeing the vision, moving toward the purpose, living the values, and working the plan. If you don't, they won't.

Don't Celebrate Too Early

Here's my advice: don't celebrate too early. Regardless of your political perspective, former president George W. Bush provided the perfect illustration of this common leadership failure. Shortly after the fall of Saddam Hussein in Iraq, President Bush flew a fighter jet onto a United States naval aircraft carrier. It was an impressive display. Upon exiting the jet, he walked in front of a huge banner that stated: "Mission Accomplished." Though the moment was well scripted and impressive, the announcement and celebration were presumptuous. An insurgency would soon erupt, taking many more lives, resources, and time than the ground war itself. This early celebration significantly hurt President Bush in the long term. While I recommend celebrating small accomplishments along the way, leaders need to be very careful about prematurely celebrating the end of the war, so to speak. As President Bush discovered, the world and circumstances can rapidly change. As they do, the church must be ready to change. I would encourage you to avoid the proclamation "Mission Accomplished." Premature announcements undercut the leader's ability to keep leading. So be careful.

> In leading, you have to make sure you're making the important turns, and then you must follow through with them.

Final Thoughts

Though it is so seldom addressed or done, the idea of staying the course is a significant issue in transitioning a church. If the leader doesn't hold the course long enough, the ministry will return to its old habits. Therefore, if you are seeking to lead the church through successful change, it's vital that you stay the course long enough for the new course to become the normal and most comfortable course for the church.

Though our church is an entirely different church today and would never retreat to the old patterns, this has only been made possible by staying the course. We've been holding our present course for long enough that it's now the only course the church knows. This is no accident. We are still working the plan that I began outlining in vision during my first talk as pastor of this church. We're able to do this without becoming irrelevant because I helped them to embrace God's principles and not specific practices. By aligning our vision to God's eternal principles rather than specific practices, we can stay the course even as we continue to change many of the ways that we do ministry.

People Will Only Follow You Around So Many Bends

Make sure that the turns you're making as a church are important ones. Some leaders change the direction of the church so often that their people are constantly seasick. They will go to a conference, come home, and start redirecting the church in accordance with what they learned. Then, after reading a new book, they'll do the same thing. What leaders must understand is that people are only willing and able to follow them around so many bends in the road. This is especially true if the people have seen no positive benefit from the previous turns. In leading, you have to make sure you're making the important turns, and then you must follow through with them. Stay the course.

You Can't Build Momentum by Cornering

In order to build momentum, you must make the important turns and then hold steady. This was the only way we were able to create momentum in our transition. We would slow down as we made a significant turn, but we would then hold steady until the church was able to gain momentum again. This is a vital aspect of transitional leadership. Too often, church leaders make so many turns that the church is never able to build any kind of momentum. As a result, the leader or the people ultimately lose hope, give up, and go back to the way things were.

Those of us who are called to lead the church can't allow this to happen. We have to make the right turns but allow the momentum to grow again. In our transition, this process took six years. I would make a turn and lose a little momentum. Then, I'd hold it so that we could gain forward momentum. I would repeat this as often as necessary with sensitivity to the church's ability to keep moving forward. After six years, we were heading in the right direction and I was able to keep the ministry moving forward with greater and greater momentum. This is when our significant growth spurt began. Avoid turning, when possible, in order to keep from cutting into the church's momentum.

Staying the Course Allows the Change to Become the Norm

If you know you're turning in the right direction, you need to stay the course. This will allow the changes to become the normal way of doing ministry. When this happens, you can mark it down. As it relates to that particular change, the church has successfully transitioned. This, of course, is the goal, but it requires staying the course.

PART 5

hope of the world

CHAPTER 15

A Life Is Waiting

Lost People Matter to God

*T*ragedy isn't a strong enough word. There aren't words to describe an atrocity of this magnitude. It was five days before Christmas. A couple of hardened criminals had staked out several jewelry stores in our area, looking for the big score. When they finally selected their target, they went to work. Pretending to have a delivery, they showed up at the doorstep of the jeweler's home. His visiting mother kindly invited them in.

While holding her at gunpoint, they waited for his three preteen children to come home from school. Upon their arrival, they made the oldest call their daddy. He was home in minutes. Threatening his life and the life of his family, they made him open the safe he had at home. Although this heist was not as profitable as robbing the store itself, it seemed safer, easier, and lucrative enough.

Oh that the story ended with only the loss of some jewelry and money. It was not to be. These lunatics wouldn't have it. One by one, they murdered everyone in the home. It was and remains an incomprehensible tragedy. We got the call from the man's relative who attended our church. They were asking for prayer, counsel, help, and guidance in working through all of the issues facing them. Of course, our church family was all over it. If the church can't be a support during times like this, there is no point. We would do whatever we could to help the family and community deal with this tragedy.

What I didn't know, until meeting with the family, was that this man and his three precious children had recently started attending our church. Because this man was experiencing some marital difficulties, he began looking for and opening up to the idea of God in his life. As a result, when the family members who attended our church invited him, he gladly came along with his three children. They fell in love with it and began attending regularly.

When meeting with the extended family, I was told that this man and his three children had accepted Christ as their personal Savior as a result of attending our church. The children had been reached through our kids' ministry. Their father had made the decision to follow Christ during one of our services. Because he had communicated this decision to his family members, they knew the service and the seat he was in when his life was eternally changed. Though it didn't change the devastation of this human tragedy, it did change everything as it related to this family's eternal destiny.

They are in heaven today because they found a church that communicated about God in a language they could understand.

At the time he began attending, we were doing a survey in our church. When I found the one he had filled out, along with all of the general information, he thanked us for making God and His truth so relevant to his life, and he encouraged us to keep up the good work. Imagine this: according to his own words, the reason this man and his children had come to faith was because our church had finally introduced them to God in a relevant way. Though religious, they had never experienced God's truth in a way that related to their everyday lives. When they did, they trusted Him and found eternal

hope. They are in heaven today because they found a church that communicated about God in a language they could understand.

The Church Is the Hope of the World—When It's Working Right

I'm eternally grateful that our church was working right when this family was invited. In light of the eternal gains in this family's life, every loss and hardship of the transition became insignificant. I was so impacted by this experience that, to this day, I keep his survey form at eye level in my study. I never want to forget what's really at stake in the church. I never want to allow the church to turn inward, for me or for others. The church is the only hope of the world, and it must continue to work right because, as always, a life is waiting.

Though this is the final chapter, I'm actually ending where the church needs to begin. Without fully understanding and embracing the value of this chapter, there is no way or reason for the church to transition. Changing a church without compromising the truth will prove to be too long and difficult for anyone who doesn't remain focused on what motivated Jesus—people in desperate need of God's forgiveness, hope, help, joy, promises, purpose, love, peace, security, and fulfillment. Unless reaching these people is their driving focus, churches will always pander to the needs and wants of those already in the church. For the church to change, it must keep the focus of Jesus as recorded in John 10:16: "I have other sheep that are not of this sheep pen. I must bring them also." In order to change, a church family must remember "it's not all about them."

Why Should We Care?

The question every church asks when confronted with the idea of transitioning to cultural relevance is "Why?" *Why should we care if our church is relevant? Why should we care that we are speaking in the language of our culture?* The answer is simple. It's the reason Jesus transitioned from heaven to earth. It's the reason Jesus builds His church. Lost people are treasured by God and must be treasured by His church.

In Luke 15:1–24, Jesus told three stories back to back to back that all teach exactly the same truth. He did this for the same reason He occasionally repeated a person's name: for emphasis. He was tired of people continually asking why He hung out with tax collectors and sinners. He was tired of people missing the point. So finally, in Luke 15, He told these three stories to make it clear what motivated His life and ministry.

The three stories were about lost things that had great worth. More than likely, you know the stories. There was a shepherd that lost one sheep out of his hundred. As a result, he left the ninety-nine in order to find the one lost sheep. When he did, he threw a party to celebrate. There was a woman that lost one of her coins. It was a significant portion of her wealth. Therefore, she put everything else in her life on hold and looked for that coin. When she found it, she called everyone she knew to celebrate. There was a dad who lost his son to self-destructive choices. While the son was gone, the father put everything on hold in his life while waiting and praying for his son's return. Jesus described the father seeing the son from a great distance as he was on his way home. It's clear he spent his life looking at the horizon for the boy to come home. When he found his son, this dad threw a huge party to celebrate.

The Common Problem

In Jesus' stories, no one questioned the excitement and celebration over finding the sheep or coin. But in the story of the lost son coming home, someone did complain about the excitement and the celebration. The elder son threw a pity party over it. Though he had been experiencing the joy, peace, security, and fulfillment of the father all along and would continue to experience them, he was ticked that the father hadn't thrown a party for him.

Here, in this last story, Jesus addressed the common problem found among those who claim to be His followers, both then and now: they begin focusing on and valuing only the insiders. He made it clear how distorted values can become. No one had a problem with celebrating a business success or financial gain. But celebrating the return and forgiveness of a wayward person was greeted with hostility. How sad. Jesus was clearly addressing the religious leaders who hated that He directed His life and ministry toward sinners. But He was also addressing today's churches that gear their ministries toward those already on the inside.

> Lost people are treasured by God and must be treasured by His church.

Unfortunately, the complaining elder son is representative of many Christian churches today. They get upset about the excitement, celebration, and expense being directed toward the people who walked away from God while they, in their minds, stayed faithful. They're upset at how these people come into and mess up their nice little comfortable churches. This reveals how far from the values of Jesus Christ many of His churches have drifted. This is the reason churches need to change. If they don't, they will compromise everything Jesus loves and values.

Three Relevant Truths

I find three relevant truths that Jesus was affirming in this passage. First, lost people are a treasure to God. Jesus leaves no room for misunderstanding why His ministry is directed to the wayward and hurting. As are the sheep, coin, and son to the shepherd, woman, and father, so lost people are a treasure to God.

Second, the value God has for lost people compelled Him to drastically reorder His world in order to find them. It makes sense that the shepherd, woman, and father would entirely reorder their lives to find or be reunited with what they genuinely valued. This is what God has done. There was only one reason for Jesus to leave heaven and come to earth: to help rescue and give hope to messed-up, rebellious sons and daughters. As 2 Corinthians 8:9 says, "For you know the grace of our Lord Jesus Christ, that though he was rich, yet for your sakes he became poor, so that you through his poverty might become rich."

Third, God rejoices more in a lost person finding Him than in anything else. Though the elder brother didn't understand this and many churches miss it as well, this is the driving reality of what God values and celebrates. As Jesus specifically stated in Luke 15:7, "I tell you that in the same way there will be more rejoicing in heaven over one sinner who repents than over ninety-nine righteous persons who do not need to repent."

Jesus' answer left no room for doubt. The reason Jesus directed His ministry toward outsiders rather than insiders was because this is what God values.

The Back Side of the Great Commission

What so many churches value and celebrate has nothing to do with what God values and celebrates. As a result, they play to the back side of the Great Commission. They don't invest in or burden themselves with reaching lost people. Of course, they rationalize this in a spiritual way. They claim that they're organizing the church to develop believers who will go out and reach unbelievers. In other words, the church gathers to worship and scatters to evangelize. But there are a lot of problems with this perspective.

It's not how the early church was organized. The early church would hold their large gatherings in the public square, where a crowd would be drawn to their worship and teaching. This is where the gospel would be preached and thousands would come to faith. They then broke off for small group in one another's homes for going deeper into worship and teaching. The most successful and impacting evangelism took place as the church was publicly gathered. This is clearly seen in the Acts of the Apostles.

How are these believers going to successfully reach unbelievers if they can't communicate God's truth in the language of the culture? If the church isn't culturally relevant, the believers from that church won't be relevant. No wonder the churches that make this claim aren't reaching anyone for Christ.

If they ever do reach a person, where is that new believer going to learn about living for God in the real world? It won't happen in a church that has no connection to or understanding of the real world. It's not happening, and it won't happen. This is an excuse for keeping their churches the way they want them. It's an excuse for why they aren't following Jesus in leaving their comfort zone in order to reveal God's truth, love, and hope in the language and context of real people's lives.

The reason Jesus directed His ministry toward outsiders rather than insiders was because this is what God values.

Now, I certainly don't want to be misunderstood on this point. The back side of the Great Commission is vital. Churches must nurture and develop new believers. As parents with an infant, the church is assigned responsibility to nurture newborn believers to fullness of faith. However, this cannot be done at the expense of reaching people for Christ. In fact, the Great Commission makes clear that the goal of developing believers is to get them following Jesus, leaving their comfort zones, and going into the world to reach more people.

Unless the church fulfills its obligation to the front side of the Great Commission, it will have no one to develop. As a result, it will start organizing around those people who are already developed. This is exactly what is happening in many churches today, and it's creating a very selfish, elder brother–like church. Jesus put the first part of the Great Commission first for a reason. The church must play to the front side if they are ever going to be able to work on the back side. The church must be driven by the unselfish value of reaching those outsiders who have yet to experience the hope that the insiders are already enjoying.

Of course, there's nothing wrong with training believers to go out and be light in the world. Every believer should be living and sharing the faith. First Peter 3:15 makes this unmistakably clear: "But in your hearts set apart Christ as Lord. Always be prepared to give an answer to everyone who asks you to give the reason for the hope that you have." It's certainly a part of the strategy of our church. However, too many churches are justifying their cultural irrelevance by claiming it's the individual believer's responsibility to light the world. As Jesus made clear in Luke 15, churches need to reorder their ministries around reaching lost people. They need to play to the front side of the Great Commission.

The Goal Is to Follow Jesus

This is exactly what Jesus did in His life and ministry. If a church is going to change without compromising, the example of Jesus is the one to follow and claim. I know it was extremely helpful to me as I led our transition. People would complain about how we were changing the church. I would immediately start comparing what we were doing to what Jesus did. They didn't like it, but they couldn't argue with it. Lost people were such a treasure to Jesus that He literally and drastically reordered His entire life to help redeem them. He rejoices more over one of them discovering and experiencing His hope than anything else. We weren't doing something unique. We were simply following Jesus.

In Luke 19:10, Jesus made it clear He came to this planet for one reason: "to seek and to save what was lost." He changed everything in His life to accomplish it. Why? Because He genuinely loved them. In spite of what they say, the reason so many churches are unwilling to change is because they don't genuinely love lost people. This needs to be a significant and constant point of evaluation for churches. Generally, they have the words down. They know all the right answers. However, it's by their fruit that we'll recognize them. How they genuinely feel about lost people is most clearly communicated through what they're doing to reach them.

> If a church is going to change without compromising, the example of Jesus is the one to follow and claim.

Unfortunately, many churches are doing and sacrificing nothing. They love, live, and sacrifice more for their buildings, traditions, and programs than they do for lost people. This makes them very poor reflections of Christ in this world. In order to change successfully, our churches must begin valuing and celebrating the same thing God does. As Jesus made clear, once and for all, He values and celebrates lost people coming to faith above all else.

Sharing Stories Motivates People

The only effective way that I've found to make this happen in the church is by sharing stories of life change. It motivates people. It makes them want to be part of those kinds of stories, even when it requires change.

When lives weren't changing through our ministry, I would raise the value of people and life change by using stories from Scripture. In the early days, I talked a lot about the church at

Antioch as it is described in Acts 11:10–21. I used this story to spark the imagination of our people to be a world-changing church someday. I'd turn to Acts 2 and highlight the three thousand people who came to Christ and ask them to imagine the stories of life change. Then I'd make it clear that the same God who showed up in Acts 2 is available to show up in our church today, if we let Him.

The best we can do is inspire a person; only God can transform one.

Today, because of our significant journey of change without compromise, I am able to share stories from our own church ministry. These stories make all the hard work of transitioning our church worth every ounce of sacrifice. For a church to get more excited about people finding Christ than anything else, they need to have it kept before them. For this reason, I consistently share stories. I share them with the staff. I share them with the elders. I share them in meetings with teachers and influencers. And I share them in our services. If I can't get the church excited about reaching people, they're not going to be excited about it. So I'm constantly stoking my own excitement so that I can fuel the church's excitement. Nothing works better than this story.

My First Letter from Rick

Dear Pastor Brad, having been to NorthRidge twice and hearing you there, I found you sincere, eloquent, and knowledgeable. Yet, that has not been near enough for me to change my thinking on either the existence or the meaning of God. I'm friends with one who attends your services and who studies often the Bible as taught by you and others. Talking with her and other people who've been "reborn to Jesus" has been an exercise in frustration. I ask hard questions and get cookie-cutter answers that, more often than not, leave me shaking my head at their narrowing perspective.

I was born Catholic, and then drifted away as I grew older, my interest in science leading me to attend more to answers of cause and effect than those of faith and prayer. In three years in the Far East during Vietnam, I had apparently (according to what Christians believe), come into contact with thousands if not millions of people doomed to a Christian hell because they had not committed themselves to Jesus. I wondered how many had not even heard of Him and yet were doomed to hell nonetheless.

In short, I've yet to be convinced of a God who has set rules which condemns most humans to a hell not of their making or understanding. I have seen *The Passion of the Christ* by Mel Gibson and found that, if even partly true, the man, Jesus, paid a heavy price for His beliefs. Yet I find it difficult to believe if even part of the movie were true, that He—that kind of man—would have created a belief system with such a narrow focus, Himself at its center, and giving no credit for good not done in His name.

I plan on attending your four weekend services in which you plan to discuss those events *The Passion* touched upon [I did the weekend series on *The Passion of the Christ* called "What If It's True?"] and I will be thinking, as I listen to you and others, of all those millions who are supposedly in hell who never heard of Jesus. If after that I think you may have some of the answers, or admit to not having all of them, I would someday like to talk to you under a tree on a warm spring day for an hour or so and give you a chance to pit your irresistible faith against my seemingly immovable objections.

This letter blew me away. What an opportunity to share God's truth with this man. The reality is that I used this man as my focus during my preparation and delivery of this series. I took great care to make sure that I presented the issues of truth in a language, context, and means that people like this could fully engage and understand, whether they accepted the truth or not.

Six Months Later, My Next Letter from Rick

I know you're probably one of the busiest men on the planet. I thought I would write you anyway. I wrote you some months ago telling you about my search for God and some of my doubts. You wrote back, and your letter to me began for me a search that goes on to this day.

Have I found God? I'm not sure. But I'm starting to think He may have found me. Although I'm unsure about my belief in God, I want you to know, I do believe in you, and I believe in your vision for NorthRidge. [Of course, in this short statement, he clearly enunciated the reason we transitioned.] I heard you speak on September 20 at your 11:15 a.m. service [this was a service where I laid out the vision for building our spiritual formation center; of course, I made it clear that the value wasn't the buildings, but people], and you made many things clear to me. I'm going to be making a donation to Phase III.

That still amazes me. No matter how I cast God's vision and values, I can't even get some Christians to give. But here was an atheist committing to give. What an encouragement!

A Little While Later, Another Letter from Rick

Pastor Brad, just a quick note to let you know that I'm glad you and NorthRidge are there. I'm the ex-atheist who's now an agnostic. [This cracked me up. He was clearly on his own spiritual journey. He just hadn't gotten to or crossed the line of faith yet.]

I'm not sure God exists, but I'm searching. If it were not for a friend introducing me to NorthRidge, I would have long ago left the rocky trail that I find the search for God to be.

NorthRidge is a revelation to one who left religion so long ago. I just wanted to thank you all for being there for me as I look for what you and so many others seem to see so clearly.

This last phrase really got me. He had obviously come to the place where he could admit that he was empty and without hope. Though his mind wasn't to the place of acceptance yet, he desperately wanted to experience the purpose, peace, and fulfillment that others at our church were experiencing. These letters encouraged me significantly. They revealed to me that, from this man's perspective and experience, our church was working. Though we were far from perfect, the reality of God's hope was shining through. The transition was successful and eternally worth it. However, his letter also saddened me. I knew that people just like him all around the world didn't have a church to attend that was committed to communicating God's truth in a language they could understand. It was one more motivation for me to start sharing our story and the lessons we learned with other churches. Every genuine church has the potential to reach people like Rick. They just have to be willing to change without compromise.

His letter continued: "NorthRidge makes the wondering about God interesting. And NorthRidge makes wondering about God often fun."

This is a guy who had completely rejected God but was coming to church for the fun. Now, there is a statement that should cause the church to ponder. I certainly did. If anyone has the right to have fun, it's the people who've been set free from the damaging effects of sin. But because of the way so many churches do ministry, they make it appear that Christianity is a curse to a boring life. This shouldn't be. After all, those without God's hope use fun as a means of hiding from reality; whereas those in Christ can have fun because their reality is awesome.

He then finished his letter this way: "So on Sundays, for the foreseeable future, I, like you, am going to be at NorthRidge."

Rick, now claiming to be an agnostic, has made great progress. In fact, over the course of the time represented by these letters, he had already made more progress than many believers and leaders in some churches had in years. Though sad, it's true.

A Couple of Months Later . . .

Pastor Brad, I don't know if you remember me or not . . . I was the agnostic who felt proud and superior not to be an atheist anymore. Remember me? I write today to tell you that I'm no longer seeking, because on December 3rd, I found God.

Though many argue that churches that change in order to become culturally relevant water down the truth, making it easier to believe, this certainly isn't true of our church and doesn't have to be true in any church. Churches can change for effectiveness in communicating God's truth without compromising it. When Rick writes in this letter that he found God, he's not talking about some watered-down, positive-attitude, self-help kind of God. He's not talking about the "all paths lead to heaven" God. He's not finding an easy God that we've made up by compromising the truth. This atheist-turned-agnostic-turned-follower-of-Jesus-Christ clearly reveals what he means by saying he found God: "I now believe that Jesus Christ was and is God's emissary to mankind and earth, that He died for our sins, which are as grains of sand upon the beach."

Of course, we didn't change this man. The best we can do is inspire a person; only God can transform one. However, by changing our church to effectively communicate God's truth in a language and cultural context that this man could relate to and understand, we created the opportunity to expose him to God's life-changing truth. Though he had rejected church for years, when we removed all the unnecessary cultural obstacles, he was finally able to see Jesus. And it has forever changed his life. Though difficult, the changes were eternally worth it.

A Recent Letter from Rick

Pastor Brad, if it were possible to tell the members and attendees of NorthRidge about NorthRidge, this is what I would say to them. It had been thirty-five years since I last stepped into a church before walking in the front door of NorthRidge and being greeted like a long-lost friend. No religious trappings on the wall, nobody dressed in pontifical robes and adornments, volunteers by the score, unpaid I was sure, to help me find my way, and a feeling in the air that something grand was about to commence. I found no altar, no pews, no wall of candles or booths like washing machines to remove the sins and stains of human existence.

I returned again for the *Passion of the Christ* series, was impressed by its logical presentation, its message concise and understandable, even to an inquisitive atheist like myself, and I began to see that not all churches were created equal, that this church was like nothing I had ever heard about in those thirty-five years, where, like the poem "Footprints," God often carried me when I wasn't even aware of it. That I had found a church like NorthRidge when I was younger, I would not have been lost those thirty-five years. I would not have sinned the way I had sinned. I perhaps would have been better able to help others, and better understood why I was doing it and why I would want to. Like a diamond in the rough, NorthRidge has been cut and polished to near perfection, but the members are constantly looking for the smallest flaw to polish even brighter, so that it may reflect truly the vision they have in providing help for us all. I know of no business, no other church, that gives so much so freely, and though asking now and again for financial support, gives so little cause for guilt to those who turn the other cheek.

What we have here is not NorthRidge, an unchanging financial vacuum cleaner that uses funds for the support of a robed and privileged elite, a gathering of moribund monotony, whose methods and message have not changed in thirty-five years. Instead we have a church teaching for the children and the troubled so that they may not have to walk in the desert of lost souls as I did those so many long and lonely years, a church that tries to change as fast as Michigan weather to keep abreast of cultural relevance so that the Word and works of God are not lost to those who had fallen asleep because they had heard it all before. Personally, I like the twenty or thirty minutes I have to wait to drive out of the parking lot. It gives me time to reflect upon the message I have heard, and to see that vast sea of untapped potential that encircles me and drives as if fleeing the ark after forty days and forty nights. That I could give more I would, to help pave the way for another five hundred cars to leave more quickly to begin God's work all over again.

Do you know there are now four ways to find direction in your life? There's magnetic north, the North Star, moss on the north side of trees and boulders, and NorthRidge. I ask you, do you truly really know what you have here? And if you do, are you doing anything to help the most remarkable diamond of NorthRidge reflect its message even more brightly in the eyes of children and the lost? I, too, was lost, and thanks to NorthRidge and those who give it life, am now found. I could not have done it without you. Without you, I would not have even tried.

Upon reading this unsolicited letter, I simply whispered words of thanks to God. Though there were times when I wondered if the hassle of leading the church through change was worth it, those thoughts have long been replaced by thousands of confirmations. Confirmations of eternally changed lives, lives that mattered to God, lives like Rick's, that may have forever been lost if this church hadn't been working. It was more than worth it.

For me, Rick's letters provide a face to those Jesus was talking about in Luke 15. All those wandering in this world so lost who are still a treasure to God. So much so, that He drastically reordered His world to seek and to save them. And when they find Him, He rejoices. Thinking that heaven is rejoicing for all that is happening these days at our church makes me smile. I now have a passion to help other pastors, leaders, and churches experience the same smile. What a wonderful world it would be if all of God's churches were touching the lives of people like Rick.

The Choice Is Yours

Though many pastors, leaders, and churches have a difficult time believing change is possible in their church, it is. If they could have seen our church when I first came, they would have never believed that a letter like Rick's could ever be written about this church. Believing our church could change may have been an impossible notion, but God has always been the God of the impossible. The problem is that His people, more often than not, forget or fail to believe. If God could do it in our church, He can do it in any church. He can do it in your church. He just needs His people, people like you, to believe in His power and to embrace His purpose and passion for the church.

People facing eternity without Christ are waiting all around the world for the church to be what Jesus called it to be—the hope of the world.

People facing eternity without Christ are waiting all around the world for the church to be what Jesus called it to be—the hope of the world. Whether it will be or won't be boils down to one thing: choice. Will we, the pastors, leaders, and people of God, choose to follow Christ or not? He left heaven to seek and save the lost. And now He's asking us to leave our comfort zones to seek and save the lost. If we don't, the church will continue to fail in its purpose and struggle for survival. If we do, we will see our churches change in ways we've never imagined. They will become what they're supposed to be . . . the hope of the world.

Though changing the church is never easy, as I've shared with you in this book, it's both possible and worth it. It's possible because with God nothing is impossible. It's worth it because lost people are a treasure to God. But the choice is yours. My prayer is that God has used this book to inspire you to make the choice you'll never regret—the choice to change your church without compromising God's truth. The reason is eternal: *a life is waiting!*

Additional Information and Resources
by Brad Powell
available online at
BradPowellOnline.com
or contact
NorthRidge Church
49555 North Territorial Road
Plymouth, MI 48170
Phone: 734.414.7777
NorthRidgeChurch.com